ADVANCES IN LEARNING AND BEHAVIORAL DISABILITIES

Volume 13 • 1999

ADVANCES IN LEARNING AND BEHAVIORAL DISABILITIES

Editors: THOMAS E. SCRUGGS
MARGO A. MASTROPIERI
Graduate School of Education
George Mason University

VOLUME 13 • 1999

United Kingdom – North America – Japan
India – Malaysia – China

Emerald Group Publishing Limited
Howard House, Wagon Lane, Bingley BD16 1WA, UK

Reprints and permission service
Contact: booksandseries@emeraldinsight.com

British Library Cataloguing in Publication Data
A catalogue record for this book is available from the British Library

ISBN: 978-0-7623-0429-5
ISSN: 0735-004X (Series)

CONTENTS

LIST OF CONTRIBUTORS

Ina van Berckelaer-Onnes	University of Leiden The Netherlands
Frederick J. Brigham	Department of Special Education University of Virginia
Lucia Cacciò	Department of Psicologia Generale University of Padova, Italy
Jane E. Cole	Greenville Junior High School Greenville, Ohio
Teresa Meade Crenshaw	Glen Allen, Virginia
Rossana De Beni	Department of Psicologia Generale University of Padova, Italy
Lois-Lynn S. Deuel	Broward County Public Schools Fort Lauderdale, Florida
Kathryn L. Fletcher	Department of Psychology University of Miami
Steven R. Forness	Neuropsychiatric Insitute University of California, Los Angeles
Beda Jean-Francois	Department of Psychology University of Miami
Kenneth A. Kavale	Division of Special Education University of Iowa

Daniela Lucangeli	Department of Psicologia Generale University of Padova, Italy
Panayota Mantzicopoulos	Department of Educational Studies Purdue University
Delmont Morrison	Department of Psychiatry University of California, San Francisco
Francesca Pazzaglia	Department of Psicologia Generale University of Padova, Italy
Ronald E. Reeve	Curry Programs in Clinical & School Psychology University of Virginia
Marcia S. Scott	Department of Psychology University of Miami
H. Lee Swanson	School of Education University of California, Riverside
Patrizio E. Tressoldi	Department of Psicologia Generale University of Padova, Italy

AN ANALYSIS OF CHANGE IN LEARNING DISABLED READERS' PHONEMIC, SEMANTIC, AND VISUAL-SPATIAL WORKING MEMORY: ADDITIONAL SUPPORT FOR AN EXECUTIVE PROCESSING DEFICIT

H. Lee Swanson

ABSTRACT

This chapter reports in detail outcomes of three studies which assess the degree of change in learning disabled (LD) readers' working memory (WM) performance. Three studies compared LD readers and various comparison groups on WM performance for phonological, visual-spatial, and semantic information under initial (no probes or cues), gain (cues that bring performance to an asymptotic level), and maintenance conditions (asymptotic conditions without cues). Study 1 compared the

Advances in Learning and Behavioral Disabilities, Volume 13, pages 1–64.

ISBN: 0-7623-0429-4

performance of LD readers, chronological age-matched, and reading level-matched (RL) children. Study 2 extended the findings by comparing severe and moderate LD readers to slow learners (children whose verbal IQ scores approximate their reading scores), and Study 3 extended the findings to LD and CA-matched readers subgrouped by severe and moderate executive processing deficits. The main findings across the three studies were that LD readers show less change in WM performance on phonological, visual-spatial, and semantic WM tasks than comparison groups. LD readers' resistance to change (as reflected from the logistic curves) was isolated to high accessibility conditions (gain conditions) when compared to reading level matched and slow learner (poor reading) groups and to high processing demand conditions (maintenance conditions) when compared to CA-matched average readers. LD readers' WM deficits are specialized to phonological and semantic tasks, however, when changes in WM performance are not considered. Taken together, the results suggest that LD readers' poor WM partially reflects constraints in executive processing above and beyond their problems in the articulatory system.

Performance differences between learning disabled (LD) and nondisabled (NLD) readers on measures of cognitive function are attributed to limitations in working memory (e.g., Siegel & Ryan, 1989; Swanson, 1993a). Working memory (WM) is defined as a processing resource of limited capacity involved in the preservation of information while simultaneously processing the same or other information (e.g., Just & Carpenter, 1992; Salthouse, 1996). It is distinguished from other forms of memory because it reflects both simultaneous processing and storage capacity (Baddeley, 1986; Just & Carpenter, 1992). These limitations have been primarily attributed to an isolated aspect of WM, holding and maintaining phonological codes (e.g., Bowey, Cain, & Ryan, 1992; Shankweiler & Crain, 1986; Hansen & Bowey, 1994), and secondarily to semantic codes (e.g., Waterman & Lewandowski, 1993; Vellutino, Scanlon, & Spearing, 1995). However, recent studies (Martin, Shelton, & Yaffee, 1994) suggest that phonological and semantic deficits can operate independently (separate capacities) of each other suggesting a multiple capacity rather than a single capacity view of WM. In addition, there are recent studies suggesting that executive processing may also contribute to the poor WM performance of LD readers above and beyond their deficits in phonological processing (e.g., Swanson & Alexander, 1997). In sum, there is no consensus about whether the primary source of difficulty in WM experienced by LD readers reflects a general storage system, the accessing of phonological information, and/or the accessing of semantic information. It is therefore possible that deficits in LD readers' WM are due to storage capacity, processing efficiency, or to both storage and processing in the retention of information related to a general (central executive) or a specific (phonological) system. The purpose of this chapter is to review three recently completed studies on these issues.

CURRENT MODEL

Recently, Swanson, Ashbaker, and Lee (1996) articulated a hypothesis that LD readers are deficient in the executive storage system of WM. They argued that previous studies that suggest LD readers' WM problems are isolated to a verbal system (such as phonological coding) utilized tasks that were not functionally equivalent to visual-spatial tasks, at least with respect to processing demands. That is, they found support for a domain-specific verbal deficit under conditions confounded by idiosyncratic processing (initial testing conditions) and conditions that enhance access to previously presented information (cued conditions), whereas deficits emerged on both verbal and visual-spatial conditions under high demand processing conditions. In their study, deficiencies in LD readers' WM performance on verbal and visual-spatial tasks were investigated by using cues to bring readers' performance to an asymptotic level. Estimates of individual differences in processing efficiency were obtained by the number of probes necessary to help subjects reinstate the memory trace and/or retrieve forgotten items. This condition, referred to as the gain condition, allowed participants to use several probes to access previously forgotten information. Such procedures provided an estimate of the information accessible in memory. Estimates of individual demands on storage were assessed by reinstating the highest level achieved successfully under gain conditions, but without probes (referred to as the *maintenance* condition). The authors assumed that if memory conditions are matched to the highest level that individual subjects can perform with help, and the items that established those levels are again readminstered, then ability group differences in recalling those same items are partially attributable to capacity (storage) limits that influence the preservation of the memory trace. They further reasoned that if LD readers are provided help to access previously presented information, then residual differences between LD and skilled readers were due to the availability of the contents within a limited capacity WM system. They found ability group differences were primarily isolated to high demand conditions (maintenance conditions) when compared to initial and high access (gain) conditions. These differences were manifested on *both* verbal and visual-spatial WM tasks, suggesting that a general storage system underlies LD readers' WM deficits.

MODELS OF CHANGE

The limitations in Swanson, Ashbaker, and Lee's (1996) conclusions are that they did not investigate the contribution of processing efficiency to *actual changes* in WM performance. It is possible that some LD readers under cued recall conditions (gain conditions) did overcome their initial processing problems, whereas others may have shown a remission of WM problems at the later retest. Both types of performances would suggest that processing inefficiencies, rather than storage, underlie performance across memory conditions. More importantly, individual differences in WM changes across conditions confound interpretations about whether to attribute ability group differences to processing efficiency or capacity. Implicit in previous analyses of observed changes in memory behavior has been the assumption that the effects of measurement errors on memory changes are generally benign and that the observed differences between LD and NLD children over processing conditions faithfully reflect processes that are stable in memory. These assumptions are questionable, and in particular it is likely that the presence of measurement errors in multiple tests of memory inflate estimates of LD-NLD group differences and therefore reflect the effects of measurement errors rather than genuine changes in memory.

For example, although processing constraints under high demand conditions may underlie most of the variance that separates LD and skilled readers under high demand conditions, there may be significant residual variance in WM between ability groups that is related to processing efficiency. One could argue that if processing conditions do not substantially change behavior on verbal tasks, but do on visual-spatial tasks, then one *cannot* assume that the residual differences between ability groups are primarily related to a general storage system (e.g., Stothard & Hulme, 1992). Simply stated, WM performance tested at three different occasions (initial, gain, and maintenance) confounds processes that lead (or fail to lead) to changes in WM. The Swanson, Ashbaker and Lee (1996) findings did not allow for an estimate of the amount of change that occurred in the LD readers under cued (gain) or maintenance conditions.

The model considered in this chapter assumes that executive processes are used to maintain associations across tasks and that a child with a learning disability cannot efficiently maintain these associations. This results in less change in WM performance across seemingly dissimilar tasks when compared to their chronologically age-matched peers. However, when excessive demands are *not* made on the executive system, performance differences between LD and NRLD readers are isolated to the verbal system. Thus, we assume that executive processing plays a major role in the degree of change that occurs in the WM performance of LD readers. Our prediction is consistent with most models of executive dysfunctions which assume there is just one central executive regardless of task and it is called into play only when the activities of multiple components of the cognitive architecture must be coordinated (e.g., Baddeley, 1990; Morris & Jones, 1990; Salthouse & Babcock, 1991). We further reason that a hallmark of an executive processing deficit is a failure to allocate resources efficiently (e.g., Baddeley, 1986). This deficit manifests itself in the selecting of retrieval strategies that enable new information to be retrieved at a later point (Shallice, 1988), and/or the switching and maintaining of a mental set (e.g., Teasdale, Proctor, Lloyd, & Baddeley, 1993). Thus, we argue that an analysis of quantitative and qualitative change in WM performance would be critical to any theory which suggests that executive processing plays a role in the reading problems. A model of change would also be helpful in understanding the pattern of performance between ability groups that reflect processing efficiency and/or capacity from a general or WM specific system. In terms of model building, there has been relatively little data collected on changes in LD readers' WM, despite general agreement that WM is a critical variable in predicting reading. This is interesting, because learning disabilities reflects, by definition, a poor responsiveness to interventions that reflect the best instructional practices.

Before we refine our model, however, some discussion of how change is analyzed in the present study is necessary. In a change analysis, the two variables of interest are the initial status and the parameters of change, in simple, a straight-line change model includes the intercept and the slope, respectively. Traditionally, the correlates related to the parameters (slopes) are of primary interest in identifying the processes associated with change (e.g., Francis, Fletcher, Stuebing, Davidson, & Thompson 1991). These parameters were investigated in the present study in two ways. First, the parameters related to differences between maintenance and initial performance were analyzed. It is assumed that an LD reader's WM span scores at the initial testing condition (time 1) can vary from the maintenance testing condition (time-1 plus some increment). Thus, change in WM performance is described as the difference between two testing times (t and $t - 1$). The degree of change is reflected in the slope relating the initial (t) to the maintenance condition ($t - 1$). The *processes* correlated with this slope line are of particular interest in testing the viability of a processing efficiency or capacity model. Specifically, a capacity hypothesis suggests that changes in performance due to procedures that increase processing efficiency are constrained by a limited capacity system. If LD and NLD readers vary in this general capacity system, then an interaction on the dependent measures related to the parameters of change (slopes related to the difference scores of maintenance and initial conditions) is expected to emerge between ability groups on measures of processing efficiency. In the present study, processing efficiency is measured by the number of probes necessary to achieve asymptotic performance (i.e., maximum performance on the gain condition). In contrast, a processing efficiency model suggests that because comparable storage ability exists between ability groups, processing efficiency measures (probe scores) would not be expected to interact with ability group on the parameters of change (i.e., slope). Support for a general system is implicated if the interactions occur across memory tasks, whereas support for a specific storage system is implicated when the interactions are isolated to a particular task (e.g., phonological task).

A second means to analyze change comes from the performance trajectory across all WM conditions. In the present design, the three WM conditions are initial, gain, and maintenance performance. With three data points, a quadratic model would perfectly reproduce all the observed trajectories. (This is a simple extension of the principle that two points determine a straight line.) Although the previous work of Swanson (Swanson, 1992; 1993b; Swanson, Ashbaker, & Lee, 1996) shows that WM performance of LD readers improves from the initial to gain conditions, it is uncertain when the maintenance conditions are presented if LD readers' WM performance falls off precipitously when compared to the NLD student. If the degree of change in the trajectories varies significantly between groups, it may be that the conditions that are designed to increase processing efficiency (probing) and retrieval of items (gain performance) yield a qualitatively different influence on LD and NLD readers' performance. Thus, two competing models can be tested. A capacity model suggests that because a general system operates across processing modalities (verbal and visual-spatial), performance change (i.e., slopes) does not vary across tasks, but does vary between ability groups. Therefore, the slopes related to a quadratic trajectory are expected to vary between ability groups, but not necessarily between verbal and visual-spatial WM tasks. In contrast, a processing efficiency model predicts comparable slopes between ability groups on the quadratic trajectory. A model which suggests that LD readers' WM deficits are isolated to a specific system predicts that the trajectories differ between groups on specific tasks. In this case, the verbal WM tasks would yield ability group differences on slopes when compared to the visual-spatial tasks.

Three studies are presented that analyze changes in the WM performance of LD readers. The rationale for the present studies can be understood within the context of Baddeley's (1986) WM model. The model consists of a limited general capacity control system, the central executive, assisted by two slave storage systems, a visual-spatial (visuo-spatial sketchpad) and a verbal (articulatory loop) system. Although all three systems include both storage and processing operations, the central executive includes nonspecialized storage space in which control operations draw information, whereas the slave systems are specialized to verbal or visual-spatial information. On the basis of this model, it seems reasonable that if individuals are provided help in overcoming processing inefficiencies, then the remaining performance differences between individuals will depend on a storage system. Further, conditions that place high demands on verbal and visual-spatial WM are more likely to draw from a general storage or central executive system (these two terms are used interchangeably in this chapter) than those conditions that place low demands on processing.

In summary, our aim in reviewing these three studies is to assess whether a general storage system underlies LD readers' WM deficits. We review whether individual differences in WM are related to processing and storage functions of a general (executive) or specific (e.g., articulatory) system. Our major assumption is that change in LD readers' WM performance is directly related to an executive system (a pervasive deficit across all WM tasks), whereas conditions that fail to take into consideration changes in performance are likely to show support for a deficit in the articulatory system (LD readers perform better on visual-spatial than verbal WM tasks relative to normal readers). To this end, Study 1 compares ability group performance on phonological visual-spatial, and semantic WM tasks. The hypothesis under investigation is that LD readers experience generalized deficits in WM conditions that make high demands on resources (maintenance conditions). Ability group differences are predicted to emerge on high demand conditions across phonemic, semantic and visual-spatial measures. More importantly, changes in

WM are assumed to be constrained by limitations in a general storage system, and therefore it was predicted that ability group interactions would emerge on the parameters related to processing efficiency across verbal and visual-spatial tasks. Study 2 tests whether the pattern of change in WM varies across poor reading groups. Although storage deficits have, been postulated to underlie differences between LD and normal readers (Swanson, Ashbaker, & Lee, 1996), the literature is unclear about whether groups matched on poor reading vary in storage or processing efficiency. Thus, no predictions were made about whether comparable capacity deficits exist between subtypes of poor readers or whether processing efficiency may be stronger in some subgroups of poor readers when compared to LD-readers. Study 3 tests whether LD readers subgrouped by executive processing performance vary in the degree of change manifested on verbal and visual-spatial WM tasks. It was predicted that if LD and NLD readers are matched on executive processing performance, then changes in WM performance would be comparable between ability groups.

STUDY 1

The hypothesis investigated in Study 1 is that changes in LD readers' WM performance are constrained by a general storage system. To examine this hypothesis, verbal and visual-spatial WM tasks were presented under three conditions: (a) without probes (cues) to assess initial performance (initial condition), (b) with probes to optimize performance (gain condition), and (c) without probes on the highest level of performance achieved under gain conditions (maintenance condition). In the present study, cuing is viewed as a procedure to reintegrate (amplify, strengthen) storage and improve retrieval of the memory trace (see Brainerd, Reyna, Howe, & Kingma, 1990). Cued retrieval also involves the activation of memory traces to produce a set of properties that might not directly correspond to the memory trace as originally stored.

Based on the systematic cuing procedures, two competing hypotheses are considered. First, if LD readers' WM deficits are due to primarily processing efficiency, then procedures that facilitate access to previously presented material ought to bring LD readers and NLD readers to approximately the same asymptotic level. On the other hand, if LD readers' WM deficits are due to storage capacity, then procedures that facilitate access to previously presented information would not bring them to the same level of performance as chronologically age-matched children.

Several measures are used to test these two competing interpretations. Processing efficiency in this study was defined as the number of probes necessary to achieve an asymptotic level (gain score), independent of the level of WM performance achieved. The number of probes used to retrieve information provides an estimate of the status of information in memory. A finding of ability group differences on the gain condition would support the inference that a failure to activate or maintain information in storage is an important determinant of reading ability. The major limitation in interpreting gain performance, however, is that there is no basis for specifying individual demands on storage. Thus, it is necessary to reinstate the highest level achieved successfully under gain conditions, but without probes (referred to as the maintenance condition). It is assumed that if memory conditions are matched to the highest level individual subjects can perform with help, and the items that established those levels are again readminstered, then ability group differences are attributable to capacity limits that influence the preservation of the memory trace.

Also considered in the analysis are *changes* in WM performance between the initial and maintenance conditions. Ability group differences in *change* are inferred from the parameter estimates (slopes) related to the difference score between the initial and maintenance conditions. The capacity hypothesis predicts that the ability group factor will interact with processing efficiency (i.e., probe score) parameter (slope estimate) that predicts the difference score. That is, if changes in WM reflect individual differences in a general capacity system, then an interaction would "qualify" any change between the initial and maintenance score. Support for a *general* capacity model occurs when a significant ability group × processing efficiency interaction emerges on both verbal and visual-spatial tasks, whereas a *specific* storage system model (i.e., ability group differences in WM are isolated to phonological information) suggests that the interactions are isolated to verbal tasks. On the other hand, if a general capacity system is comparable between reading groups, measures of processing efficiency would not interact with the ability group factor. That is, if changes in WM are primarily predicted by processing efficiency (the number of probes necessary to achieve the gain score), then no significant interaction would be expected to emerge between the predictors of ability group and processing efficiency.

Methods

Participants

Eighty-four (84) children participated in this study. All children's primary language was English. Some of the sample was drawn from a standardization of WM measures (Swanson, 1995), whereas others were drawn from private schools that provide services primarily for children with dyslexia. CA-M and RL children were primarily drawn from upper-middle class public schools. Mean chronological age was 12.82 (SD = 1.98) for LD readers ($N = 22$; 13 males, 9 females), 13.49 (SD = 1.73) for chronological age matched (CA-M) children ($N = 32$; 16 males, 16 females), and 6.83 (SD = .89) for reading-level matched children ($N = 30$, 14 males, 16 females). For LD students to be included in this study, their Full Scale WISC-R or WISC III scores during had to be greater than 85. Although the reported IQ scores by school psychologists indicated all LD readers were > 85, we did not have access to those scores. No significant differences were found between LD and CA-Matched children on age, $F < 1.0$.

To be defined as normal-achieving, the child had to have Reading and Arithmetic subtest percentile scores on the Wide Range Achievement Test (WRAT) greater than 45. To be defined as a LD reader, the child's percentile score on the reading subtest of the WRAT had to be less than 25 (standard score < 90). All children were administered the reading and arithmetic subtest from the Wide Range Achievement Test (Jastak & Wilkenson, 1984). Ethnicity of the sample was 82 percent Anglo-European, 5 percent Afro-American, 8 percent Hispanic, and 2 percent other.

Learning disabled readers were matched as closely as possible to younger average achieving children on raw scores from the reading subtest of the WRAT-R. Significant differences in raw scores were found between the three reading groups in word recognition and mathematics. A Tukey Test indicated that significant differences emerged between groups for reading: chronologically age-matched (CAM; M = 61.23, SD = 9.29) > reading level-matched (RL; M = 28.16, SD = 7.01) and LD readers (LD-R; M = 27.40, SD = 7.76), RL = LD-R; and mathematics: CAM (M = 32.46, SD = 10.81) > LD-R (M = 28.77, SD = 5.60) > RL (M = 18.24, SD = 4.60). Standard scores for the reading and mathematics were 81.88 (SD = 5.41, range 66 to 87) 92.56 (SD = 6.52, range 85 to 108); 98.81 (SD = 8.26, range 90 to 114), 107.55 (SD = 9.76; range 80 to 126); 108.58 (SD = 7.41; range 98 to 124), 108.62 (SD = 13.98, range 85 to 134) for LD-R, RL and CAM children, respectively. Thus, as in Siegel and Ryan (1989), the LD children suffered both in reading and arithmetic. As stated "it is difficult to find RD children who do not also have problems with arithmetic, particularly when calculation is involved, because of the required reading of number and symbols in the tasks" (p. 975). No significant difference ($p > .05$) was found between the CAM and LD-R group in chronological age. Because the groups were comparable in the proportion of males and females, this factor was not considered further.

Working-Memory Battery

This study draws from previous work (Swanson, 1992, 1993b, 1996) which has developed a number of WM tasks that have similar or common formats, but involve different types of information. The WM tasks were designed to conform with Baddeley's (1986) definition that they "require simultaneous processing and storage of information" and "measure various contents" (pp. 34–35). A critical feature of the WM tasks is that they require the maintenance of some information during the processing of other information. Consistent with Daneman and Carpenter's WM measures (1980), the processing of information is assessed by asking children simple questions about the to-be-remembered material (storage + processing demands), whereas storage is assessed by accuracy of item retrieval (storage demands only). The process question generally requires a simple recognition of new and old information, and is analogous to Daneman and Carpenter's task which requires a yes/no response to previously presented information. It is important to note, however, that the difficulty of the processing question remains constant within task conditions, thereby allowing the source of performance differences to reflect increases in storage demands. A previous study with a different sample (Swanson, 1992) has established the construct validity and reliability of the measures.

Working memory tasks were divided into those that required the recall of phonemic, semantic, and visual-spatial information.

Rhyming (also referred to as the Phonological Task)

The purpose of this task is to assess the child's recall of acoustically similar words. The child listens to sets of words that rhyme. Each successive word in the set is presented every two seconds. There are nine word sets that range from two to 14 monosyllabic words. Before recalling two the words, the subject is asked whether a particular word was included in the set. For example, the subject is presented the words "lip-slip-clip" and then asked if "ship" or "lip" was presented in the word set. The subject is then asked to recall the previously presented words ("lip-slip-clip") in order. The dependent measure is the number of sets recalled correctly (range of 0 to 9).

If the child omits, inserts or incorrectly orders the words, a series of probe responses are presented. Probe responses continue until the child can no longer provide the correct response. For example, consider the sample item "car-star-bar-far" (Item #3) and the process question "which word did I say—jar or star?" Based on the error, the probe sequence may proceed as follows:

Consider the Probe Sequence:

1. The last word in the sequence was "far." Now can you tell me all the words in order?
2. The first word in the sequence was "car." Now can you tell me all the words in order?
3. The middle words in the sequence are "star" and "bar." Now can you tell me all the words in order?
4. All the words in order are "car-star-bar-far." Now can you tell me all the words?

For each set not recalled in the correct order or for items left out or substituted, the experimenter provides a series of hints based on the error that is closest to Probe 1. That is, probes go from the least obvious hint (Probe 1) to the next explicit hint that facilitates recall of the answer. Once the appropriate hint has been identified, based on the location of the error, probes are presented in order until the correct sequence is given. For example, suppose the child for Item #3 responds "car-bar-far." The child obviously left out a word in the middle so the experimenter would provide a hint related to the middle words (Probe 3 in this case). If Probe 3 does not provide the correct response, the experimenter would then move to Probe 4. In contrast, if the child responds initially by saying only "car," the sequence would begin with Probe 1 and proceed through all probes until the correct response is given. If a correct response does not occur after the probing, the task is discontinued and the next task is administered.

Sematic Association Task

The purpose of this task is to determine the child's ability to organize words into abstract categories. The child is presented a set of words (one every two seconds), asked a process question, and asked to recall the words that go together. For example, some words to be categorized (for Set no. 3) include: shirt, saw, pants, hammer, shoes, nails. The child is directed to retrieve the words that go together (i.e., shirt, pants, and shoes; saw, hammer, and nails). The process question is "Which word, 'saw' or 'level,' was said in the list of words?" Thus, the task requires the child to transform information that has been encoded serially into categories during the retrieval phase. The child is told that the words can be recalled in any temporal order within a particular category, provided the words are related to the appropriate category. The range of difficulty is two categories of two words, to five categories of four words. The dependent measure is the number of sets recalled correctly (range of 0 to 8). Based on the type of error, the Probe Questions may include the following sequence:

1. The child is told the categories and the final word that appears in the list within each category of the words (e.g., tools and nails; clothes and shoes) and then asked to recall all the words.
2. The child is told the category names and the first word within that category appears in the list (e.g., tools and saw, clothes and shirt).
3. The child is told the word category and each middle word in the category (e.g., tools and hammer, clothes and pants).
4. The child is presented all words in the original order and asked to recall words by category.

Visual Matrix Task

The purpose of this task is to assess the child's ability to remember visual sequences within a matrix. The child is presented a series of dots in a matrix and is allowed five seconds to study the matrix. The matrix is removed and the child is asked a process question, namely, "Are there any dots in the first column?" To insure the understanding the concept of column, the experimenter points to the first column on a blank matrix (a grid with no dots). After answering the process question, the child is asked to draw the dots in the correct boxes on the blank matrix. The task difficulty ranges from a matrix of 4 squares and 2 dots to a matrix of 45 squares and 12 dots. The dependent measure was the number of matrices recalled correctly (range of 0 to 11). If an error occurs, probe questions are implemented. Probe procedures follow the same format as the other two tasks, except that the matrices are represented as columns that reflect recency, primacy, and middle positions. For example, when probing for errors that occurred in the recency position, the experimenter draws dots on a blank matrix in the appropriate last columns and says "Now can you tell me where the rest of the dots go?"

Dependent Measures

Along with initial testing scores; gain, maintenance, and probe scores were obtained. To measure gain performance, WM was tested under conditions that use a series of graduated probes to enhance item accessibility. A gain score, or asymptotic level, is defined as the highest score that is obtainable under probing conditions. Maintenance performance was established by readministering the highest item on the gain condition, but without probes. Maintenance performance was established after all three tasks under initial and gain conditions were administered. The maintenance score reflects the stability of the asymptotic level after the probing condition has been removed. This measure was scored dichotomously so that if the gain score was not maintained, the initial score was assigned to the child. If the gain score was maintained, the maintenance score matched the gain score. A probe score was the number of hints needed to achieve the gain score. All children were administered tasks in which initial, probe, gain, and maintenance scores were determined. All items on WM tasks were administered until probing did not improve performance. For children who were not able to respond correctly to the process question (< 1% of the sample) on a particular item, item recall was not requested and their response was scored as reflecting the last series of items recalled correctly.

Procedure

Each subject was tested individually by graduate students. All examiners were trained prior to the testing of children. Total testing time on the three tasks was approximately 30 minutes per student. All items for the initial condition were administered until (a) a process question was missed or (b) an error in retrieval occurred. If an error in retrieval occurred (a child omitted, inserted, or incorrectly ordered the numbers, dots, words, related to the appropriate task), probes were administered. The only stipulation for instituting the probing condition was that the process question be answered correctly. Probes were administered based on the type of error made (i.e., whether the error is related to recency, primacy, or middle items), and probing procedures continued until all targeted items cannot be recalled correctly.

After all three tasks administered under initial and gain conditions, are readminstered the items for the highest successful set (highest item established under gain conditions) for each task. The general instructions were "These items were presented to you earlier—I want to see what you can remember this time without hints."

Order effects were tested in an earlier pilot study. Thirty normal-achieving subjects (ages 7–12) were administered the tasks that included six different presentation orders. Children in groups of five were randomly assigned to one of the presentation orders. An analysis of variance on the factor of presentation order was not significant, $F < 1$. Thus, tasks were administered in the following order: Rhyming, Visual Matrix, Semantic Association.

Results

Table 1 shows the means and standard deviations for the dependent measures. Prior to analyzing scores across the three conditions, effect sizes were calculated to determine if probing conditions influenced performance. Effect sizes were calculated for gain scores as ES = ([Mean of gain-mean of initial]/standard deviation of initial scores) and for maintenance scores as ES = ([Mean of maintenance-mean of initial performance]/standard deviation of initial scores). According to Cohen (1977), effect sizes less than or equal to .10 are small, between .30 and

Table 1. Working Memory Performance as a Function of Task, Condition and Ability Group (Study 1)

	LD		*CA-Matched*		*RL Matched*		
	M	*SD*	*M*	*SD*	*M*	*SD*	*F-ratio*
			Initial				
Rhyming	2.09	1.01	2.48	1.09	2.13	1.33	.98
Visual Matrix	3.77	.92	4.58	1.14	2.33	1.02	35.62** CA > LD = RL
Semantic	1.68	1.21	2.61	1.56	2.26	1.68	2.46
			Gain (Cued)				
Rhyming	2.72	1.63	4.00	1.29	3.10	1.49	5.60* CA > RL = LD
Visual Matrix	4.36	1.21	6.62	2.07	3.53	2.11	21.69** CA > RL = LD
Semantic	1.95	1.46	4.65	1.47	3.63	2.08	16.48** CA > RL > LD
			Maintenance				
Rhyming	2.45	1.14	3.06	1.18	2.76	1.52	1.39
Visual Matrix	4.04	1.21	5.37	1.28	3.06	1.87	17.48** CA > RL = LD
Semantic	1.81	1.29	3.64	1.74	3.13	2.11	6.90** CA > RL, CA > LD, RL > LD
			Probe				
Rhyming	2.13	3.87	3.62	2.56	2.50	2.09	
Visual Matrix	2.36	3.78	3.48	3.20	1.90	3.32	
Semantic	1.22	2.77	3.62	2.77	2.33	2.92	

.50 are medium, and greater than .80 are large. As can be calculated from Table 1, probing procedures had an impact on all tasks for all reading groups. The results indicated that the effect sizes for gain performance on phonemic, visual-spatial, and semantic tasks were .62, .64. and .22 for LD readers, .72, 1.16, .83 for reading matched, and 1.39 1.72, and 1.30 for CA-matched children, respectively. The results indicate that the effect size for maintenance performance on phonemic, visual-spatial, and semantic tasks were .35, .29. and .11 for LD readers, .47, .71, .52 for reading matched and .52, .64, and .66 for CA-matched children, respectively. Thus, the CA group improved approximately 1 1/2 standard deviations in performance on the gain condition, whereas the RL group improved approximately 3/4 standard deviations and the LD-R group improved 1/2 standard deviation. One notable exception was the semantic condition for LD-R children in which the effect size was extremely low. The RL and CA group improved approximately 1/2 of a standard deviation on the maintenance condition, whereas the LD group improved approximately 1/4 standard deviation. Thus, all groups were responsive to probes (to cues). The mean number of probes for each group is shown in Table 1. A MANOVA for the group effect on the number of probes used to achieve gain performance for the three tasks was not significant.

A Multivariate Analysis of Variance across task scores indicated that a significant reading group effect occurred for the initial, gain, and the maintenance conditions. As shown in Table 1, the majority of univariate analyses were significant.

Trend Analysis

It was predicted that ability groups would differ across the three conditions and that a quadratic trend would capture most of the performance. Figure 1 illustrates the quadratic trend for all three ability groups. To determine if the degree of change varied statistically between ability groups, span scores from the initial, gain, and maintenance conditions were submitted to a repeated measures polynomial analysis of variance. Meredith and Tisak (1990) indicate that repeated measures polynomial analysis of variance models are special cases of Latent Growth Models in which the factor means are of interest. The design was a 2 (ability group) × 3 (condition: initial, gain, maintenance) ANOVA with repeated measures on the last factor as function of the type of tasks (phonological, visual-spatial, semantic).

Phonological Task

The group main effect and memory condition effect was significant. As shown in Figure 1, a Tukey test indicated that gain scores were significantly higher than maintenance and initial scores (Gain > initial = maintenance). The interaction of ability group × condition was also significant. The tests of simple effects are shown in Table 1, and indicate that ability group differences are isolated to the gain conditions (Tukey Test indicated CA > RL > LD). Ability group differences were

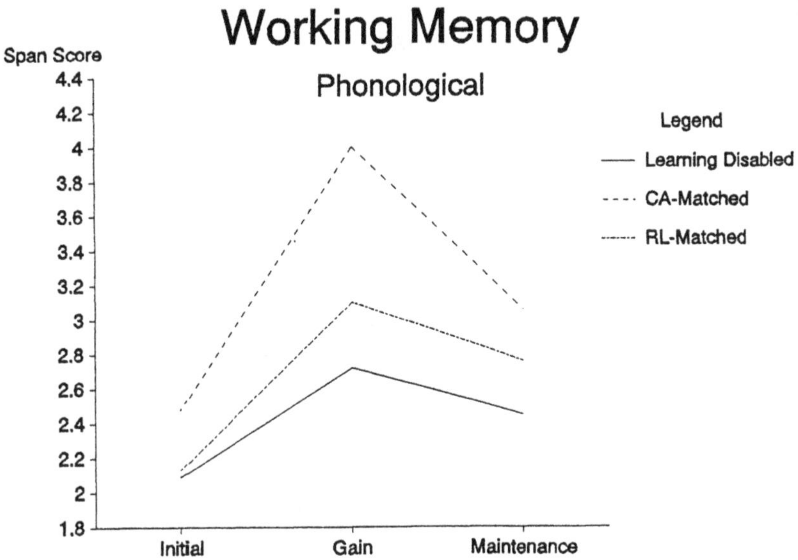

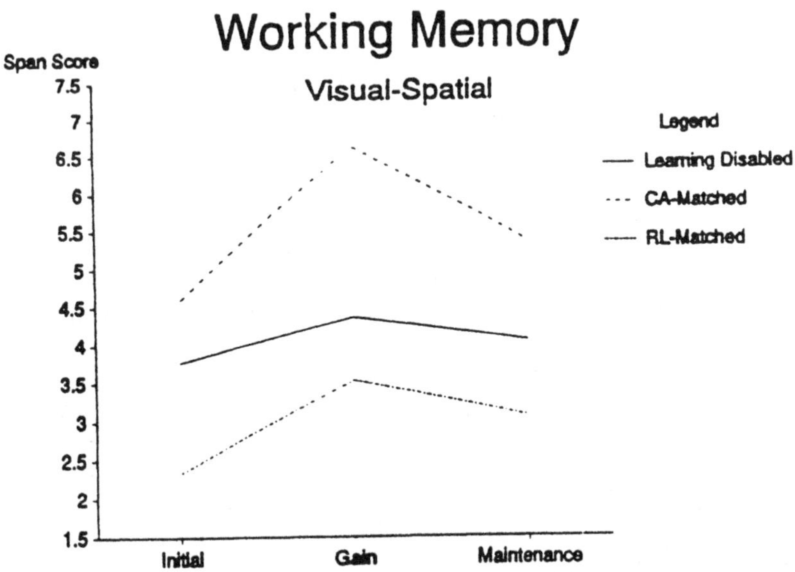

Figure 1. Mean Span Scores for Study 1 as a Function of Ability Group, Condition, and Type of Task (continued)

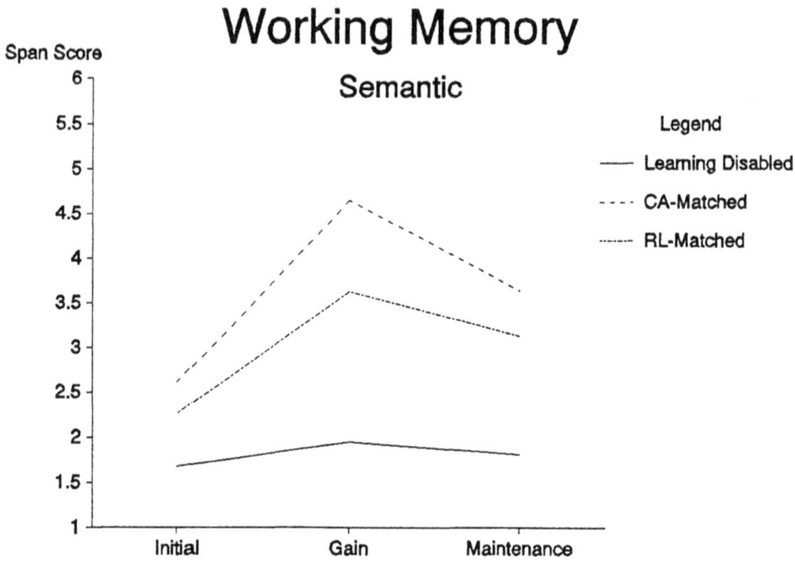

Figure 1. Continued

greater on gain than initial conditions, but comparable between initial and maintenance conditions.

To determine if the interactions primarily reflect a quadratic trend, polynomial contrasts were made. The linear effect was significant, suggesting a trend of improvement across testing conditions from the initial condition. This trend accounted for 25 percent of the variation (SS = 11.05 / SS = 43.75 for main effect of condition). The slopes did not vary significantly between groups on the linear trend. The quadratic components accounted for 75 percent of the variance. As predicted, the slope varied between groups on the quadratic trend. As shown in Figure 1, the curvature is steeper for the CA-M children when compared to the LD-R group. No significant differences were found between LD and RL in the curvature; but significant differences emerged between CA-M and LD-R children. A significant difference was also found between CA and RL children. The total group mean quadratic estimate was −1.38 (SD = .39). Removing the LD-readers from the total sample decreased the down curve [M = −.42, SD = .32)], whereas systematically removing the CA and RL from the total sample (i.e., leaving LD's in the analysis) increased the down curve (M = −.77, SD = .39; M = −1.70, SD = .55, respectively). Taken together, the results indicate less change in the LD group.

Visual-spatial Task

A significant effect emerged for ability group, memory condition, and the ability group × memory condition interaction. Tests of simple effects indicated ability group differences emerged on initial condition [significant differences ($p < .05$) in mean scores on the Tukey Test indicated CA > LD > RL], gain conditions (Tukey Test indicated CA > LD = RL), and maintenance conditions (CA > LD = RL). Ability group contrasts between the initial and gain conditions were significant, but not between the initial and maintenance conditions, $F < 1.0$. For the polynomial contrast, the linear effect was significant, and accounted for 21 percent (SS = 14.05 / SS = 65.41 for main effect of condition) of the variation. The quadratic trend (SS = 51.40 / SS = 65.41) accounted for 78 percent of the variance. The slope estimates varied between groups on the quadratic trend, but not the linear trend, $F < 1$. For the quadratic trend, no significant differences in slope estimates were found between LD and RL. A significant difference was found between CA and RL and between CA-M and LD readers. The mean total group quadratic estimate was –.91 (SD = .26). Removing the LD readers from the total decreased the down curve [M = –.12, SD = .13; M = –.13, SD = .23, respectively), whereas removing the RL group increased the estimate (M = –1.78, SD = .45). This latter finding again suggests that less change occurred for the LD readers.

Semantic Task

The ability group effect was significant, as was the main effect for condition, and the ability group × condition interaction. Tests of simple effects indicated ability group differences emerged on gain conditions (Tukey Test yields CA = LD > RL), and maintenance conditions (Tukey Test Indicated CA = LD < RL), but not initial conditions. Ability group differences were greater on gain than initial conditions, and maintenance than initial conditions, and between gain and maintenance conditions. For the polynomial contrast, the mean effect was significant for the linear trend, and accounted for 30 percent of the variation. The quadratic trend accounted for 69 percent of the variance. The slopes varied significantly between groups on the quadratic and linear trend. A significant difference in slopes was found between LD and RL groups for the linear and quadratic trend. A significant difference in slopes was also found between LD and CA for the linear, and quadratic trend. A significant difference in slopes was also found between CA and RL for the quadratic trend, but not for the linear trend. The total group quadratic mean estimate was –1.40 (SD = .28). Removing the LD group from the total decreased the down curve [M = –.13, SD = .26)], whereas systematically removing the CA from the total sample increased the curve (M = –1.11, SD = .25). Removing the RL group from the total sample increased the estimate (M = –2.06, SD = .39). Taken together, the results clearly indicate that less change emerges in the LD group when compared to the other groups. The LD group consistently decreased (toward 0) the slope estimate for phonological, visual-spatial, and semantic tasks.

Between Task Comparisons

Of interest was whether ability group differences are greater on the phonological measures than semantic and visual spatial measures, and whether those differences interact with processing conditions. The first question was addressed by investigating whether a two-way interaction emerges between ability group × type of task (i.e., phonological, visual-spatial), whereas the other is investigated by determining whether a three-way interaction emerges between ability group × type of task and type of memory condition (initial, gain, maintenance). Because the span scores reflect different scaling, all span scores were converted to z-scores, based on the total sample. These z-scores were submitted to a 3 (ability group: CAM, LD-F, RL) × 3 (condition: initial, gain, maintenance) × 3 (Task: Phonological, Visual-Spatial, Semantic) ANOVA, with repeated measures on the last two factors. Because the scores were transformed to z-scores within tasks across conditions, no differences related to the task main effect would be expected to emerge. Figure 2 shows the mean z-score performance across processing conditions.

As would be expected from the preceding analyses, a significant effect ability group main effect emerged. The ability group × condition interaction was also significant. When compared to initial conditions, ability group differences were greater on gain, but statistically comparable on maintenance scores. A follow-up analyses of these interactions within task were addressed in the previous tests of main effects.

A significant ability group × type of task interaction emerged. The three-way interaction was not significant. As shown in Figure 2, when compared to phonological tasks, ability group differences were more pronounced for visual- spatial, and semantic tasks. As shown in Figure 2, LD readers showed lower performance on semantic than phonological conditions, whereas visual-spatial performance was higher than phonological and semantic conditions. The CA-M children have comparable performance between phonological and semantic conditions, but higher performance in the visual-spatial when compared to the phonological and semantic condition. The RL children have comparable phonological and semantic performance, but substantially lower visual-spatial performance when compared to the semantic and phonological task.

Summary

The purpose of the previous analysis was to determine if a general system underlies changes in LD readers' performance across memory conditions. Inferences about a general system are bolstered when performance patterns between ability groups are comparable across tasks and under high demand conditions. On this issue, the important results from the previous analysis related to LD readers across phonological, visual-spatial, and semantic tasks are (a) effect sizes for gain and maintenance conditions are higher for CA and RL controls than LD readers,

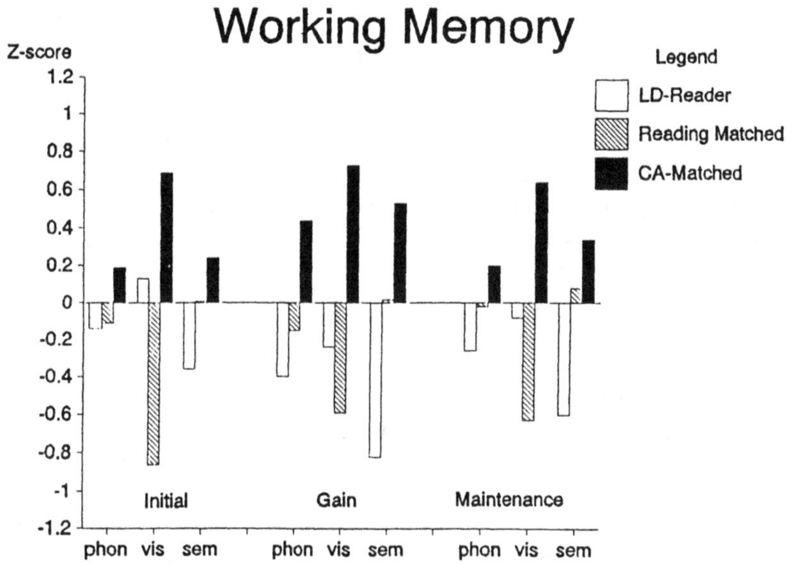

Figure 2. Mean Z-scores for Study 1 as a Function of Ability Group, Condition, and Type of Task

(b) memory span scores for the gain condition are higher for CA controls than LD readers, and (c) the slopes related to quadratic trends are steeper (suggesting less change) for LD readers when compared to CA and RL controls.

The results in support of a general system deficit in LD readers are not convincing, however, because ability group differences were also isolated to particular tasks when compared to LD readers. The results on specific span measures (subsidiary systems) were: (a) memory span scores for the initial conditions are higher for CA controls, but lower for than RL controls on the visual-matrix task, (b) RL controls are comparable in performance on phonological and visual matrix tasks and superior on semantic tasks, (c) memory span scores for the maintenance conditions are higher for CA controls on visual matrix and semantic tasks, but comparable to RL controls on visual spatial tasks, (d) RL children are superior on the semantic tasks, and (e) differences in performance are larger on visual-spatial and semantic tasks when compared to the phonological conditions for CA and RL children.

Hierarchical Regression Analysis

When compared to normal readers, LD readers were penalized more on the semantic than on the phonological task. The lack of statistical differences between LD and CA's on the phonological task when compared to other tasks may reflect interference in the phonological system on rhyming tasks for NLD readers (see

Shankweiler & Crain, 1986 for a review). Therefore, further analysis was necessary given the extensive literature separating LD-readers from average readers on phonological measures. We further analyzed the criterion variables under the three conditions (initial, gain, maintenance) by refraining the reading-matched design. Serious artifacts (e.g., regression confounds) related to reading matched designs are reviewed in Stanovich and Siegel (1994), and therefore regression-based designs are suggested to augment with the current analysis. A reframing was also necessary because it is difficult to attribute processing deficits only to reading because the LD-R group also suffers difficulties in arithmetic when compared to CA-M children, suggesting more generalized achievement deficits in the LD-R group.

Our regression design begins by partialing out the linear trend of reading and math raw scores on the WRAT-R from the criterion variable. The criterion variable (WM span) is regressed on the WRAT-R reading and mathematics scores, thus removing the variance in the criterion measure (e.g., phonological task) associated with achievement level. Subsequent to entering the WRAT-R reading and math level, simultaneous contrasts reflecting group classifications are entered into the equation. The contrasts are considered nonorthogonal (Keppel & Zedeck, 1989) and entered simultaneously into the equation. One contrast is the differences in reading between LD and non LD readers (LD-R versus CA-M & RL children) and the other contrasts children of comparable word recognition to LD-readers. The coding for the first contrast is –1 for CA-M and RL children and +1 for LD-R children. A positive beta weight for this contrast indicates that the performance of LD-R children exceeds that of the other children without reading difficulties on the criterion variable (e.g., rhyming) after partialing out the effects of reading and mathematics. The second contrast is coded as –1 for RL and +1 for LD-R and 0 for CA-M children. A positive beta weight for this contrast indicates that LD-R children outperformed the RL on the criterion variable when the effects of WRAT-R reading and mathematics and the other contrast are removed.

The interpretation of this design is straight forward. A developmental lag-model predicts that subject classification (LD versus NLD) is irrelevant once the reading (or math level) level of the subject is taken into account. Conversely, if either contrasts are significant in the equations in which reading level has been partialed out, then this would suggest that LD readers suffer processing deficits independent of their reading level. Our results are shown in Table 2.

The important results shown in Table 2 are as follows. First, achievement measures are significantly related to differences in WM for all conditions and type of tasks. The R^2 is consistently higher on gain conditions across all tasks. Second, when achievement is partialed from the analysis, the LD contrast variable (LD versus RL & CA-M) is significant on the maintenance condition for the phonological task. We cannot explain this finding except that this condition may have caused more interference in processing in.the NLD than LD readers. Third, when achievement is partialed from the analysis, the RL group is it an advantage on the

Table 2. Regression Results for Working Memory Tasks as a Function of Initial, Gain and Maintenance Conditions (Study 1)

	Rhyming			*Visual Spatial*			*Semantic*		
	Init.	*Gain*	*Main*	*Init.*	*Gain*	*Main*	*Init.*	*Gain*	*Main*
Entry Order									
Achievement									
1. Reading & Math (RS)									
R^2	.09	.19	.09	.27	.32	.27	.09	.28	.15
F-Ratio	3.79*	9.94**	3.92*	14.98**	18.99**	15.08**	4.09*	15.52**	7.05**
Contrast Variables									
2. LD-R vs. CA & RL contrast									
B	ns	.81	1.40*	–.72	–.48	–.04	.77	.65	.65
3. LD-R vs. RL contrast									
B	ns	–.82	–1.32*	1.03*	.56	.22	–.82	–.90*	–.84*
Complete Model									
R^2	.09	.23	.19	.46	.35	.32	.14	.41	.25
F-Ratio	3.78*	6.03**	4.62**	16.93**	10.69*	12.65**	3.22	13.49**	6.30*

Notes: * $p < .05$, ** $p < .001$.

phonological and semantic tasks for the maintenance condition when compared to the LD-R group. In contrast, the LD-R group is at an advantage for maintenance conditions when compared to the RL children on the visual-spatial task.

Finally, the results generally support a deficit model in verbal WM among poor readers. The results appear to reflect a visual-spatial processing strength for LD readers on visual-spatial tasks, and deficits on phonological and semantic tasks when compared to younger skilled readers. In general, the results suggest that LD readers are inferior to younger skilled readers when matched on word recognition. These differences are isolated to the verbal system (phonological and semantic) under high demand (maintenance) conditions.

Change Analysis

The previous results suggest that a verbal system, and not a general system, is involved in LD readers' WM performance. In addition, the previous results are problematic to an executive processing hypothesis because reading and mathematic performance partialed out most of the variance that separates LD and NLD readers (LD versus CA-M & RL). Thus, we sought to determine if the non significant contrast variable (LD versus CA-M & RL) may be related to the functions of executive processing. Executive processing has at least two roles: (a) access LTM stores (e.g., Baddeley, 1990; Cantor & Engle, 1993) and (b) allocate limited resources to initiate and coordinate cognitive operations (e.g., Baddeley, 1986). It is possible that the previous analysis removed all differences related to LTM access. Thus, to determine if the contrast variable may be sensitive to the coordination and allocation of resources, an analysis of changes in WM performance was instigated. More specifically, we have yet to analyze the correlates of change and whether those correlates are related to processing efficiency or processing constraints (capacity). Further, the relationship between change in WM and predictors (reading, mathematics, LD classification, asymptotic performance, processing efficacy) has not been addressed.

To address the above issues, an unbiased measure of change was computed. Willet (1994) suggests that the difference between initial and final scores provides an unbiased measure of change. Two basic strategies to measure change can be applied to difference scores (e.g., Rogosa, Brandt, & Zimowski, 1982; Rogosa & Willett, 1985; Willett, 1994). One involves the calculation of the gain scores (the difference between each subjects observed initial and final or maintenance score) which becomes the dependent variable in the regression analyses of the relationship between change and predictors of change. The second method is to treat the final (maintenance) score as the dependent variable and include the initial score as a predictor in regression analyses, thus controlling for initial status. We selected the first approach. The primary reason for using the first approach is the minimization of estimation bias in the interpretation of results (see Rogosa & Willett, 1985 for review). In contrast, the control-for-initial-status approach leads to a biased parameter estimation because the inclusion of the initial score as a covariate in subsequent regression models only imperfectly controls for true prior status (Rogosa, Brandt, & Zimowski, 1982). The control-for-initial- status method addresses a more complex question concerning the relationship between maintenance conditions and selected predictors of change if all subjects had started out equal. It is not possible, however, to control for initial status simply by including the observed initial score. Therefore, the control-for-initial-status strategy leads to a specification bias that negates the ability to draw conclusions about inter-individual differences in change (Rogosa & Willett, 1985).

Thus, an unbiased measure of change in WM as a function of ability group was computed by calculating the difference score between the maintenance and initial performance. The correlates related to this index were investigated. Three correlates were considered: processing efficiency as reflected in probe scores, item accessibility as reflected in WM performance for the gain conditions, and processing efficiency in the context of item accessibility as reflected in both the probe and gain scores.

In the present analysis, we used ordinary least squares regression analyses to construct a series of hierarchical models. The technique allowed us to fit the models to the data and to simultaneously test for the effects of ability group on each variable. In this regression model, we examined the effect of reading and mathematics achievement and LD classification, and then added asymptotic (gain scores) and processing efficiency (probe) scores as predictors. Although the previous analysis indicated LD classification was not significant (when reading and math were entered into the analysis), we have yet to determine if the LD classification variable is related to change in WM. Table 3 presents the fitted regression estimates for a series of models examining the relationship between ability group and changes in WM. Interactions between predictors were investigated, and retained where significant. Model 1 of Table 3 contains the regression coefficient estimates and the standard error estimates for a model containing reading, mathematics, and LD classification (LD versus CA-M & RL). As shown, the main effect model that includes achievement and the LD classification variable did not account for significant variance in difference scores for the phonetic, visual-spatial, and semantic task. However, the intercept (initial status) and mathematics score was significant for the phonological task. In general, children varied in initial status (intercepts), but the changes (regression coefficients) among children were statistically comparable.

Table 3. Predictors of Change (difference between maintenance and initial score) in Working Memory in Learning Disabled and Nondisabled Reader (Study 1)

	Model							
	1		*2*		*3*		*4*	
	Estim.	*SE*	*Estim.*	*SE*	*Estim.*	*SE*	*Estim.*	*SE*
Phonological Information Predictors								
Diagnostic Indicators								
Intercept	.60**	.25	.45	.25	.57**	.22	.12	.28
Word Recognition	.009	.005	.008	.006	.007	.006	.004	.005
Arithmetic	–.021*	.010	–.021*	.010	–.020*	.01	–.014	.008
LD	–.10	.10	–.19	.20	–.04	.11	–.14	.25
Responsive Indicators								
Asym Per. (AP)	—	—	.07	.06	—	—	.08	.11
LD * AP	—	—	.03	.06	—	—	.02	.10
Proc. E. (PE)	—	—	—	—	.04	.02	.74***	.15
AP*E	—	—	—	—	—	—	–.12***	.02
LD*E	—	—	—	—	–.02	.02	.52***	.14
LD*AP*PE	—	—	—	—	—	—	–.09***	.02
R^2	.08		.10		.11		.38	
df	3,79		5,77		5,77		9,73	
F	2.25		1.62		2.06		4.87**	

(continued)

Table 3. Continued

	Model							
	1		2		3		4	
	Estim.	*SE*	*Estim.*	*SE*	*Estim.*	*SE*	*Estim.*	*SE*
Visual-Spatial Information Predictors								
Diagnostic Indicators								
Intercept	.44	.42	–.07	.65	.42	.37	.15	.65
Word Recognition	.012	.011	–.003	.011	.005	.01*	.002	.010
Arithmetic	–.017	.086	–.023	–.010	–.02	.02	.015	.014
LD	–.18	.18	–.41	.55	–.009	.18	.06	.59
Responsive Indicators								
Asym Per. (AP)	—	—	.25*	.12	—	—	.001	.15
LD * AP	—	—	.04	.12	—	—	–.05	.15
Proc. E. (PE)	—	—	—	—	.15*	.04	–.43	.36
AP*PE	—	—	—	—	—	—	.12	.07
LD*PE	—	—	—	—	–.09	.04	–1.06**	.36
LD*AP*PE	—	—	—	—	—	—	.17	.07
R^2	0.4		.15		.30		.41	
df	3,79		5,77		5,77		9,73	
F	1.18		2.66		6.66**		5.72**	
Semantic Information Predictors								
Diagnostic Indicators								
Intercept	.20	.41	–.01	.42	.29	.36	.72*	.37
Word Recognition	–.001	.011	–.008	.01	–.009	.009	–.01	.008
Arithmetic	.015	.018	.005	.017	.008	.01	–.006	.014
LD	–.36	.18	.095	.30	–.06	.18	–.35	.27
Responsive Indicators								
Asym Per. (AP)	—	—	.20	.11	—	—	–.01	.11
LD * AP	—	—	–.11	.10	—	—	.05	.63
Proc. E. (PE)	—	—	—	—	.14*	.05	1.72	1.39
AP*PE	—	—	—	—	—	—	–.41	.34
LD*PE	—	—	—	—	–.13*	.05	2.18	1.39
LD*AP*PE	—	—	—	—	—	—	–.56	.34
R^2	.09		.20		.32		.50	
df	3,78		5,76		5,76		9,72	
F	2.49		3.78		7.20**		8.14**	

Notes: LD = classification-LD vs. NLD (CA-M & RL-Matched)
Estim. = Parameter Estimates,
SE = Standard Errors
AP = Asymptotic Performance-Gain Scores
PE = Processing Efficiency-Probe Scores

As shown in Table 3, Model 2 adds the highest performance on WM tasks (asymptotic or gain performance) to the baseline model, as well as the LD* Asymptotic (gain score) classification interaction. The addition to the baseline model was significant improvement for the processing of semantic information (R^2 = .09 vs. .20), but not for other types of information. There were no significant interactions. Model 3 in Table 3 adds probes and the related interactions to the baseline model. As shown, this model substantially improves the R^2 and a significant LD* processing efficiency interaction emerged for the semantic tasks. The model accounted for 30 percent of the variance.

Model 4 in Table 3 adds asymptotic (gain) performance, processing efficiency (probe scores), and the related interactions to the baseline model. As shown in Table 3, this model was significant for the processing of phonological, visual-spatial, and semantic information. The LD × processing efficiency interaction was significant for phonological, visual-spatial, and semantic information.

Taken together there are four important findings in Table 3. First, the R^2 for changes in WM is nonsignificant for the baseline model that includes the intercept (initial status), achievement, and the classification variable. That is, although these variables were important in the previous regression analysis testing a deficit or lag model, these variables do not play a significant role in predicting change. Second, the model that adds processing efficiency (probes) to the base captures about 30 percent of the variance in the visual-spatial and semantic condition. This model was not significant for the phonological tasks. Third, when item accessibility (asymptotic performance) was added to the base model no significant predictors of change emerged for any task. Finally, significant parameter estimates for the processing × LD interaction emerge across tasks for the complete (baseline, gain, probes and related interactions) model. The significant interaction provides tentative support for a storage hypothesis. That is, as suggested by the ability group × processing efficiency interaction across all tasks, processing efficiency is constrained in LD groups.

Categorical Modeling and Individual Analysis

Questions may be raised that our span scores suffer from scaling problems (e.g., floor effects on the phonological tasks). Thus, initial, gain, and maintenance performance was reanalyzed in terms of categorical variables. The initial scores were categorized in terms of high or low scores (high and low threshold; scored as 1 and 0 respectively) based on the average scores of the LD group. Those participants who had gain scores higher than their initial scores reflected change (scored as 1), whereas those participants who had initial scores that matched their gain scores were scored as no change (scored as 0). Subjects who had maintenance scores the same as their gain conditions were scored as change (1) and those who had maintenance scores that were the same as the initial scores where scored as no change (0). As shown in Table 4, performance was separated into six categories across the WM conditions. Six rather than eight (2 × 2 × 2) response categories were coded because a low initial-low gain-high maintenance category, or a high initial-low gain-high maintenance category was not possible based on the scoring system for analysis. A maximum-likelihood estimation is used because it treats all zero frequencies as structural zeros (see SAS Institute, 1989; p. 463).

Table 4 provides a profile analysis for six patterns of change in the analysis. The legend at the bottom of Table 4 provides the binary information to interpret the six patterns. As shown, the patterns of change varied among ability groups and tasks. The weakest pattern of change (*profile 1*-low initial score and no change and *profile 4*-high initial score and no change) was characteristic of LD readers for the verbal (phonemic and semantic) and visual spatial tasks. A weak profile of change emerged for the RL matched children on the visual-spatial task, whereas a positive model of change emerged on the phonological tasks.

We were concerned with how well the best fitting parameters of a categorical model predicted functions in WM across the three conditions. Categorical scores were submitted to a maximum likelihood analysis (SAS CATMOD procedure). For each model, a maximum log likelihood statistic was calculated and various models

Table 4. Percentage of Children Whose Scores Change and the Change Profile (Study 1)

	Patterns of Change						
Profile	1[a]	2	3	4	5	6	X^2 *(6)*
Phonological (Rhyming)							18.62**
LD	27	0	5	36	14	18	
RD	10	16	6	16	6	43	
CA	0	9	3	9	37	40	
Visual-Spatial							42.93**
LD	5	0	0	63	18	13	
RD	53	7	7	13	10	10	
CA	0	0	6	25	41	28	
Semantic							28.76**
LD	45	0	0	27	14	14	
RD	13	10	7	30	10	30	
CA	0	12	16	13	38	21	

Note: [a]patterns of change

	Initial	*Gain*	*Maintenance*		*Initial*	*Gain*	*Maintenance*
1.	0	0	0	2.	0	1	0
3.	0	1	1	4.	1	0	0
5.	1	1	0	6.	1	1	1

0 denotes low initial score (low threshold) or no change from initial score
1 denotes high initial score (above threshold) or positive change from initial score

were compared by seeing how this statistic changed when individual terms are *deleted* from the saturated model, using the likelihood ratio test. In our change analysis, predictors included ability group (LD, RL, and CA-M) and changes in category across the three memory conditions (status for the initial conditions, and change or no change for the gain [asymptotic] and maintenance conditions). The dependent variable was a repeated measurement factor of time of testing, (linear combination of the parameters, i.e., log of each response probability with the log probability of the last response category).

Because we are interested in ability group differences as a function of change in WM, we focused primarily on whether the removal of the interaction terms from the model made a *nonsignificant* difference in the predictive power of the model. That is, the goal of categorical modeling is to find a nonsaturated model in which the residual is nonsignificant. The "fully saturated" model contains three main effects for the initial condition [high vs. low WM span score (a score of 1 was assigned if a span score was above 1 for the phonological and semantic tasks and above 2 for the visual-spatial task) and 0 (i.e., a span score at or below 1 for phonological and semantic and at or below 2 for the visual-spatial task)], gain condition (improvement or nonimprovement from initial score vs. stable performance, scored as 1 and 0, respectively), and maintenance condition (improvement or nonimprovement from the initial condition, scored as 1 and 0, respectively) and the interactions with ability group and the three factors (the full model yields 14 contrasts and 21 parameter estimates). The maximum log likelihood statistic for the saturated model in Table 5 (e.g., 301.01 for phonological task) provides an index of how well the best fitting parameters predict WM classification for these ability groups. Three competing model were considered.

The first model contained all the terms, except the interactions related to initial status (initial score). Comparing the maximum log likelihood statistic for this model allowed us to evaluate whether initial status accounted for a significant proportion of the variance in change, i.e., whether initial status had any effect on the shape of the change curve. Model 2 contained all the terms of the saturated model, except the interactions related to gain performance. Model 3 removes all the interactions related to maintenance condition from the saturated model. Support for a specific model is found when the removal of an interaction yields a nonsaturated model in which the residual is nonsignificant. As shown in Table 5, Model 1 made no important contributions to change. Model 2 (minus gain main effects and interactions) best captures changes in performance for all three WM tasks. Model 3 captured change for the visual-spatial and semantic tasks, but not the phonological tasks.

The important findings related to the categorical modeling are that initial scores do not contribute to a model of change. Change across categories is best reflected in Model 2 which removes the interactions related to ability group performance on the gain condition. For this sample, it appears that children's initial and maintenance categories have little value in evaluating change in WM over the course of the three conditions.

Table 5. Parameter Estimates for Working Memory Obtained from Logistic Curves (Study 1)

	Total Sample Maximum Log		
	Likelihood	x^2	*p*
Phonological			
1. Full model	301.01	—	1.00
2. Model-minus initial interactions	251.64	12.74	.05*
3. Model-minus gain interactions	244.83	5.93	.11–
4. Model-minus maintenance-interactions	251.86	12.96	.05*
Visual-Spatial			
1. Full model	301.01	—	1.0
2. Model-minus initial interactions	219.51	10.03	.12
3. Model-minus gain interactions	212.87	3.39	.49–
4. Model-minus maintenance interactions	213.13	3.65	.81
Semantic			
1. Full model	301.01	—	1.0
2. Model-minus initial interactions	264.75	14.73	.02*
3. Model-minus gain interactions	257.62	7.78	.16–
4. Model-minus maintenance interactions	254.63	4.78	.78

Discussion

As expected, when the parameters of change are not analyzed, the WM memory deficits of LD readers are isolated to a verbal system. However, the findings suggest a general pattern of processing constraints for the LD-readers when changes in WM performance are considered. Support for this assumption is based on three findings. First, the correlates of change were comparable across types of WM tasks. That is, the regression analysis of difference scores yields a LD × processing efficiency interaction (see Table 3) for phonological, visual-spatial, and semantic tasks. Thus, the LD* processing efficiency interaction related to difference scores was pervasive across WM tasks. Second, categorical modeling suggested that most of the variance related to changes in WM across phonological, visual-spatial and semantic tasks can be accounted for by removing the ability group × gain score interactions from the fully saturated model. Finally, the curvilinear trend analysis suggested that LD-R differences emerged on the slopes across all memory conditions when compared to controls. Less change emerged for LD readers, when compared to the other groups.

STUDY 2

The pervasively weak change in LD readers' performance across tasks implies that a general storage system underlies their WM deficits. These results cannot be easily reconciled with the notion that a failure to make changes in LD readers' WM performance is isolated to a phonological system (articulatory loop). Functional dissociations (visual-spatial WM performance exceeds verbal WM performance for LD readers) emerged only when the analysis of performance change was *not* considered. On this account, we argued that the similarity between verbal and visual-spatial-tasks—the degree of change—involves some kind of conscious monitoring of information or material in memory, a characteristic of the central executive.

A competing interpretation to Study 1 findings is that performance across WM tasks does not reflect a common characteristic of a changing state, but rather reflects variations in the demands on phonological processing. On the surface, however, the results are difficult to reconcile with the prevalent view that WM problems of LD readers are isolated to the phonological system (e.g., Stanovich & Siegel, 1994). This is because when semantic and phonological performance was compared (after a similar scaling of the tasks, i.e., span scores were converted to z-scores), LD readers were more depressed on semantic when compared to phonological tasks, whereas the superior performance for CA children relative to LD readers was comparable across semantic and phonemic conditions. Previous studies report that poor readers are less influenced by the phonological similarity effects than good readers (Libermann, Mann, Shankweiler, & Werfelman, 1982), but other studies suggest that this effect disappears when memory span is overloaded. Thus, to investigate the influence of phonological processing on the degree of change that occurs in WM, we subgrouped poor readers on word recognition level.

Because proficiency in word recognition has been directly related to phonological awareness (e.g., Siegel & Ryan, 1989), we assumed that by matching poor readers on word recognition level there would be comparable changes in WM performance on verbal WM tasks if phonological processing underlies performance. Previous studies suggest that LD readers share similar phonological deficits with other poor readers (Stanovich & Siegel, 1994). Thus, if ability groups share a similar phonological problem, it will be possible to determine if LD readers' resistance to changes on verbal WM is the result of an articulatory or executive system. That is, matching ability groups on word recognition, as well as presenting WM tasks under low (e.g., initial and gain conditions) and high demand conditions (i.e., maintenance conditions), should yield comparable degrees of change if phonological processing underlies performance.

The purpose of Study 2 was to determine if performance changes in WM vary between LD readers and other children who are poor readers. To this end, three subgroups were created: (1) LD children with severe reading problems, (2) LD children with moderate reading problems, and (3) slow learners (referred to in the literature as poor readers, Stanovich & Siegel, 1994) Slow learners were children who achieved low reading scores that approximated their standardized intelligence score. The slow learners and severe LD readers were matched statistically on word recognition ability. We reasoned that if the articulatory system is the major contributor to LD readers' WM problems, rather than executive processing, then recall should be comparable to slow learning children under conditions that place demands on verbal coding, but not under conditions that place demands on visual-spatial coding. Because of their higher IQ and mathematics scores, one would predict an advantage in WM performance for LD readers when compared to slow learners on visual-spatial tasks. Likewise, if phonological coding underlies resistance to change in LD groups, then comparable patterns of change should occur between LD and slow learners on verbal, but not visual-spatial conditions.

In sum, if changes in verbal WM are related primarily to a phonological system in LD readers, then the following results are expected: (a) poor readers matched on word recognition would not differ in performance on verbal WM tasks, and (b) the parameters of change (slopes) would be comparable between poor readers on verbal (semantic and phonological), but not visual spatial tasks. Thus, an ability group × processing efficiency would emerge for the visual-spatial task, whereas no such interaction is expected to occur for the phonological or semantic tasks on measures of change (e.g., difference score between initial and maintenance conditions).

Method

Participants

Forty children with reading problems participated in this study. Children were subgrouped into LD readers of average verbal intelligence with severe reading disabilities (LD-R), slow learning children with low average verbal intelligence and reading (SL), and those children with moderate learning disabilities (LD-M). Mean chronological age was 11.15 (SD = 2.10) for LD readers (LD-R; $N = 13$; 10 males, 2 females), 10.51 (SD = 2.56) for slow learning children (SL; $N = 12$; 9 males, 3 females), and 10.56 (SD = 1.85) for LD children with moderate reading disabilities (LD-M; $N = 17$, 11 males, 6 females). All children were administered the reading and arithmetic subtest from the Wide Range Achievement Test (Jastak & Wilkenson, 1984), and Peabody Picture Vocabulary Test. Ethnicity of the sample was 100 percent Anglo-European. Significant differences in standard scores were found between the three groups in verbal intelligence (PPVT-R), word recognition, and mathematics. A Tukey Test indicated significant differences ($p < .05$) in standard scores between groups for:

1. Reading: LD readers (LD-R; M = 74.39, SD = 7.03) = slow learners (SL; M = 80.45, SD = 9.88) < LD-moderate (LD-M; M = 90.69, SD = 5.77);
2. Mathematics: LD-R (M = 78.66, SD = 8.53) = SL (M = 77.76, SD = 7.25) < LD-M (M = 85.02, SD = 4.63); and
3. Verbal IQ: LD-R (101.29, SD = 5.82) = LD-M (M = 106.21, SD = 10.93) > SL (M = 91.39, SD = 5.56).

The LD-M group was better in reading and mathematics than the other two groups. The slow learners matched the psychometric characteristics described in Siegel (1992) and Shaywitz, Fletcher, Holahan, and Shaywitz (1992) of poor readers whose cognitive performance was statistically comparable to LD readers. These two groups are also referred to as IQ-reading discrepancy groups in which the LD-readers have discrepancies (high differences in IQ and reading scores) and the poor readers have IQ scores that approximate their reading scores. The difference in discrepancies (verbal IQ minus reading) was significant between ability groups, $F(2,39) = 10.81, p < .01$. A Tukey Test indicated significant mean standard score differences: LD-R (M = 27.73, SD = 8.23) > LD-M (M = 15.51, SD = 10.73) = SL (M = 10.93, SD = 8.72). The difference in standard scores between Verbal IQ and mathematics was not significant $F(1,39) = 2.81, p > .05$.: LD-R(24.15, SD = 9.76) = LD-M (M = 21.19, SD = 11.73; SL (M = 14.29, SD = 7.86). The groups were comparable in the proportion of males and females, $X^2(2, N = 40) = 1.27, p > .05$, and therefore this factor was not considered further.

Method and Procedures

Same as Study 1.

Results

Table 6 shows the means and standard deviations for the dependent measures. Effect sizes were calculated for gain scores as ES = ([Mean of gain-mean of initial]/standard deviation of initial scores) and for maintenance scores as ES = ([Mean of maintenance-mean of initial performance]/standard deviation of initial scores). As can be calculated from Table 7, probing procedures had an impact on all tasks for all reading groups. The results indicated that the effect size gain performance on phonemic, visual-spatial, and semantic tasks was 2.63, 1.68 and 3.34 for LD-R, 3.42, 3.55, 1.13 for SL learners and 2.07, 2.73, and 1.06 for LD-M children, respectively. Thus, all groups improved approximately 1-3 standard deviations in performance on the gain condition. The results indicated that the effect size for maintenance performance on phonemic, visual-spatial, and semantic tasks was 1.72, .61, and 2.73 for LD-R, 1.92, .67, .92, for SL and .22, 0, and .66 for LD-M children, respectively.

The LD-M group showed the least amount of improvement on maintenance conditions (M < 1/2 standard deviations). Maintenance was weak for all groups on the visual spatial conditions. In general, all groups were responsive to probes (cues). A MANOVA for the group effect on the number of probes used to achieve gain performance for the three tasks was not significant, $F(6,74) = .68, p > .05$. The mean number of probes for each group is shown in Table 7.

Table 6. Working Memory Performance as a Function of Task, Condition and Ability Group (Study 2)

	LD-Severe		*Slow Learner LD-M*		*F-Ratio*		
	M	*SD*	*M*	*SD*	*M*	*SD*	
			Initial				
Rhyming	1.07	.75	1.83	.38	1.41	.79	3.73*
				SL > LD-S; SL = ILD-M; LD-S = LD-M			
Visual Matrix	3.61	.86	3.66	.49	3.52	.62	.15
Semantic	.38	.50	1.33	1.61	1.41	1.32	2.91
			Gain (Cued)				
Rhyming	3.07	.75	3.16	.39	3.05	.24	.18
Visual Matrix	5.07	1.25	5.41	.90	5.23	1.09	.30
Semantic	2.07	1.60	3.16	1.40	2.82	1.55	1.70
			Maintenance				
Rhyming	2.38	1.26	2.58	.79	1.58	1.01	3.84*
				SL > LD-M; SL = LD-S; LD-S = LD-M			
Visual Matrix	4.15	1.40	4.00	1.04	3.52	.62	1.50
Semantic	1.76	1.78	2.83	1.46	2.29	1.99	1.10
			Probe				
Rhyming	1.76	2.65	2.16	3.37	2.52	2.45	.27
Visual Matrix	1.77	2.31	2.33	2.60	2.88	3.60	.52
Semantic	1.92	2.59	3.66	2.74	3.23	2.19	1.72

Within Task Comparisons

Span scores were analyzed, via an Analysis of Variance, represented factorially as a 3 (*ability group*: LD-R, SL, LD-M) × 3 (*condition*: initial, gain, maintenance) design with repeated measures on the last factor as a function of the type of WM task.

For phonological tasks, a significant effect emerged for ability group, the memory condition effect, and the ability group × condition interaction. The memory condition main effect is expected in that gain scores were higher than initial and maintenance scores, and the maintenance score did not vary substantially from the initial scores. Significant simple effects for ability group emerged for the initial, and maintenance task, but not for the gain task. A Tukey test indicated that significant ($p < .05$) ability group differences emerged on the initial condition (LD-R < SL, LD-M = LD-R & SL) and maintenance condition (LD-M < SL, LD-R = LD-M & SL).

Table 7. Regression Results for Working Memory Tasks as a Function of Initial, Gain and Maintenance Conditions (Study 2)

	Rhyming			*Visual Spatial*			*Semantic*		
	Init.	*Gain*	*Main*	*Init.*	*Gain*	*Main*	*Init.*	*Gain*	*Main*
Entry Order									
Achievement									
1. Reading & Math (RS)									
R	.14	.12	.15	.24	.01	.05	.15	.26	.10
F-Ratio	2.18	2.77	3.38*	.83*	.05	1.02	3.14*	6.72**	2.27
Contrast Variables									
2. LD-R & LD-M vs. SL contrast									
B	–.47	.08	–83*	–.09	–.08	–.55	–.01	–.71*	–.73*
3. LD-R vs. SL contrast									
B	.13	–.24	.61	–.007	–.05	.52	–.26	.44	.47
Complete Model									
R	.26	.15	.29	.05	.02	.10	.21	.39	.24
F-Ratio	3.10*	1.66	3.81	.49	.21	1.07	2.47	5.48**	2.82*

Notes: * $p < .05$, ** $p < .01$
(RS) = Raw Scores

Ability group differences were higher on the maintenance than initial conditions. The first-degree (linear) polynomial was significant, and accounted for 20 percent of the variation. The quadratic trend accounted for 80 percent of the variance. The total group mean quadratic estimate was .38 (SD = .73). The slopes varied between groups on the linear, but not the quadratic trend. As shown in Figure 3, the linear trend (the tendency to be higher on the maintenance and gain conditions when compared to initial conditions) is the not same for the ability groups. The drop off in performance is higher for the LD-M group when compared to the LD-S and SL group. No significant differences in slopes were found between the LD-R and SL children, $F < 1.0$; but slope differences emerged between LD-R and LD-M children. No significant differences in slopes were found between LD-M and SL groups.

For the visual spatial WM task, the only significant effect was the main effect for condition. The first-degree (linear polynomial) was significant, but accounted for only 3 percent of the variation (SS = 1.73/SS = 62.85 for main effect of condition). The quadratic trend accounted for 97 percent of the variance. The total group mean quadratic estimate was 1.70 (SD = .46).

For the semantic WM tasks, the only significant effect was the main effect for condition. The first-degree trend (linear polynomial) was significant, and accounted

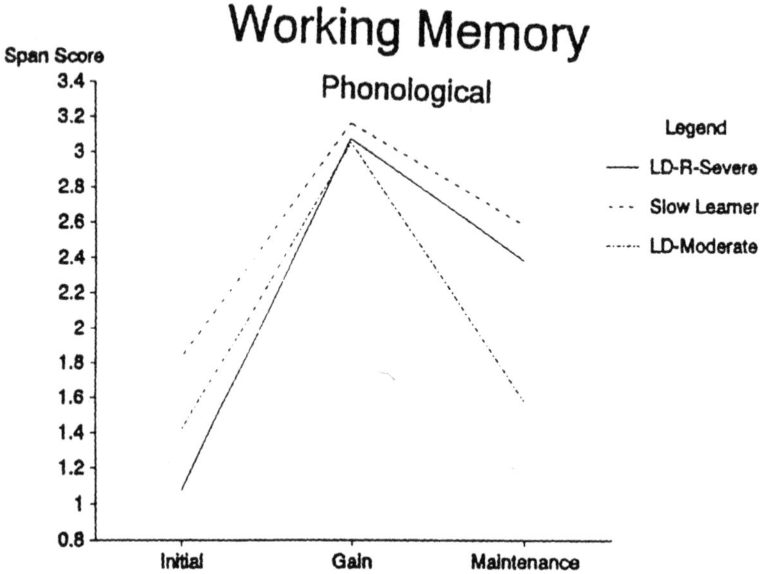

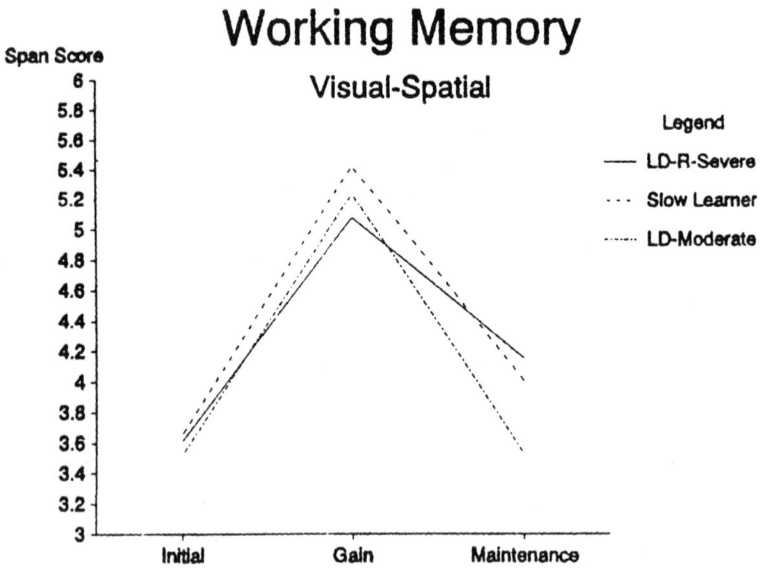

Figure 3. Mean Span Scores for Study 2 as a Function of Ability Group, Condition, and Type of Task (continued)

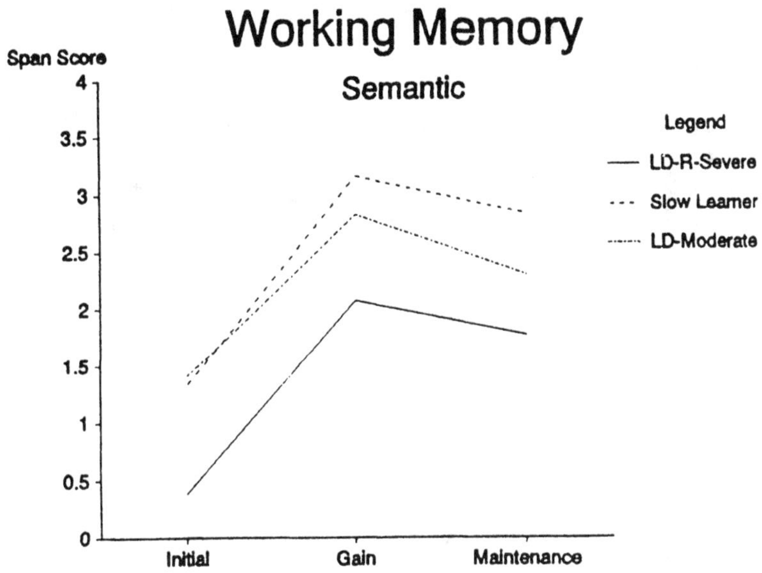

Figure 3. Continued

for 53 percent of the variation. The quadratic trend accounted for 46 percent of the variance. The total group quadratic estimate was –.80 (SD = 1.09).

Across Task Comparisons

Of interest was whether ability group differences are greater on the phonological measures than semantic and visual spatial measures, and if those differences interact with processing conditions. All span scores were converted to z-scores, based on the total sample. The mean z-scores as a function of ability groups, condition, and type of task are shown in Figure 4. These z-scores were analyzed, via a MANOVA represented factorially as a 3 (ability group: LD-R, SL, LD-M) × 3 (condition: initial, gain, maintenance) × 3 (type of task: phonemic, visual-spatial, semantic), with repeated measures on the last two factors. The only significant effect to emerge was the ability group × memory condition interaction. When compared to the initial conditions, ability group differences were greater on the maintenance conditions, but comparable on gain conditions. A Tukey Test indicated that scores were higher for the SL on the maintenance conditions (SL > LD-R > LD-M).

In summary, the analyses indicate that differences between readers are isolated to phonological information. When compared to slow learners, the LD-R children are at a disadvantage for initial conditions, and the LD-M children are at a

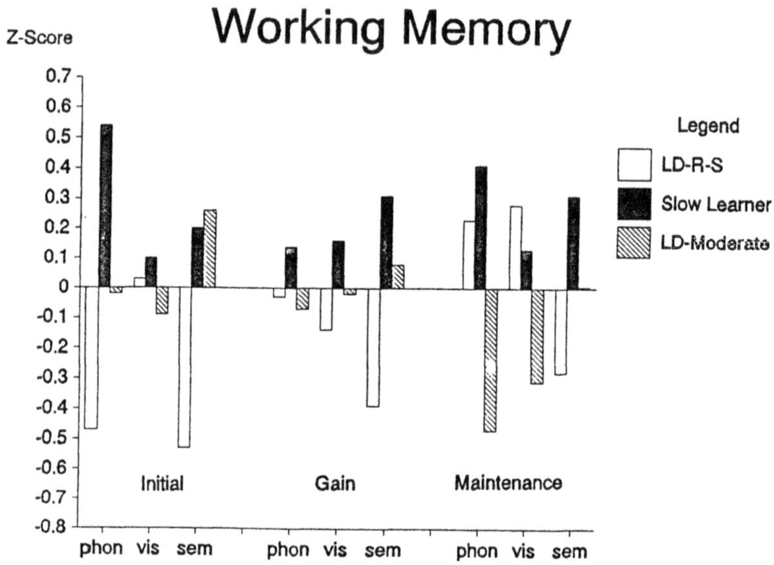

Figure 4. Mean Z-scores for Study 2 as a Function of Ability Group, Condition, and Type of Task

disadvantage for maintenance conditions. The slopes related to the quadratic trend across tasks are comparable between the SL and LD-R ability groups.

Hierarchical Regression Analysis

As in Study 1, the criterion variables under the three memory conditions (initial, gain, maintenance), were submitted to regression design which partialed from the criterion variable the linear trend of WRAT-R reading and mathematics. Subsequent to entering the achievement scores, simultaneous contrasts reflecting group classifications are entered into the equation. One contrast is the difference in poor readers who have a severe discrepancy between reading and verbal IQ (LD-R vs. LD-M & SL) and the other contrasts children of statistically comparable reading scores (LD-R versus SL). The coding for the first contrast is −1 for SL and LD-M children and +1 for LD-R children. The second contrast is coded as −1 for SL and +1 for LD-R and 0 for LD-M children.

Table 7 shows two important findings. First, reading and math level accounted for significant variance in performance for the gain conditions that included the recall of phonological and semantic information. Second, although the direction of the beta weight suggests an advantage for slow learners when compared to the two LD reading groups, the majority of the beta weights were nonsignificant. However, a significant beta weight emerged on maintenance conditions for the phonological and semantic tasks indicating that slow learners perform better on the high demand conditions than LD groups.

Change Analysis

Difference Scores

As in Study 1, change in WM was the difference score between the maintenance and initial WM performance. The regression analyses were the same as Study 1 The contrast variable of interest was between the slow learners and the LD readers matched on word recognition. We again examined the effect of reading and mathematics achievement and then added asymptotic performance (gain scores) and processing efficiency (probe scores) as predictors. Interactions between predictors were investigated, as well, as retained where significant. Table 8 presents the fitted regression estimates to a series of models examining the relationship between student characteristics and responsiveness to changes in WM. The models tested are the same as Study 1.

Table 8. Predictors of Change (difference between maintenance and initial score) in Working Memory in Learning Disabled and Nondisabled Readers (Study 2)

	Model							
	1		2		3		4	
	Estim	*SE*	*Estim*	*SE*	*Estim*	*SE*	*Estim*	*SE*
Phonological Information Predictors								
Diagnostic Indicators								
Intercept	4.41*	1.97	–1.63	2.09	2.49	1.73	1.67	11.38
Word Recognition	–.09**	.01	–.06**	.01	–.08**	.01	–.04**	.01
Arithmetic	.05*	.02	.02	.018	–.06**	.02	.037	.029
LD vs. SL	–.12	.22	.17	1.06	–.19	.23	–4.01	2.76
Responsive Indicators								
Asym Per. (AP)	—	—	1.59**	.30	—	—	–.002	1.40
LD * AP	—	—	–.03	.33	—	—	1.39	.94
Proc. E. (PE)	—	—	—	—	.22**	.04	–.5	.34
AP*PE	—	—	—	—	—	—	.06	.10
LD*PE	—	—	—	—	.06	.06	–.17	.10
LD*AP*E	—	—	—	—	—	—	ns	ns
R^2	.40		.73		.63		.74	
df	3,36		5,34		5,34		9,30	
F	8.80**		17.22**		8.59**		11.09**	

(continued)

Table 8. Continued

	Model							
	1		*2*		*3*		*4*	
	Estim	*SE*	*Estim*	*SE*	*Estim*	*SE*	*Estim*	*SE*
Visual-Spatial Information Predictors								
Diagnostic Indicators								
Intercept	1.66	1.04	1.07	1.24	1.22	1.13	.78	1.67
Word Recognition	–.02*	.006	–.02*	.01	–.02*	.05	–.016	.01
Arithmetic	.04	.01	.003	.01	.01	.01	.002	.01
LD vs SL	–.04	.12	–.30	.61	–.01	.18	–.70	1.02
Responsive Indicators								
Asym Per. (AP)	—	—	.13	.08	—	—	.11	.19
LD * AP	—	—	—	.11	—	—	.17	.21
Proc. E. (PE)	—	—	—	—	.04	.03	.10	.24
AP*PE	—	—	—	—	–.01	.05	–.01	.04
LD*PE	—	—	—	—	—	—	.52	.70
LD*AP*PE	—	—	—	—	—	—	.07	.11
R^2	.10		.18		.16		.24	
df	3,36		5,34		5,34		8,31	
F	1.41		6.55		1.32		1.08	
Semantic Information Predictors								
Diagnostic Indicators								
Intercept	4.69	2.67	4.13	2.44	1.66	2.11	2.37	2.30
Word Recognition	–.01	.026	–.04	.02	–.02	.02	–.04	.02
Arithmetic	.02	.03	–.01	.03	.008	.02	.01	.03
LD vs SL	–.36	.30	–.67	.75	–.03	.38	–.83	.87
Responsive Indicators								
Asym Per. (AP)	—	—	.42*	.14	—	—	.18	.26
LD * AP	—	—	.15	.22	—	—	.36	.32
Proc. E. (PE)	—	—	—	—	.35**	.07	.14	.22
AP*PE	—	—	—	—	—	—	.02	.06
LD*PE	—	—	—	—	–.03	.09	.23	.29
LD*AP*PE	—	—	—	—	—	—	–.09	.07
R^2	.08		.27		.46		.53	
df	3,36		5,34		5,34		9,30	
F	.98		2.61*		5.85**		3.82**	

Notes: Estim.= Parameter Estimates
SE = Standard Errors
AP = Asymptotic Performance-Gain Scores
PE = Processing Efficiency-Probe Scores

The important results in Table 8 are as follows. First, there are no interactions that emerge related to change across task conditions. Given that no main effects emerge related to the LD-R versus SL contrast, the results suggest that both groups are statistically comparable in the processing of information. Second, the base model is significant only for the phonological tasks. This model was improved by 30 percent when entering gain scores, and accounted for a substantial amount of the variance when entering gain and processing efficiency (probe) scores together (74 percent of the variance). Reading level contributes significantly to change scores across all models for the phonological task. Third, *no* significant model emerged for the visual-spatial condition. As with the phonological tasks, no significant ability group interactions emerged. Finally, for the semantic task, the complete model accounted for 65 percent of the variance. The process models were a substantial improvement from the base model for gain (accessibility) performance alone (increment in R^2 of .27), processing efficiency (probe scores) alone (increment in R^2 of .38), and accessibility and processing efficiency combined (increment in R^2 of .45). In sum, the results suggest that the shape (as reflected in the quadratic estimate) and the increments of change (as reflected in the difference scores) are comparable between groups matched on word recognition ability for phonological, visual-spatial and semantic tasks.

Categorical Modeling

It should be noted that the previous trend and regression analysis focus on the changes across groups of subjects. The disadvantage of this analysis is that change within group is not taken into consideration. That is, within group, intraindividual change is considered error in the analysis (see Francis et al., 1991 for discussion). To the extent that change occurs within groups, the three groups were next analyzed across discrete categories of change. As in Study 1, performance was separated into six categories across the WM conditions. The profile analysis of change is shown in Table 9. For the phonological list, a significant difference emerged. Forty-one percent of the moderate LD readers showed a profile of high change on the gain condition, but no change on the maintenance conditions (profile 2) when compared to the other groups. None of the severe LD readers reflected profile 6 (high initial-high gain-high maintenance), whereas 25 percent of the slow learners and 18 percent of the moderate LD readers reflect this profile.

For the visual-spatial task, no significant ability group differences emerged in profiles. Approximately 50 percent of the subjects within ability groups showed no changes in performance (profiles 1 and 4). For the semantic task, no significant differences emerged in profiles. The profiles that reflected a high degree of change were infrequent (profiles 5 & 6) for all ability groups.

Categorical scores were submitted to a maximum likelihood analysis following the procedures outlined in Study 1. Parameter estimates were obtained by maximum (log) likelihood function with respect to unknown model parameters. Again, we

Table 9. Percentage of Children Whose Scores Change and the Change Profile (Study 2)

	Patterns of Change						
Profile	*1*[a]	*2*	*3*	*4*	*5*	*6*	X^2 *(6)*
Phonological (Rhyming)							15.46**
LD-SR	31	0	38	23	08	0	
SL	41	0	17	0	17	25	
LD-M	41	41	0	0	0	18	
Visual Spatial							6.42
LD-R	24	0	07	24	15	30	
SL	25	0	0	17	41	17	
LD-M	35	0	0	24	41	0	
Semantic							7.99
LD-R	46	0	54	0	0	0	
SL	8	8	59	17	8	0	
LD-M	12	41	17	12	6	12	

Notes: *$p < .05$

[a] patterns of change

	Initial	*Gain*	*Maintenance*		*Initial*	*Gain*	*Maintenance*
1.	0	0	0	2.	0	1	0
3.	0	1	1	4.	1	0	0
5.	1	1	0	6.	1	1	1

0 denotes low initial score or no change from initial score

1 denotes high initial score or positive change from initial score

were concerned with how well the best fitting parameters of a model predict functions in WM across the three conditions. As shown in Table 10, an interaction model related to gain scores contributed substantial to change across phonemic, visual-spatial, and semantic tasks. Change across categories was best reflected in Model 2 which removes the interactions related to ability group on the gain condition (0 or 1). That is, when interactions related to the *availability* of information (gain scores) are removed from the full model, reading group changes are comparable across phonological, visual-spatial, and semantic conditions.

Discussion

Three important findings emerged. First, recall differences in semantic and phonemic information exist between LD and slow learners. The results related to the hierarchical regression model that partialed out achievement indicated that processing deficits for LD-readers were isolated to semantic and phonological information under high demand (maintenance) processing conditions when compared to slow learners. No advantage was found for visual-spatial processing for

Table 10. Parameter Estimates for Working Memory Obtained from Logistic Curves (Study 2)

	Total Sample Maximum Log		
	Likelihood	*p*	X^2
Phonological			
1. Full model	150.50	—	1.00
2. Model-minus initial interactions	141.64	41.93	.001**
3. Model-minus gain interactions	115.86	16.30	.06
4. Model-minus maintenance interactions	124.72	25.16	.001*
Visual-Spatial			
1. Full model	135.19	—	1.0
2. Model-minus initial interactions	112.84	5.30	.62
3. Model-minus gain interactions	109.90	2.36	.79
4. Model-minus maintenance interactions	119.25	11.71	.03
Semantic			
1. Full model	150.50	—	1.0***
2. Model-minus initial interactions	135.07	33.33	.001**
3. Model-minus gain interactions	113.68	11.94	.15
4. Model-minus maintenance interactions	119.88	18.14	.05

LD readers once the effects of arithmetic and reading were partialed in the analysis. Thus, the WM performance differences between LD readers and SL learners were primarily isolated to the high demand (maintenance) verbal conditions.

Second, no significant ability group differences emerged on the visual-spatial task. We predicted that if phonological coding primarily underlies ability group differences, then ability group differences in favor of the LD readers would be manifested on visual-spatial tasks, but comparable to the slow learners on the verbal conditions. Support for phonological core deficits would suggest that comparable performance would have occurred on the verbal conditions, but not the visual-spatial system. Such was not the case in this study.

Finally, an analysis of difference scores and quadratic trends suggests that processing efficiency is *comparable* between LD readers and slow learners matched on word recognition ability. However, when the data are resealed into categorical scores, the categorical modeling suggests that changes in categories are best predicted by the ability group interactions related to the gain conditions. However, when the LD-M group is removed from the categorical modeling analysis, the results indicate that the slow learners exhibited the same degree of changes across the three tasks as severe reading LD children. That is, the findings suggest a general pattern of processing that is comparable between LD and slow learners matched on reading ability.

STUDY 3

The results of Study 1 suggest that when compared to CA-matched children and younger skilled readers, that LD readers' WM performance reflects general constraints in processing, whereas the results of Study 2 suggest that when compared to poor readers, LD readers' WM performance reflects a general processing inefficiency. That is, an interaction between ability group × processing efficiency measures (e.g., probe scores) across phonological, semantic, and visual-spatial tasks on parameters related to difference scores occurred in Study 1, whereas no such interaction occurred in Study 2. The previous studies assume that LD readers' WM deficits, at least as reflected in terms of changes in WM performance, are related to a general system.

No doubt, the conclusion that a general system is involved in the depressed change scores of LD readers is not obligatory. The previous results may not be due to a general system, but simply to the fact that LD readers generally do worse than their counterparts because of lower verbal and visual-spatial WM spans and the size of the differences depends on the difficulty of the task. In addition, one can argue that reading group differences on the tasks in Study 1 and 2 do not reflect limitations in a nonspecialized general storage system (central executive system), but two specialized systems. In the previous studies, both verbal and visual-spatial tasks reflect some similarities on the gain (cued) conditions (all cues are related to serial order) that bring subjects to an asymptotic level. Thus, by using the cuing procedures, it may be argued that the integrity of each system (verbal and spatial) is emphasized, rather than a common system. The present study was designed to elucidate whether reading group differences in WM are related to a general or an isolated storage system.

In this study we reasoned that if WM deficits between reading groups are due to a general system, then reading group differences in WM should be reduced (or made comparable) when executive processing is partialed out in the analysis. This assumption is based on the Baddeley's (1986) notion that the articulatory and visual-spatial storage system have resources that operate independent of the executive system. To this end, the present study used the Sentence Span Task (Daneman & Carpenter, 1980) as an indicator of ability group differences in functional WM capacity. In this task, subjects are required to read a series of sentences for comprehension while retaining the last word of each sentence for later recall. The proportion of words retained is used as a measure of functional capacity during reading (Daneman, 1987; Daneman & Carpenter, (1983). This measure reflects not only the overall capacity of the memory system, but also the efficiency of the component reading processes (e.g., Dixon, Lefevre, & Twilley, 1988). Two subgroups on LD and NLD readers were matched on functional WM capacity. Based on the matching procedures, two competing interpretations of ability group differences can be assessed.

One interpretation is that the degree of change in WM demonstrated in LD readers reflects the independent contribution of an isolated peripheral storage system. That is, when global processing efficiency is controlled (as reflected when LD and NLD readers are matched on functional WM capacity), then residual differences that occur between reading groups are directly related to specialized verbal and visual-spatial storage systems. The rationale for these assumptions is twofold. First, a specialized activity of the central executive, resource monitoring, is reflected in the processing and storage demands on the Sentence Span Measure. The Sentence Span Measure is also correlated with visual-spatial WM (Turner & Engle, 1989) suggesting a unified construct, sensitive to processing capacity. Thus, when ability groups are matched on this general processing measure, one would expect recall differences to be directly attributed to specialized resources (verbal and/or visual-spatial).

Second, based on Baddeley's (1986, 1990) WM model, there is a unidirectional capacity transfer (central executive > verbal and visual-spatial). This implies that when demands on functional WM capacity are controlled, via the matching of children on WM capacity, the variance in performance attributed to the central executive in providing resources to the peripheral systems is also controlled. If no performance differences emerge between ability groups, then the specialized pools are not contributing a substantial amount of variance to task performance. In short, support for the peripheral storage hypothesis would be found if ability groups with comparable functional WM capacity differ in performance on the verbal or visual-spatial condition.

Based upon a previous study (Swanson, 1993a, Study 2), we anticipate no ability group differences will emerge on the semantic, phonological, and visual-spatial tasks for the ability groups matched on sentence span performance. This is because executive processing has been controlled. However, the literature is unclear about whether poor and average readers matched on low span scores exhibit the same profile of change on WM tasks. We assume that although LD-readers and average readers are equated on executive processing, they may show different patterns in performance changes across verbal, visual-spatial, and semantic tasks. This is because LD readers' limited resources are constrained by structural limitations (limitations related to neuropsychological inefficiencies), whereas average readers with poor executive processing may reflect functional problems (poor strategic allocation of resources—Carpenter & Just, 1989). A hypothesis supporting qualitative differences in processing is supported if the interactions between: ability groups matched on executive processing emerge on measures of change.

Method

Participants

Seventy-five children participated in this study. Classification of LD children was similar to Study 1. The LD sample was subgrouped into high and low executive processing as measured by the Sentence Span Task. Mean chronological age was 11.06 (SD = 2.17) for LD readers with severe executive-processing deficits (LD-S; *N* = 20; 16 males, 4 females), 11.49 (SD = 1.97) for LD-moderate executive processing ability (LD-Moderate; *N* = 16; 13 males, 3 females), 10.72 (SD = 2.25) for CA-Matched children-moderate executive processing ability (CA-M; *N* = 26, 14 males, 6 females) and 12.37 (SD = 2.64) for CA-Matched children-average (CA-A; *N* = 20, 13 males, 7 females). No differences were found between ability groups related to chronological age. All children in the LD groups and all children in the CA-M group were administered the reading and arithmetic subtest from the Peabody Achievement Test, Peabody Picture Vocabulary Test, and the Performance IQ test from the WISC-R. Unfortunately only six children in the CA-average group were administered these psychometric measures. However, school records and group administered tests as indicated by the school district indicated that children in this group were average or above average readers. Ethnicity of the sample was 93 percent Anglo-European and 7 percent Hispanic.

Significant differences in standard scores were found between the four groups on verbal intelligence (PPVT-R), and word recognition, reading comprehension, and mathematics, on the PIAT-R, and the sentence span measure. A Tukey Test indicated significant differences ($p < .05$) in standard scores between groups for:

1. Reading recognition: LD readers-severe (LD-S; M = 81.98, SD = 4.54) = LD moderate (LD-Moderate; M = 82.24, SD = 6.41) < CA-matched (CA-Moderate; M = 104.97, SD = 8.78) = CA-Average (CA = A *N* = 6, M = 113.07, SD = 7.28).
2. Reading comprehension: LD readers-severe (LD-S; M = 88.44, SD = 7.31) LD moderate (LD-M; M = 82.20, SD = 11.55) < CA-matched-M (CA-Moderate; M = 110.53, SD = 8.05) = CA-Average (CA = A *N* = 6, M = 114.05, SD = 10.82).
3. Mathematics LD-S (M = 98.64, SD = 8.14) = LD-Moderate (M = 93.55, SD = 8.85) < CA-Moderate (M = 108.59, SD = 11.58) CA-Average < (CA = A *N* = 6, M = 115.05, SD = 9.24).
4. Verbal IQ: LD-S (93.53 SD = 5.99) < LD-Moderate (M = 102.726, SD = 9.92) < CA-Moderate (M = 115.69, SD = 15.72) = CA-Average (CA-A *N* = 6, M = 117.01, SD = 6.15).

For the sentence span measure, children in the severe LD-executive processing deficiency group (LD-S) achieved a processes score of 1 and a span score of 0 (0 reflects recall of sets of less than 2 sentences). Thus, all children were assigned a span score of 0. The mean and standard deviations span scores for the remaining groups were 1.50 (SD = .51) for LD-Moderate group, 1.75, (SD = .44) for the CA-Moderate and 2.75, (SD = .48) for the CA-A group. A Tukey test indicated significant differences emerged between groups on the sentence span measure, LD-S < LD-Moderate = CA-Moderate < CA-A). The important findings related to the classification variables were that both the LD groups were statistically comparable on reading, mathematics and intelligence, and the LD-Moderate and CA-Moderate group were statistically comparable on the Sentence Span Measure (all *ps* > .05).

Procedures

Same as Study 1, except that the Sentence Span task was administered to classify ability groups.

Sentence Span Task

The Sentence Span Task, adapted from Daneman and Carpenter (1980), was used to establish the existence of reading group differences in memory span. Materials for the Sentence Span Task were composed of 17 unrelated declarative sentences, seven to ten words in length. The sentences were randomly arranged into sets of two, three, four, or five with two sets at each level. An example of the sentences at the three-sentence level would be:

1. We waited in line for a *ticket.*
2. Sally thinks we should give the bird its *food.*
3. My mother said she would write a *letter.*

In order to ensure that children comprehended the sentences and did not merely treat the task as one of verbal memory for the last words only, they were required to answer a question at the end of each presentation set. Questions referred to a randomly selected sentence in the set with the restriction that the probe was not related to the last sentence. For example, for the three sentence set above, children were asked "Where did we wait?"

The administration of the Sentence Span Task was conducted individually. Four practice trials were presented, and for each trial the entire set of sentences was first read aloud to the child, who was then asked to verbally recall the last word of each sentence in the set in correct order. Sentences were presented approximately at the rate of one word per second. The comprehension question was then asked and the child answered verbally. The dependent measure was the span level as measured by Daneman and Carpenter (1980; 1983) and was the largest set size for which correct recall of all the last words in each set occurred. Test-Retest reliability on the measure is .92 (Swanson, 1992).

Results

Ability Group Differences

Table 11 shows the means and standard deviations for the dependent measures. Effect sizes were calculated for gain scores as ES = ([Mean of gain-mean of

Table 11. Working Memory Performance as a Function of Task, Condition and Ability Group (Study 3)

	LD-S (N = 20)		LD-M (N = 16)		CA-A (N = 20)		CA-M (N = 20)		
	M	*SD*	*M*	*SD*	*M*	*SD*	*M*	*SD*	*Ratio*
					Initial				
Rhyming	2.05	.68	1.75	.93	2.05	.79	2.65	1.18	3.21*
						CA-A > LD-M & LD-S & CA-M			
Visual Matrix	3.65	1.66	3.87	1.31	3.75	1.99	3.90	1.20	.10
Semantic	.85	. 74	1.43	1.15	1.95	1.39	1.75	1.16	3.56*
						CA-M > LD-S & LD-M & CA-A			
					Gain (Cued)				
Rhyming	2.30	.73	2.25	.93	2.65	.67	2.85	1.31	1.98
Visual Matrix	3.95	2.11	4.12	1.50	5.20	1.82	4.40	1.66	1.84
Semantic	1.05	.60	1.75	1.23	2.80	1.85	2.00	.97	6.62**
						CA-A > LD-S			
						CA-A = LD-M & CA-M			
					Maintenance				
Rhyming	2.25	.71	2.06	1.06	2.25	.85	2.80	1.15	2.11
Visual Matrix	3.85	1.95	3.87	1.31	4.25	2.02	4.00	1.37	.22
Semantic	.85	.74	1.62	1.31	2.20	1.57	1.80	1.10	4.33**
						CA-A > LD-S			
						CA-M = LD-M & CA-M			
					Probe				
Rhyming	.60	1.35	1.50	3.57	1.00	1.71	.40	.99	1.11
Visual Matrix	.85	1.75	.62	2.20	3.00	3.67	.80	1.85	4.19*
						CA-M > LD-S = CA-A = LD-M			
Semantic	.35	.93	.50	1.50	1.35	2.39	.30	.73	2.04

initial]/standard deviation of initial scores) and for maintenance scores as ES = ([Mean of maintenance-mean of initial performance]/standard deviation of initial scores). As can be calculated from Table 11, probing procedures had an impact on all tasks for all reading groups.

The results indicated that the effect size for gain performance on phonological, visual-spatial, and semantic tasks were .36, .18, and .26 for LD-S, .53, .19, .27 for LD-Moderate, .79, .72, .60 for CA-A, and .16, .41, and .21 for CA-Moderate children, respectively. The results indicated that the effect size on the maintenance conditions for phonological, visual-spatial, and semantic tasks were .29, .12 and .0 for LD-S, .33, .0, .16 for LD-Moderate, .26, .25, .17 for CAA, and .12, .08, and .04 for CA-Moderate children, respectively. Thus, only the LD-Moderate group improved approximately 1/2 standard deviations in performance on the gain condition and less than 1/4 standard deviations for the gain condition. Changes on the gain and maintenance conditions were weak for all groups on the visual-spatial conditions. In general, these groups were less responsive to probes (cues) than in the previous studies. This finding may be related to the homogeneity among groups in the present study. Further, a MANOVA for the group effect on the number of probes used to achieve gain performance for the three tasks was significant. The mean number of probes for each group is shown in Table 11. The ANOVA was significant for the visual-spatial task, but not the phonological task or semantic task. A Tukey test indicated that the LD-S group was less responsive ($p < .05$) to probes in the visual-spatial conditions when compared to the other three groups.

A Multivariate Analysis of Variance of WM span scores as a function of condition (initial, gain, maintenance) indicated a significant ability group effect occurred for initial, gain, and maintenance conditions. As shown in Figure 5, initial, gain, and maintenance scores differed between ability groups. For the initial conditions, the ANOVA was significant for the phonological, and the semantic task, but not for the visual-spatial task, $F < 1.0$. A Tukey test indicated that significant differences ($p < .05$) emerged between groups for the phonological (LD-Moderate = LD-S = CA-A < CA moderate) and semantic (LD-S < CA-Moderate = LD-Moderate < CA-A) tasks.

For the gain conditions, the ANOVA was significant for the semantic task, but not for the phonological and visual-spatial task. A Tukey test indicated significant differences between groups for the semantic task (LD-S < CA-Moderate = LD-Moderate < CA-A).

For the maintenance conditions, the ANOVA was significant for the semantic WM task, but not the phonological and visual-spatial task. A Tukey Test indicated that significant differences ($p < .05$) emerged between groups for the semantic task (LD-S < CA-Moderate = LD-Moderate < CA-A).

Trend Analysis

To determine if ability groups differed across initial, gain, and maintenance conditions, the span scores were analyzed, via an ANOVA represented as a 4 (*ability group*: LD-S, LD-Moderate, CA-Moderate, CA-A) × 3 (*condition*: initial, gain, maintenance) factor design with repeated measures on the last factor. Each ANOVA was computed as a function of the type of WM task. The trends in performance are shown in Figure 5. For the phonological task, a significant effect emerged for ability group, condition, but *not* for the ability group × memory condition interaction. As expected, scores were high on the gain when compared to the other conditions (gain > initial; maintenance > initial; gain > maintenance). We tested the hypothesis that the first-degree (linear) polynomial from initial to gain score was significant. The linear effect was significant and accounted for 30 percent of the variation. The quadratic components accounted for 69 percent of the variance. The total group

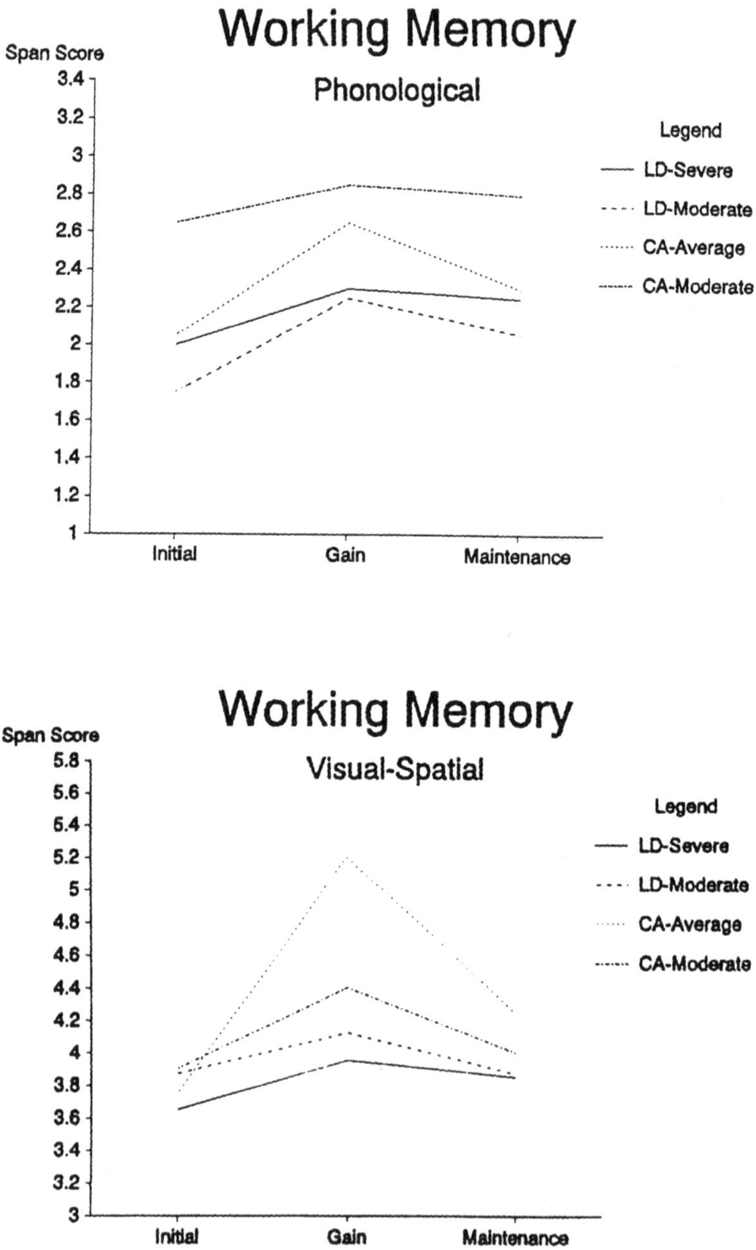

Figure 5. Mean Span Scores for Study 3 as a Function of Ability Group, Condition, and Type of Task (continued)

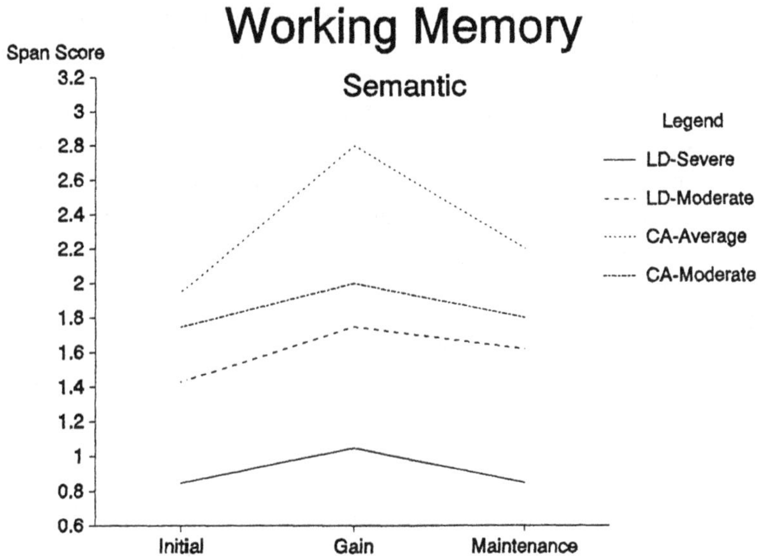

Figure 5. Continued

quadratic mean estimate was –1.43 (SD = .56). Removing various groups to determine contribution to the estimate was not done because the interaction were not significant.

For visual-spatial tasks, a significant effect emerged for memory condition, and the ability group × memory condition interaction. No significant differences emerged between the ability groups. Test of simple effects reported earlier indicated no significant differences in means scores. Ability group differences were greater at initial than gain condition, whereas the ability group contrast between initial and maintenance was not significant. A Tukey test indicated that a greater difference emerged for the CA-Moderate group when compared to the other group on initial than gain and maintenance conditions (CA-Moderate > LD-A = LD-Moderate = LD-S). The linear effect across conditions was significant, but accounted for only 10 percent of the variation. The slopes between groups on the linear effect did not vary between groups. The quadratic component accounted for 90 percent of the variance. As expected from the significant interactions, the slopes varied between groups on the quadratic trend. A removal of the CA-Moderate group from the slope analysis yielded a nonsignificant difference between the remaining ability groups, suggesting that the degree of change was higher from the CA-Moderate group when compared to the other groups. The total group quadratic estimate was –1.28 (SD = .33), indicating that WM changes curved down. Removing the CA-Moderate group from the total sample decreased the down curve [M= –.94, *SD* = .24)].

For the semantic tasks, a significant effect emerged for group, memory condition, and the group × memory condition interaction. Ability group differences emerged on initial (LD-S < LD-Moderate = CA-Moderate < CA-A), gain (LD-S < LD-Moderate = CA-A < CA-Moderate), and maintenance conditions (LD-S < LD-Moderate < CA-A = CA-Moderate). When compared to the initial conditions, ability group differences were greater on the gain, then the maintenance conditions. The first-degree linear polynomial was significant, but accounted for only 9 percent of the variance. The quadratic trend accounted for 91 percent of the variance. Ability group differences emerged related to the slope. The removal of the CA-Moderate group from the slope analysis yielded a nonsignificant difference between the remaining groups, suggesting that the degree of change was higher from the CA-Moderate group when compared to the other groups. The total group quadratic estimate was –1.24 (SD = .36), indicating that WM changes curved down. Removing the CA-Moderate group from the total decreased the down curve [M = –.92, SD = .39)].

Of interest was whether ability group differences are greater on the phonological measures than on the semantic and visual spatial measures, and if those differences interact with processing conditions. As in the previous two studies, all span scores were converted to z-scores, based on the total sample. The mean z-scores are shown in Figure 6. These z-scores were analyzed, via a MANOVA, represented factorially

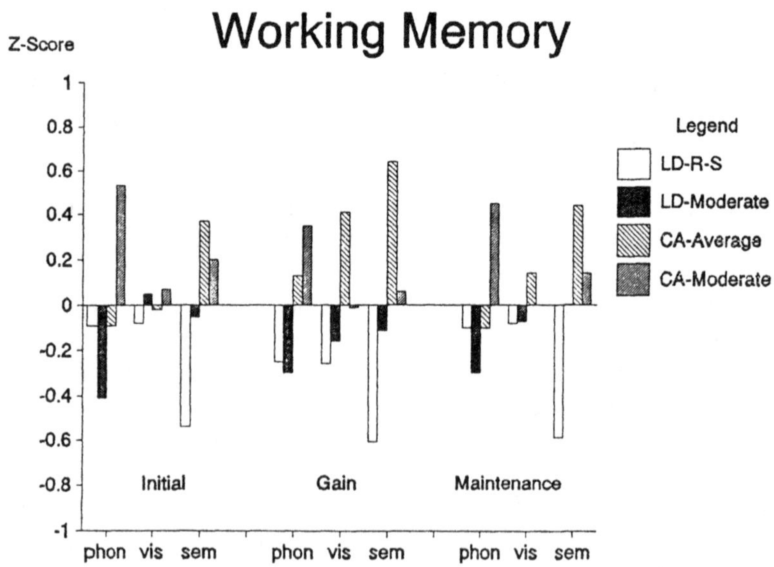

Figure 6. Mean Z-scores for Study 3 as a Function of Ability Group, Condition, and Type of Task

as a 4 (ability group: LD-S, LD-Moderate, CA-Moderate, CAA) × 3 (condition: initial, gain, maintenance) × 3 (type of task: phonological, visual-spatial, semantic) factor design, with repeated measures on the last two factors. The only significant effects to emerge were the main effect for ability group and the ability group × memory condition interaction. A Tukey Test indicated that the Span Score (M z-scores = −.44, −.19, .34, .25, for LD-S, LD-Moderate, CA-Moderate, CA-A, respectively)) was higher for the NLD group (CA-Moderate = CA-A > LD-Moderate > LD > S). These findings are qualified by the interactions. When compared to the initial conditions, ability group differences were significantly comparable on the gain conditions, and maintenance conditions, $F < 1$. When compared to gain conditions, ability group differences were significantly greater on the maintenance conditions. A Tukey Test indicated that scores were higher for the CA-Matched groups than LD groups on the maintenance conditions (CA-Moderate = CA-A > LD-S = LD-Moderate).

Hierarchical Regression Analysis

As in Study 1 and 2, a regression design partialed from the criterion variable the linear trend of reading recognition and mathematics level. Also entered into the regression was reading comprehension performance. An advantage of this procedure is that trends can be detected in the data, even though reading scores are missing in some of the average readers. Subsequent to entering the reading level, simultaneous contrasts reflecting group classifications are entered into the equation. One contrast is the difference in achievement between LD and NLD readers (LD-S & LD-Moderate vs. CA-Moderate & CA-A) and the other contrasts children of different word reading scores but comparable in executive processing (LD-Moderate versus CA-Moderate). The coding for the first contrast is −1 for LD-S and LD-Moderate and +1 for average readers children. A negative beta weight for this contrast indicates that the performance of LD-Moderate and LD-S children is inferior to that of NLD children on the criterion variable (e.g., rhyming). The second contrast is coded as −1 for CA-Moderate and +1 for LD-Moderate children with executive processing difficulties and 0 for CA-A and LD-S children. A positive beta weight for this contrast indicates that LD-Moderate children- outperformed the CA-Moderate on the criterion variable when the effects of reading and math and the other contrasts are removed. If the results are explained primarily as a function of achievement, cognitive performance is significantly related to reading and mathematics, but by neither contrast. If either contrasts are significant in the equations in which reading and mathematics level has been partialed out, then this would suggest that LD children suffer processing deficits independent of their reading and mathematics level. The hierarchical regression modeling with the order of presentation varied is shown in Table 13.

The important results shown in Table 12 are as follows. First, the reading and mathematics measures did not account for significant variance in the regression

Table 12. Regression Results for Working Memory Tasks as a Function of Initial, Gain and Maintenance Conditions (Study 3)

	Rhyming			*Visual Spatial*			*Semantic*		
	Init.	*Gain*	*Main*	*Init*	*Gain*	*Main*	*Init.*	*Gain*	*Main*
Entry Order									
Achievement									
1. Reading (recognition & comprehension) & Math									
R	.08	.12	.06	.05	.07	.04	.09	.11	.08
F-Ratio	1.63	2.38	1.30	.91	1.38	.73	1.78	2.24	1.69
df(3,55)									
Contrast Variables									
2. CA-Matched VS LD Contrast									
B	–.24	–.51	ns	ns	–.17	–.18	–.72*	–.60**	–1.01**
3. Moderate NLD vs. Moderate LD									
B	ns	.17	ns	ns	ns	ns	ns	–.17	.23
Complete Model									
R	.09	.15	.06	.05	.09	.06	.24	.21	.26
F-Ratio	1.48	1.89	1.29	.91	1.29	.81	4.17**	3.65*	3.68**
df(5,53)									

Notes: * $p < .05$ ** $p < .01$

models, suggesting the WM deficits are independent of reading and mathematics. Second, the contrast between the two ability groups matched on executive processing yielded no significant effects. The contrast variable that globally compared LD and NLD children contributed significant variance to the regression model, but this contribution was limited to the initial and maintenance conditions on the semantic tasks. Finally, the complete model was significant only for the semantic task.

In sum, the results support the hypothesis that ability groups matched on executive processing are statistically comparable in performance on phonological, semantic, and visual-spatial measures. These findings emerge whether reading is left to vary (as indicated in the MANOVA) or whether achievement is partialed from the analysis (as indicated by the regression analysis). Thus, support is found for the notion that a general system plays a role in separating LD and NLD readers in WM performance.

The next analysis determined whether the patterns of change between the two matched groups differed. Although the two groups (LD-Moderate vs. CA-Moderate) are matched on executive processing, the role that a general system plays in WM change may vary between the two groups. That is, similar to the prediction in Study 1, we investigate whether general processing or a general storage system accounts for the ability group differences.

Table 13. Predictors of Change (difference between maintenance and initial score) in Working Memory in Learning Disabled and Nondisabled Readers (Study 3)

	Model							
	1		2		3		4	
	Estim	*.SE*	*Estim.*	*SE*	*Estim.*	*SE*	*Estim.*	*SE*
Phonological Information Predictors								
Diagnostic Indicators								
Intercept	.60	.88	.08	.81	.79	.56	.33	.52
Word Recognition	.009	.012	.01	.01	.008	.007	.006	.007
Arithmetic	-.005	.008	-.005	.007	-.006	.005	-.003	.005
Comprehension	-.007	.01	-.009	.01	-.008	.007	-.007	.006
LD Moderate vs. CA Moderate	.09	.16	-.32	.43	-.027	.11	.03	.23
Responsive Indicators								
Asym Per. (AP)	—	—	.29**	.11	—	—	.05	.07
LD * AP	—	—	.19	.14	—	—	.01	.09
Proc. E. (PE)	—	—	—	—	.28**	.03	-.29	.16
AP*PE	—	—	—	—	—	—	.02**	.05
LD*PE	—	—	—	—	-.09*	.04	-.14**	.04
LD*AP*PE	—	—	—	—	—	—	.00	.00
R^2	.03		.24		.64		.73	
df	4,54		6,52		6,52		9,49	
F	.41		2.87**		15.67**		14.78**	
Visual-Spatial Information Predictors								
Diagnostic Indicators								
Intercept	-1.64	1.16	-1.57	1.21	.60	1.41	1.30	1.18
Word Recognition	-.001	.016	-.003	.017	-.01	.01	-.02	.01
Arithmetic	.01	.011	.009	.01	.001	.001	.001	.009
Comprehension	.07	.01	.007	.01	.007	.013	.008	.013
LD	-.07	.22	-.13	.50	-.09	.20	-.13	.52
Responsive Indicators								
Asym Per. (AP)	—	—	.08	.05	—	—	.05	.06
LD * AP	—	—	.04	.11	—	—	.01	.06
Proc. E. (PE)	—	—	—	—	.18**	.03	.47	.32
AP*PE	—	—	—	—	—	—	-.04	.05
LD*PE	—	—	—	—	.02	.07	1.31*	.55
LD*AP*PE	—	—	—	—	—	—	.18	.08
R^2	.05		.09		.35		.45	
df	4,54		6,52		6,52		10,48	
F	.78		.94		4.67**		4.06**	

(continued)

Table 13. Continued

	Model							
	1		2		3		4	
	Estim	*.SE*	*Estim.*	*SE*	*Estim.*	*SE*	*Estim.*	*SE*
Semantic Information Predictors								
Diagnostic Indicators								
Intercept	.51	.68	.61	.66	.41	.45	–.73	.47
Word Recognition	.006	.009	.005	.009	–.002	.007	.002	.007
Arithmetic	.006	.006	–.009	.006	.002	.004	.003	.004
Reading Comp.	–.003	.009	–.001	.008	.004	.006	.001	.006
LD Moderate vs. NLD Moderate	.09	.13	–.38	.20	–.06	.08	.08**	.16
Responsive Indicators								
Asym Per. (AP)	—	—	.02	.05	—	—	.01	.04
LD * AP	—	—	.25*	.09	—	—	.01	.07
Proc. E. (PE)	—	—	—	—	.03	.03	.14**	.07
AP*PE	—	—	—	—	—	—	–.03	–.07
LD*PE	—	—	—	—	.45	.06*	–.13**	.24
LD*AP*PE	—	—	—	—	—	—	.16***	.06
R^2	.05		.20		.65		.7280	
df	4,54		6,52		6,52		10,48	
F	.67		2.20		16.34**		12.29**	

Notes: LD = Classification-LD-severe reading vs. moderate & SL-LD
Estim. = Parameter Estimates
SE = Standard Error
AP = Asymptotic Performance-Gain Scores
PE = Processing Efficiency-Probe Scores

Change Analysis

The difference score between the maintenance and initial performance was submitted to an ordinary least squares regression analyses in a series of hierarchical models. The procedures were the same as Study 1 and 2. We examined the effect of reading and mathematics achievement and then added asymptotic (gain) performance and processing efficiency (probe scores) as predictors. Interactions between predictors were investigated, as well as retained where significant. Because of the predictions related to executive processing, the ability group contrast included subjects matched on executive processing (LD-Moderate versus CA-Moderate). Table 13 presents the fitted regression estimates for a series of models examining the relationship between student characteristics and responsiveness to changes in WM.

The important results reported in Table 13 are as follows. First, the base model is not significant for any of the tasks. Second, all base models were improved by at least 30 percent when processing efficiency (probe) scores were entered into the model. The processing efficiency model alone (probe scores) was substantially better than the access model (gain scores) alone. The best model for the three tasks included the full model. Finally, an ability group × processing efficiency interaction occurred in the full model for all three tasks. These findings suggest that executive processing is qualitatively different between the LD-M and CA-M group in predicting change. A competing interpretation is that the interaction reflects fundamental differences in language between ability groups, particularly phonological coding. Thus, the regression analyses were computed with the change scores related to phonological coding (difference between maintenance and initial scores for the phonological-rhyming list) partialed out in the models for semantic and visual-spatial information. The significant ability group × probe interaction was retained for the visual-spatial difference score, estimate = 1.18, SE = .51, and semantic difference score, estimate = .12, SE = .24, for the full model. This finding suggests that the interactions were not due primarily to phonological coding.

As in studies 1 and 2, we categorized performance into six categories across the WM conditions. The profiles of change are shown in Table 14. For the phonological and visual-spatial tasks, no significant profile differences emerged between ability groups. The majority of children show a nonchange profile (patterns 1 and 4). For the semantic task, a significant difference emerged in profiles by ability group. Certain patterns of change (patterns 2, 3, 5, and 6) were more frequent for the CA-Moderate group when compared to the other ability groups.

Categorical scores were submitted to a maximum likelihood analysis following the procedures outlined in Study 1. Parameter estimates were obtained via a maximum (log) likelihood function, with respect to unknown model parameters. As shown in Table 15, interactions related to the maintenance conditions contributed substantial variance to a model of change across phonological, visual-spatial, and semantic measures. Change across categories is best reflected in model 4 which removes the interactions related to ability group on the maintenance condition.

Discussion

Three important findings emerged. First, LD and NLD readers matched on the sentence span measure perform comparably on visual-spatial, semantic and phonological WM measures on the difficult processing (maintenance) conditions. These findings were stable even when differences related to reading were partialed from the analysis. This finding replicates the previously reported differences between LD and NLD readers (Study 1).

Second, an analysis of change scores reflects a consistent pattern. The regression analysis of difference scores yields a LD × processing efficiency interaction (see Table 13) for the phonological, semantic and visual-spatial conditions. These

Table 14. Percentage of Children Whose Scores Change and the Change Profile (Study 3)

	Patterns of Change						
Profile	*1*[a]	*2*	*3*	*4*	*5*	*6*	X^2 *(9)*
Phonological (Rhyming)							4.79
LD-SR	05	0	05	75	05	10	
LD-M	12	6	12	70	0	0	
CA-A	05	10	0	55	10	0	
CA-M	05	0	5	75	5	10	
Visual Spatial							14.25
LD-R	25	0.	0	55	5	15	
LD-M	6	0	0	81	13	0	
CA-A	10	10	10	40	20	10	
CA-M	05	05	0	75	10	05	
Semantic							21.19*
LD-R	70	20	0	10	0	0	
LD-M	30	13	6	44	0	0	
CA-A	20	15	5	40	15	05	
CA-M	20	15	5	60	0	0	

Notes: [a]patterns of change

	Initial	*Gain*	*Maintenance*		*Initial*	*Gain*	*Maintenance*
1.	0	0	0	2.	0	1	0
3.	0	1	1	4.	1	0	0
5.	1	1	0	6.	1	1	1

0 denotes low initial score or no change from initial score

1 denotes high initial score or positive change from initial score

interactions in the semantic and visual-spatial conditions were retained, even when changes in phonological processing were partialed out in the analysis. The interactions support the notion the executive processing in the LD readers reflects a Constraint in storage.

Finally, in contrast to Study 1, the results of categorical modeling suggest that most of the variance related to changes in WM can be accounted for by interactions related to ability group × maintenance scores. As shown in Table 15, profiles of change (categories) across conditions are best modeled by ability group changes in the maintenance condition, suggesting that ability group differences are related to high demand conditions.

Taken together, the results support the notion that LD readers' WM problems are not primarily due to isolated deficits in the verbal system, but rather reflect a general storage system. In addition, the findings suggest a general pattern of processing that is different for LD-readers when compared to average readers who are matched on

Table 15. Parameter Estimates for Working Memory Obtained from Logistic Curves (Study 3)

	Total Sample Maximum Log Likelihood	X^2	*p*
Phonological			
1. Full model	272.34	—	1.00
2. Model-minus initial interactions	211.66	59.17	.001**
3. Model-minus gain interactions	207.45	54.96	.001**
4. Model-minus maintenance interactions	159.88	7.24	.77
Visual-Spatial			
1. Full model	272.34	—	1.0
2. Model-minus initial interactions	207.63	43.79	.001
3. Model-minus gain interactions	203.54	39.70	.001
4. Model-minus maintenance interactions	170.07	6.23	.79
Semantic			
1. Full model	272.34	—	1.0***
2. Model-minus initial interactions	205.06	31.00	.001***
3. Model-minus gain interactions	213.80	39.74	.001***
4. Model-minus maintenance interactions	183.09	9.03	.708

executive processing ability. An important finding is that moderate span LD readers are statistically comparable in recall to their span matched NLD reading counterparts on WM performance. However, they vary in processing efficiency under conditions that maximize item accessibility, suggesting qualitative differences among ability groups in how executive processing allocates resources.

GENERAL DISCUSSION

The results were interpreted as support for a model which suggests that an executive system plays a major role in accounting for the deficiencies noted in LD readers' WM performance. The findings supporting the notion that LD readers' WM difficulties are related to an executive system are: (1) LD readers show less change (as reflected in effect size scores, slopes in the quadratic curve, and profile patterns related to categorical modeling) across visual-spatial and verbal WM tasks than average readers (Study 1), (2) processing efficiency interacts with LD-NLD readers across phonological, visual-spatial, semantic tasks-(Study 1 & 3), and (3) matching LD and average readers matched on executive processing yield nonsignificant ability groups differences on verbal and visual-spatial tasks under high demand conditions (Study 3). In addition, the findings that argue against the notion that ability groups differences are isolated primarily to the articulatory system were (a) LD readers were more depressed on semantic than phonological tasks when compared to NLD readers (Study 1 & 2), (b) LD readers performed poorer on semantic than phonological tasks when compared to slow learners (Study 2), (c) no processing advantage was found for LD readers when compared to other poor readers on visual-spatial measures (Study 2), and (d) patterns of change were comparable between poor and LD readers across WM measures (Study 2).

The results also clarify the role of processing efficiency and general storage as a source of WM deficiencies in LD readers. The results indicated that LD readers' resistance to change (as reflected from the logistic curves derived from categorical modeling) across phonological, visual-spatial and semantic conditions are isolated to gain conditions (high accessibility conditions) when compared to reading level matched and slow learner groups and to maintenance conditions (high demand conditions) when compared to CA-matched average readers. These findings suggest that when LD readers are compared to reading-level matched and poor readers (slow learning group) they suffer from limitations in WM due to processing inefficiencies (accessibility), whereas limitations in change when compared to CA-matched average readers reflect a general storage system (i.e., information availability). Overall, the results suggest that although the LD readers' WM performance can be modified on phonological, visual-spatial, and semantic measures, as suggested by the effect size scores, the LD reader remains at a clear disadvantage when compared to their same age normal-achieving counterparts. The findings are comparable to those of Swanson (e.g., Swanson, 1984, 1989, 1993, 1993b; Swanson, Asbaker, & Lee, 1996) indicating that LD children suffer capacity deficits across an array of WM memory measures. The findings also compliment those of Engle (e.g., Engle, Cantor, & Carullo, 1993; Turner & Engle, 1989) which suggest that WM is a relatively stable characteristic in poor and good readers.

Competing Model

A theoretical problem emerges in the present study when one considers how to reconcile specific verbal memory processing deficits (e.g., phonological coding) commonly attributed to LD readers (Cohen, 1981; Siegel & Ryan, 1989; Stothard & Hulme, 1992; Vellutino, 1979) with the notion that they also suffer a deficiency in the central executive system. One means of reconciling this issue is to suggest that problems in specific activities of the central executive system can exist in LD readers independent of their problems in low-order processing (Swanson, 1989, 1993a). Another possibility is to suggest that a generic storage system may indirectly account for low-order processing deficits (especially on language-related tasks). For example, in Baddeley's (1986) model the central executive system is an undifferentiated generic system which stores information that is used to support low-order systems. However, if the executive system is over taxed it cannot contribute resources to low-order processing. This assumption is consistent with the notion that a limited capacity WM system plays a role in the translation of phonemic and orthographic codes into a semantic representation while simultaneously storing the output from previous processing.

There are two major alternative interpretations of the present results that must also be considered. The first option is related to the increasing skepticism about the usefulness of resource-allocation models that invoke a central processing mechanism (e.g., Brainerd & Reyna, 1989). This option suggests that LD children are less resistant to *interference* (see Brainerd & Reyna, 1993; Dempster, 1991 for discussion of this model). For example, the process questions in the current tasks may constitute a very temporary competing condition with storage. Further, because the WM tasks vary considerably in the number of processing questions (e.g., compare the phonological task with the visual-spatial task) the subjects are exposed to, the pervasiveness of LD children's poor performance across such diverse measures may reflect a general interference condition. As a consequence, LD readers may have difficulty preventing unnecessary information from entering WM and, therefore, are more likely to consider alternative interpretations of material (such as asked for in the processing questions) that are not central to the task when compared to NLD readers. This interpretation fits within several recent models that explain individual differences in memory performance as related to inhibitory mechanisms (e.g., Brainerd & Reyna, 1989, 1993; Dempster, 1991; Hasher & Zacks, 1988), without positing some form of a capacity deficit.

Although we see the above model as a viable alternative to the results, we have three reservations. First, only subjects who answered the process question correctly were analyzed. That is, if a process question was missed, the child's recall of previously stored information was not requested. This procedure is different from previous studies (e.g., Daneman & Carpenter, 1980) which have allowed a dissociation between the process question (i.e., it is not necessary for subjects to answer the process question correctly) and retrieval question in the analyses. Thus, there was an experimenter imposed association between the process and retrieval question for the same set of inputs. This control also provides feedback to subjects related to the interpretation and/or relevance of the material to be remembered. Further, a post-hoc analysis of the protocols did not indicate that irrelevant information from the process question was more likely recalled by LD than NLD children. That is, if ability group differences are due to an ability to resist interference for irrelevant items, then higher levels of recall of irrelevant information should emerge with LD readers. Such was not the case in this study. Second, if LD children suffer more interference (i.e., diminished inhibition in that a large number of traces are simultaneously active) than NLD children, then one would expect the probing to narrow significantly the alternative interpretations of items in memory when compared to NLD children. That is, inefficiencies in inhibiting traces or competition effects should be reduced more in LD than NLD children. Further, one would predict that a procedure which gives feedback on the relevancy of a response should lead to a substantial increase in memory performance in the group with the diminished inhibitory efficiency. Such was not the case in this study. Finally, it seems to us that the concept of "interference" can be tied to a resource allocation model. That is, capacity constraints may underlie individual differences in inhibitory efficiency. This ha's been suggested in the literature on depression and WM (e.g., Ellis, 1990), as well as on aging and WM (e.g., Hasher, Stoltzfus, Zacks, & Rypma, 1991). In short, LD readers may use more capacity than NLD readers to inhibit or resist potential interference from irrelevant items.

The second option for interpreting the results suggests that LD children suffer functional WM problems (e.g., a lack of flexibility in coordinating various memory stores) rather than processing constraints related to a particular store. In this view, the executive processing system of LD children may or may not have the same storage capacity as NLD children, but an important source of individual differences in children is an inability to coordinate and/or compensate for the processes they have. This option differs from the processing vs. storage issue by emphasizing the coordination of processes. It also differs from the divided attention among relevant and irrelevant information view as discussed above. In support of this assumption, Yee, Hunt, and Pellegrino (1991) have argued that complex tasks (i.e. dual or multiple tasks situations) are more likely to reflect the coordination of processes- than the more common assumption that they require divided attention between competing memory traces (also see Carlson, Wenger, & Sullivan, 1993, for a testing of this notion). Thus, although individual differences in WM may reflect a situation in which information is poorly encoded and maintained, individual differences also occur in how subjects switch between and coordinate sources of information. For example, LD children may be forced to represent word information in a visual-spatial form, rather than leave it in a articulatory form, or visa versa, and this coordination across different representations is particularly difficult for LD children. This interpretation is especially appealing because the articulatory form of information has been found deficient in LD readers (e.g., Crain & Shankweiler, 1990). We believe, however, that the major limitation of this option in interpreting the present results is that it does not eliminate a resource allocation model. This is because one can speculate that resource trade-offs can exist between storage and response execution processes (Carlson, Wenger, & Sullivan, 1993). Simply stated, there is a cost in switching and/or coordinating across multiple memory traces.

Contributions to the Literature

One contribution this study makes to the memory literature is that an analysis of change may help untangle processing efficiency vs. general capacity interpretations of LD readers' WM performance. It appears to us that processing efficiency and capacity are not either/or constructs, but reflect shared variance. That is, the degree to which processing influences WM performance is constrained by capacity. Likewise, capacity constraints are related to how much efficient processing can actually change behavior. On this assumption, one can argue that if ability groups vary in the degree (or rate) of change, then we would expect an interaction between processing efficiency and ability group on measures of change. That is, if processing conditions (probes) do influence genuine changes in WM, then the magnitude of these changes would be constrained by a reduction in capacity. Thus, an ability group interaction emerges because the influence of processing efficiency is primarily mediated by constraints in storage. That is, we assumed that if ability group differences exist in WM capacity, the degree of change would not be the same for ability groups across processing conditions. Our results are in line with this assumption.

No doubt, a contrasting interpretation of this interaction related to ability group and processing efficiency on measures of change can be considered. A contrasting view is that ability groups are comparable in WM capacity, but the LD readers are less efficient processors of information. Similar to the capacity hypothesis, a processing efficiency hypothesis would predict a different trajectory, that is, the degree of change (slopes) is not comparable between LD and NLD groups. As in the capacity hypothesis, an interaction would emerge between the parameters of change and ability group. However, if process efficiency underlies the difference between ability groups, then more change (as reflected in a steeper slope) should emerge in the LD group. Such was not the case in this study. In the present study, the results showed clearly that probes influenced performance in both groups, but the memory performance of the LD child was less accelerated than the NLD readers (the slopes were steeper for NLD than LD children).

Second, LD readers are deficient in semantic coding. There has been some suggestion in the literature that LD readers' semantic coding is superior when compared to their phonological processing abilities (e.g., Siegel, 1993; Waller, 1976). As shown in Figures 2, 4, and 6, however, the severe LD readers' semantic processing is more depressed than phonological processing on initial, gain and maintenance conditions (see Figure 6). In addition, the CA-matched reader exhibits no depression in performance related to semantic conditions (see Figure 2). An exception to this finding occurs when CA-matched readers were divided into average and moderate executive processing subgroups (see Figure 6). A slight depression in phonological processing emerges for the ability group with average executive processing. Interestingly, a similar effect occurred for the slow learners (poor readers) (see Figure 4). Although researchers in the area of learning disabilities view the processes related to semantic memory as an outgrowth of problems in phonological memory, the present study, along with other studies outside the domain of reading (e.g., Martin, Shelton, & Yaffee, 1994), suggests that these two processes may at times operate independently of each other.

In summary, future research must focus on the interaction between executive and lower order processing during the act of reading to disentangle the alternative interpretation of the results. The results clearly suggest, however, that LD children experience generalized deficits related to changes in WM performance. These deficits emerged across task conditions, suggesting that the source of individual differences related changes in WM are isolated to an executive processing system.

ACKNOWLEDGMENT

Some portions of this new work occur in Swanson, Ashbaker, and Lee (1996) and Swanson (manuscript). Prior reports of this working memory project occur in Swanson (1992, 1995, 1996).

REFERENCES

Baddeley, A. D. (1986). *Working memory*. London: Oxford University Press.

Baddeley, A. D. (1990). *Human memory*. Oxford, England: Oxford University Press.

Bowey, J. A., Cain, M. T., & Ryan, S. M. (1992). A reading-level design study of phonological skills underlying fourth-grade children's word reading difficulties. *Child Development, 63*, 999–1011.

Brainerd, C. J., & Reyna, V. F. (1989). Output interference of dual task deficits in memory development. *Journal of Experimental Child Psychology, 47*, 1–18.

Brainerd, C. J., & Reyna, V. F. (1993). Memory independence and memory interference in cognitive development. *Psychological Review, 100*, 42–67.

Brainerd, C. J., Reyna, V. F., Howe, M. L., & Kingma, J. (1990). The development of forgetting and reminiscence. *Monographs of the Society for Research in Child Development, 55*, Whole No. 222.

Cantor, J., & Engle, R. W. (1993). Working memory capacity as long-term memory activation: An individual-differences approach. *Journal of Experimental Psychology: Learning, Memory, and Cognition, 19*, 1101–1114.

Carlson, R. A., Wenger, J. L., & Sullivan, M. A. (1993). Coordinating information from perception and working memory. *Journal of Experimental Psychology: Human Perception & Performance, 19*, 531–548.

Cohen, J. (1977). *Statistical power analysis for the behavioral sciences*. New York: Academic Press.

Cohen, R. L. (1981). Short-term memory deficits in reading disabled children in the absence of opportunity for rehearsal strategies. *Intelligence, 5*, 69–76.

Crain, S., & Shankweiler, D. (1990). Explaining failures in spoken language comprehension by children with reading disabilities. In D. A. Balota, G. B. Flores d'Arcais, & K. Rayner (Eds.), *Comprehension processing in reading* (pp. 539–555). Hillsdale, NJ: Lawrence Erlbaum.

Daneman, M., & Carpenter, P. A. (1980). Individual differences in working memory and reading. *Journal of Verbal Learning and Verbal Behavior, 19*, 450–466.

Daneman, M., & Carpenter, P. A. (1983). Individual differences in integrating information between and within sentences. *Journal of Experimental Psychology: Learning, Memory, & Cognition, 4*, 561–584.

Dempster, F. N. (1991). Inhibitory processes: A neglected dimension of intelligence. *Intelligence, 15*, 157–173.

Dixon, P., LeFevre, J., & Twilley, L. C. (1988). Word knowledge and working memory as predictors of reading skill. *Journal of Educational Psychology, 80*, 465–472.

Ellis, H. D. (1990). Depression deficits in memory: Processing initiative and resource allocation. *Journal of Experimental Psychology: General, 119*, 60–62.

Engle, R., Cantor, J., & Carullo, J. (1993). Individual differences in working memory and comprehension: A test of four hypotheses. *Journal of Experimental Psychology: Learning, Memory, and Cognition, 18*, 972–992.

Federal Register. (1977). The rules of a regulatory for implementing P.L. 94-142. Washington, DC: U.S. Government Printing Office.

Francis, D. J., Fletcher, J. M., Stuebing, K. K., Davidson, K. C., & Thompson, N. M. (1991). Analysis of change: Modeling individual growth. *Journal of Consulting and Clinical Psychology, 59*, 27–37.

Hansen, J., & Bowey, J. A. (1994). Phonological analysis skills, verbal working memory, and reading ability in second-grade children. *Child Development, 65*, 938–950.

Hasher, L., Stoltzfus, E. R., Zacks, R. T., & Rypma, B. (1991). Age and inhibition. *Journal of Experimental Psychology: Learning, Memory, & Cognition, 17*, 163–169.

Hasher, L., & Zacks, R. T. (1988). Working memory, comprehension, and aging: A review and a new view. In G.H. Bower (Ed.), *The psychology of learning and motivation: Advances in research and theory, Vol. 22* (pp. 193–225). San Diego, CA: Academic Press.

Jastak, S., & Wilkenson, G. (1984). *Wide range achievement test-revised.* Wilmington, DE: Jastak Associates.

Just, M. A., & Carpenter, P. A. (1992). A capacity theory of comprehension: Individual differences in working memory. *Psychological Review, 99*, 122–149.

Keppel, G., & Zedeck, S. (1989). *Data analysis for research designs: Analysis of variance and multiple regression/correlation approaches.* New York: W.H. Freeman & Co.

Liebermann, I. Y., Mann, V. A., Shankweiler, D., & Werfelman, M. (1982). Children's memory for recurring linguistic and nonlinguistic material in relation to reading ability. *Cortex, 18*, 367–375.

Martin, R. C., Shelton, J. R., & Yaffee, L. S. (1994). Language processing and working memory: Neuropsychological evidence for separate phonological and semantic capacities. *Journal of Memory & Language, 33*, 83–111.

Meredith, W., & Tisak, J. (1990). Latent curve analysis. *Psychometrika, 55*, 107–122.

Morris, N., & Jones, D. M. (1990). Memory updating in working memory: The role of the central executive. *British Journal of Psychology, 81*, 111–121.

Rogosa, D. R., Brandt, D., & Zimowski, M. (1982). A growth curve approach to the measurement of change. *Psychological Bulletin, 90*, 726–748.

Rogosa, D. R., & Willett, J. B. (1985). Understanding correlates of change by modeling individual differences in growth. *Psychometrika, 50*, 203–228.

Salthouse, T. A. (1996). The processing-speed theory of adult age differences in cognition. *Psychological Review, 103*, 403–428.

Salthouse, T. A., & Babcock, R. L. (1991). Decomposing adult age differences in working memory. *Developmental Psychology, 27*, 763–776.

SAS Institute, Inc., (1989). *SAS/STAT User's Guide, Version 6, Fourth Edition, Volume 1.* Cary NC: SAS Institute Inc.

Shallice, T. (1988). *From neuropsychology to mental structure.* New York: Cambridge University Press.

Shankweiler, D., & Crain, S. (1986). Language mechanisms and reading disorder. *Cognition, 24*, 139–168.

Shaywitz, B. A., Fletcher, J. M., Holahan, J. M., & Shaywitz, S. E. (1992). Discrepancy compared to low achievement definitions of reading disability: Results from the Connecticut Longitudinal Study. *Journal of Learning Disabilities, 25*, 639–648.

Siegel, L. S. (1988). Evidence that IQ scores are irrelevant to the definition and analysis of reading disability. *Canadian Journal of Psychology, 42*, 201–215.

Siegel, L. S. (1992). An evaluation of the discrepancy definition of dyslexia. *Journal of Learning Disabilities, 25*, 618–629.

Siegel, L. S. (1993). Phonological processing deficits as the basis of a reading disability. *Developmental Review, 13*, 246–257.

Siegel, L. S., & Ryan, E. B. (1989). The development of working memory in normally achieving and subtypes of learning disabled. *Child Development, 60*, 973–980.

Stanovich, K. E., & Siegel, L. S. (1994). Phenotypic performance profile of children with reading disabilities: A regression-based test of the phonological-core variable-difference model. *Journal of Educational Psychology, 86*, 24–53.

Stothard, S., & Hulme, C. (1992). Reading comprehension difficulties in children. The role of language comprehension and working memory. *Reading and Writing, 4*, 245–256.

Swanson, H. L. (1984). Effects of cognitive effort and word distinctiveness on learning disabled and nondisabled readers' recall. *Journal of Educational Psychology, 76*, 894–908.

Swanson, H. L. (1989). Central processing strategy differences in gifted, average, learning disabled and mentally retarded. *Journal of Experimental Child Psychology, 47*, 370–397.

Swanson, H. L. (1992). The modifiability and generality of working memory in skilled and less-skilled readers. *Journal of Educational Psychology, 84*, 473–488.

Swanson, H. L. (1993a). Executive processing in learning disabled readers. *Intelligence, 17*, 117–149.

Swanson, H. L. (1993b). Working memory in learning disability subgroups. *Journal of Experimental Child Psychology, 56*, 87–114.

Swanson, H. L. (1995). Cognitive Processing Test. Austin, TX: PRO-ED.

Swanson, H. L. (1996). Individual and age-related differences in children's working memory. *Memory & Cognition, 24* (1), 70–82.

Swanson, H. L. (manuscript). *An analysis of change in learning disabled readers working memory.*

Swanson, H. L., & Alexander, J. (1997). Cognitive processes that predict reading in learning disabled readers: Revisiting the specificity hypothesis. *Journal of Educational Psychology.*

Swanson, H. L., Ashbaker, M. H., & Lee, C. (1996). Learning-disabled readers' working-memory as a function of processing demands. *Journal of Experimental Child Psychology, 61*, 242–275.

Teasdale, J. D., Proctor, L., Lloyd, C. A., & Baddeley, A. D. (1993). Working memory and stimulus-independent thought: Effects of working memory loan and presentation rate. *European Journal of Cognitive Psychology, 5*, 417–433.

Turner, M. L., & Engle, R. W. (1989). Is working memory capacity task dependent? *Journal of Memory and Language, 28*, 27–154.

Vellutino, F. (1979). *Dyslexia: Theory and research.* Cambridge, MA: MIT Press.

Vellutino, F., Scanlon, D. M., & Spearing, D. (1995). Semantic and phonological coding in poor and normal readers. *Journal of Experimental Child Psychology, 59*, 76–123.

Waller, T. G. (1976). Children's recognition memory for written sentences: A comparison of good and poor readers. *Child Development, 47*, 90–95.

Waterman, B., & Lewandowski, L. (1993). Phonologic and semantic processing in reading-disabled and nondisabled males at two age levels. *Journal of Experimental Child Psychology, 55*, 87–103.

Willett, J. B. (1989). Questions and answers in the measurement of change. In E. A. Rothkopf (Ed.), *Review of research in education, Vol. 15* (pp. 345–422). Washington, DC: American Educational Research Association.

Willett, J. B. (1994). Measuring change more effectively by modeling individual change over time. In T. Husen & T. N. Postlethwaite (Eds.), *The international encyclopedia of education.* Oxford, England: Pergamon.

Yee, P. L., Hunt, E., & Pellegrino, J. W. (1991). Coordinating cognitive information: Task effects and individual differences in integrating information from several sources. *Cognitive Psychology, 23*, 615–680.

A COMPARISON OF THE COGNITIVE CAPABILITIES OF YOUNG CHILDREN WITH MILD MENTAL RETARDATION OR LEARNING DISABILITIES

Kathryn L. Fletcher, Marcia S. Scott,
Lois-Lynn S. Deuel, and Beda Jean-Francois

INTRODUCTION

Children classified as having a learning disability (LD) or mild mental retardation (MMR) constituted more than half of all children who required special educational services in the mid 1980s (Hallahan, Keller, & Ball, 1986). Furthermore, the number of children classified as LD has been steadily growing while the number of those classified as educable mentally handicapped (EMH), most of whom have mild mental retardation, has diminished only slightly (Office of Special Education and Rehabilitation Services, 1989, cited in Slavin et al., 1991). One prevalent issue in special education is the extent to which children with LD and children with MMR are different (e.g., Polloway, Patton, Smith, & Buck, 1997). Some investigators have

Advances in Learning and Behavioral Disabilities, Volume 13, pages 65–93.

ISBN: 0-7623-0429-4

argued that there are few differences between these two exceptional groups which impact educational instruction (Hallahan & Kauffman, 1976; Neisworth & Greer, 1975). Research demonstrating that similar teaching techniques are effective for both groups seems to provide support for this argument (e.g., Algozzine, Korinek, Morsink, & Algozzine, 1988; Finn & Resnick, 1984; Polloway, Epstein, Polloway, Patton, & Ball, 1986; Ysseldyke, O'Sullivan, Thurlow, & Christenson, 1989). Furthermore, observational research has found that the behaviors of teachers and exceptional students with different categorical labels (e.g., LD, MMR, or emotional handicaps) within the classroom are similar (Algozzine, Morsink, & Algozzine, 1988; O'Sullivan, Marston, & Magnusson, 1987; Ysseldyke, Thurlow, O'Sullivan, & Christenson, 1989).

Researchers have also argued that a classification scheme in which these two groups are viewed as being more similar than different should be devised (MacMillan, Sipperstein, & Gresham, 1996). For example, MacMillan, Sipperstein, and Gresham (1996) argue that children with MMR are more similar to children with LD than children with moderate and severe forms of mental retardation, mainly because both groups exhibit mild cognitive deficits within a school context. According to MacMillan, Sipperstein, and Gresham (1996), the major difference between children with LD and children with MMR is that children with LD demonstrate deficits within a specific domain (i.e., usually reading), whereas children with MMR demonstrate a more generalized deficit across domains. These authors have suggested the use of the term "Generalized Learning Disability" to characterize children currently described as having MMR, which would signify a stronger congruence between children with LD and children with MMR. However, children in these two groups would still need to be differentially identified in a reliable manner to determine the services necessary to address their particular pattern of cognitive deficits.

To date, however, there is limited information available that has systematically compared the performance of LD and MMR children on cognitive tasks (Berger & Reid, 1989; Brown & Palincsar, 1982; Wiss, 1986). Gresham, MacMillan, and Bocian (1996) compared the performance of children with LD, children with low achievement, and children with MMR on the WISC-III subtests and the Wide Range Achievement Test (i.e., reading, arithmetic, and spelling). In this study, children with LD performed significantly better than the children with MMR on every subtest of the WISC-III and all three WRAT domains. Whereas this study suggests that the level of cognitive performance of LD and MMR children are different, conclusions are tentative given that these assessments were also used to classify children into these exceptional groups. In fact, Gresham, MacMillan, and Gresham (1996) conclude that additional research to examine the cognitive strengths and weaknesses of children with LD and MMR on tasks other than those used to define each group is necessary. The cognitive abilities of LD and MMR children has mainly been investigated by comparing these two groups separately to normally-achieving (NA) children and not directly to each other.

Although there is no single study which has contrasted the performance of NA, LD, and MMR children on a variety of cognitive tasks, individual studies have compared the cognitive performance of NA, LD, and MMR school-aged children on certain cognitive tasks such as listening (Wood, Buckhalt, & Tomlin, 1988), concept utilization (Wiss, 1986), analogy (Swanson, Christie, & Rubadeau, 1993), central processing (Swanson, 1989, 1990), story recall (Wolman, van den Broek, & Lorch, 1997), rhyme (Scott, Perou, Greenfield, & Swanson, 1993), taxonomic information (Scott & Greenfield, 1992), and oddity (Scott, Greenfield, & Partridge, 1991; Scott, Perou, Greenfield, Partridge, & Swanson, 1993). With the exception of story recall and analogy tasks, in each study the NA children performed more accurately than the LD children. On the other hand, in each study, the LD children performed more accurately than the MMR children. Even though there are problems comparing results across different studies, there is a consistent pattern on most of these cognitive tasks of the NA children performing at higher levels than the LD children and the LD children performing at higher levels than the MMR children.

The majority of this research, however, has been conducted with school-aged exceptional children, mainly because in the past children were not identified for special education placement until the early school grades. The passage of Public Law 99-457 (Part B), which mandates free and appropriate educational services to all three- through five-year-old children with disabilities, has increased the number of young exceptional children now identified and served in the public school system. This population includes some young children classified as LD and MMR. Unfortunately, little research about the cognitive strengths and weaknesses of young children with LD or MMR has been conducted. So while researchers have argued that LD and MMR school-aged children are more compatible than previously assumed (MacMillan, Sipperstein, & Gresham, 1996), there is no information about the extent to which young children classified as having LD or MMR are either similar or different. This is especially surprising since this is important information for the design of appropriate intervention and educational services.

It might be expected that these two groups are more similar before the early formal school years, before children may have developed coping skills and strategies for their cognitive deficiencies. And yet, children classified as MMR or LD, by definition, have demonstrated significant differences in cognitive capabilities as measured by a standardized intelligence test. Thus, one might expect some differences to be observed if these groups are compared on a variety of cognitive tasks. Patterns found in performance similarities and differences may begin to provide a profile of the cognitive abilities of these young exceptional children. There may also be important qualitative differences in the cognitive performance of preschool children with LD or MMR. Such information would provide valuable assistance in the design of appropriate educational interventions for children in these exceptional groups.

The purpose of this chapter is to compare the cognitive performance of children with MMR, children with LD, and NA children on a broad selection of cognitive tasks. Sets of cognitive tasks were presented to children from each of these groups in three different studies. There are a number of commonalities between the three studies reported. The first two studies evaluated a battery of tasks, each of which was a potential component of a new cognitive screening test. Those cognitive tasks that were selected as components of the new screening test were examined in Study 3. Samples in each study consisted of three groups of four- and five-year-old children; one consisting of NA children, one of children with LD, and one of children with MMR. The exceptional students were all recruited from the same school district and were enrolled in EMH or LD classes. The procedure for identifying and classifying children as EMH or LD is described in detail in Scott, Deuel, Claussen, and Sanchez (1993) and Scott and colleagues (1996). The IQ data for the students with MMR and LD were obtained from computerized school records. For the samples with MMR, only children with IQs between 50 and 69 were included. All participating children with LD had a full scale IQ of at least 80.

Exceptional children were matched to NA children on age, race/ethnicity and gender. Most of the NA children were attending private preschools but some five-year-olds in each study were attending public school kindergarten classes. The schools were geographically dispersed throughout the entire county and the participating children came from one of the following racial/ethnic groups: Black/non-Hispanic; White/non-Hispanic; or White/Hispanic.

The data from all three studies were examined using the same data analysis plan. First, the absolute performance of the children on the major dependent measures was analyzed. These were the primary analyses. Based on the performance of school-aged children with NA, LD, or MMR (e.g., Scott & Greenfield, 1992), it was expected that in all three studies, the pattern NA > LD > MMR would be present on all dependent measures. Thus, one-tailed tests of planned comparisons of adjacent groups were made, that is, NA > LD and LD > MMR, given a significant group effect.

Subsequent to the primary analyses, a series of secondary analyses were computed in order to more fully explore the similarities and differences reflected in the primary analyses. Finally, the individual tasks from the batteries were ordered for difficulty from the easiest to the hardest in terms of percentage correct, separately for each group. This permitted a final comparison of the three educational groups in terms of the relative difficulty of the cognitive tasks.

STUDY 1

Method

Participants

Of the 98, four- and five-year-old children in this study, 22 were classified as MMR, 27 as LD and 49 as NA. The mean chronological ages for the MMR, LD and NA groups were 60.6 (range = 49–71), 59.8 (range = 48–71), and 60.0 (range = 49–71), respectively. The mean full scale IQ score for the MMR group was 61.1 (range = 55–68) and for the LD group was 98.3 (range = 82–126). Ninety-two percent of the LD sample had full scale IQs greater than 85 and 44 percent had full scale IQs greater than or equal to 100. As one would expect given the distribution of male and female children in the exceptional student population, there were more males (37) than females (12) in the MMR and LD groups. As the NA group was matched on this variable, the same distribution was observed, that is, 37 males and 12 females. The number of White/non-Hispanic, White/Hispanic and Black/non-Hispanic children in the MMR group was six, eight, and eight, respectively. Similar data for the LD group was 9, 14, and 4. The sum of these, 15, 22, and 12 represents the distribution of race/ethnicity for the NA group.

Cognitive Battery and Instructions

Children were seen individually by one of two testers for a single session. For all but the word task, which was a verbal task, colored pictures or letters were pasted onto 21.6 cm × 33.0 cm white posterboard cards that were then covered with clear contact paper. The eight tasks are briefly described here in the order in which they appeared in the battery.

Picture recall task. The children were shown memory cards on which from one (level 1) to eight (level 8) unrelated pictures were displayed. There were two memory tests for each level. The testers named each of the pictures on each memory card once and then turned the card over so the pictures were no longer visible to the children. The children were then asked to recall as many of the pictures as they could. Failure level was the first level at which children failed to recall one or more of the to-be-remembered pictures on both tests at that level.

Taxonomic generation task. The children were shown five cards, on each of which were displayed two exemplars from one of five categories, for example, fruit. The testers named each of the exemplars and with the exemplars in view, asked the children to name as many other (e.g., fruits) as they could.

Taxonomic information task. Following pretraining with exemplars of a telephone, the children were shown a sequence of five cards. On each card were four exemplars from one of five categories, for example, clothing. The children were asked to tell how the items in each category were the same (alike), and then how they differed from one another (not the same). The scoring procedure for this task is detailed in Scott, Greenfield, and Sterental (1986). In general, each discreet piece of information that was correct or was true of most category exemplars, was awarded a point.

Standard oddity. This task consisted of nine, three-picture arrays, on each of which were displayed two identical and one different picture. The children were asked to point to the different picture, the one that didn't belong, that didn't have a buddy. Incorrect responses were corrected on no more than three arrays.

Oddity variations task. This task consisted of several different oddity arrays. For one type, three different three letter-group word problems constructed of upper or lower case red letters were constructed. Either the (1) initial or (2) final letter was different (four cards) or (3) the odd array was a reversal of the other two, as in tip versus tip versus pit (two cards). For these problems, the children were asked to point to the different group of letters. There were also two *complementary pair oddity* displays, as in fish, fish bowl, shirt, and two *orientation oddity* displays, for example, two arrows pointing up and one pointing down. For these 10 oddity problems, the children were asked to find the picture that didn't belong with the other two, the one that was all alone. There was no correction for this task.

Picture rhyme task. A target picture was centered at the top of each of four cards and two semantically unrelated choice pictures, one whose name rhymed with the target picture, appeared on the bottom. Based on pilot data, the rhyming cards presented to the four-year-olds were different from those cards presented to the five-year-olds. The testers named all three pictures and the children were asked to point to the picture on the bottom whose named sounded like the target picture.

Picture pointing task. The children were shown four cards, on each of which was displayed a six-picture set, and were told to point to each picture just one time. Their pointing sequence earned a score of 3 for a reading order sequence, 2 for a sequence that was systematic but not in a reading order, 1 for a nonsystematic sequence without an error and a 0 if one or more errors (i.e., repetitions or omissions) were committed.

Word meaning task. The children were asked to define the words "car" and "orange," as in "What does car mean? What is an orange?" The children's responses were scored and awarded 3, 2, 1, or 0 points depending upon the abstractness and uniqueness of the response. A zero was given if the response had nothing to do with either car or orange.

All of the children were tested in English except for 10 White Hispanic preschoolers who by teacher report knew little English. For those students, the battery was administered in both Spanish and English to ensure understanding, and responses from the child in either English or Spanish were accepted. A tester who was fluent in both English and Spanish did all the testing in Spanish. Greater details about samples, procedures and tasks are available in Scott and colleagues (1996).

Results

Primary Analyses

The eight tasks and dependent measures are listed in Table 1 and are grouped according to whether the task was a generating (production) or identification task. The picture recall task was grouped with the generating tasks, even though the set of to-be-remembered items was given to children, because (a) children had to access and produce the items from their memory, a processing act which at this age must place a significant demand on the children, and (b) the possible responses were not "out there" in front of them as in the typical identification task. The picture pointing task, on the other hand, was grouped with the identification tasks because (a) it demanded only a minimal contribution from the children, and (b) in a factor analytic study of a battery which included the picture pointing task, this task loaded on the same factor as the other identification tasks and not on the factor associated with the generating tasks (Tu, Scott, Mason, & Urbano, 1997).

Employing a MANOVA with groups as an independent variable and performance on the identification tasks and generating tasks as the two dependent measures,

Table 1. Means and SDs for the Performance of the Three Educational Groups on the Eight Tasks in Study 1

	NA *N* = 49		*LD* *N* = 27		*MMR* *N* = 22
			Generating Tasks		
Taxonomic Generation					
total # of exemplars	14.0 (9.1)	>	4.9 (5.5)	>	0.9 (1.3)
Taxonomic Information					
# of same descriptors	2.2 (2.1)	>	0.9 (1.4)	>	0.2 (0.7)
# of different descriptors	3.9 (3.1)	>	1.2 (1.9)	>	0.1 (0.3)
Word Meaning					
total points	6.3 (4.1)	>	3.2 (3.2)	>	1.6 (2.2)
Picture Recall					
failure level	3.8 (1.0)	>	2.9 (0.8)	>	2.1 (0.7)
			Identification Tasks		
Picture Pointing					
quality score	6.8 (2.4)	>	5.2 (3.0)	>	2.6 (2.2)
Picture Rhyme					
# correct/4	3.1 (1.1)	>	2.4 (0.9)	=	2.0 (1.0)
Oddity Variations					
# correct/10	5.8 (2.0)	>	4.6 (1.9)	=	4.3 (1.3)
Standard Oddity					
# correct/9	7.9 (2.1)	>	6.9 (2.6)	>	5.6 (2.4)

there was an overall significant effect of groups, $F(4, 188) = 22.33$, $p < .001$. Follow-up univariate tests revealed that these significant group differences were present for both types of tasks, $Fs(2, 95) > 23.69$, both $ps < .001$.

Generating tasks. The significant effect associated with generating tasks was further explored by examining the impact of groups on each of the five generating measures. The overall MANOVA was significant, $F(10, 182) = 8.64$, $p < .001$, as were all five univariate tests, all $Fs(2, 95) > 12.32$, all $ps < .001$. When the NA and LD groups and the LD and MMR groups were compared, all ten contrasts were significant, all $ps < .05$. For every measure, the NA group performed at a higher level than the LD group and the LD group performed at a higher level than the MMR group (see Table 1).

Identification tasks. The group effect for the identification tasks was also explored for the individual tasks. A MANOVA with group and the four dependent measures, was associated with an overall significant effect, $F(8, 184) = 6.76$, $p < .001$ and there was a significant effect for each of the four univariate follow-up analyses, all $Fs(2, 95) > 7.32$, all $ps < .001$. The follow-up of group contrasts resulted in significant group differences, $ps < .05$, for all but two of the contrasts, i.e., the LD versus MMR comparisons for the picture rhyme and oddity variations tasks. These two comparisons were not reliable, $ps > 05$.

Secondary Analyses

Generating tasks. The differential mean performance of the three groups on the first three generating tasks is, in part, reflecting differences in the proportion of children in each of the three groups who were unable to generate a single scoreable response. As can be seen in Table 2, when the children had to provide exemplars and information about simple categories and concepts, few children from the NA group could not comply at least in a minimal fashion. In contrast, a high percentage of children from the LD and MMR groups could not generate even a single acceptable response. Within the exceptional groups, the percentage of young children classified as MMR who failed to generate a single acceptable response was greater on all measures than the percentage of children with LD who failed to do so.

In order to evaluate these differences between the NA and LD groups as well as the LD and MMR groups on the first four generating measures (except the picture recall test), a series of eight chi-square analyses were computed comparing adjacent groups on the number of children generating no scoreable response versus the number of children generating at least one or more scoreable responses. All four of the NA versus LD contrasts were significant, $\chi^2(1, N = 76) > 6.19$, $ps < .02$, indicating that a greater proportion of the children classified as LD failed to generate a single acceptable response. All the LD versus MMR contrasts were significant, $\chi^2(1, N = 49) > 4.08$, $ps < .05$, except for the comparison of these two exceptional

Table 2. The Percentage of Children in the Three Educational Groups Who Were Unable to Generate a Single Scorable Response on the Taxonomic and Word Meaning Tasks in Study 1

	NA	*LD*	*MMR*
Taxonomic Generation	4	30	59
Taxonomic Information			
Same Descriptors	29	59	91
Different Descriptors	12	67	91
Word Meaning	10	33	54

groups on the word meaning task, $p > .10$. Clearly, on these generating tasks, the inability of many exceptional children to respond at all is a major factor differentiating them from the NA children and is also operating to differentiate the children with LD from the children with MMR in most cases.

To further explore the differences among the three groups on the picture recall task, we compared the level at which the children failed and the level at which they committed their first error. For the majority of NA (53%) and LD (59%) children, a failure to demonstrate perfect recall on one of the recall tests at a given level did not signal failure on the other test item at that level. However, the majority of children with MMR (77%) did fail at the same level at which they committed their first recall error(s). The adjacent groups were contrasted on separate chi-square analyses with the children being grouped into those who made their first error and failed at the same level versus those who failed at a higher level. The NA versus LD contrast was not significant, $\chi^2(1, N = 76) < 1.0$, $p > .10$, but the LD versus MMR comparison was, $\chi^2(1, N = 49) = 6.61$, $p < .02$. Even though the overall level of performance was low on this picture recall task, the LD group performed more like the NA children, than like their MMR same age peers.

Identification tasks. An additional look at the picture pointing task can be made by examining the total number of errors (omissions or repetitions) made by each of the children over the four arrays. The error data were used to sort the children into one of two groups; those making no errors and those making one or more errors. The majority of the NA children (69%), and nearly half (48%) of the LD children did not make a single error, but only 14 percent of the MMR children were errorless. When the children were grouped into those who did and did not make any errors, chi-square analyses revealed that the number of NA and LD children in each group was not significantly different, $\chi^2(1, N = 76) = 3.33$, $p > .05$, while the LD versus MMR comparison was reliable, $\chi^2(1, N = 49) = 6.57$, $p < .02$. On this categorical distribution of errors, the young LD group was more like NA than MMR children.

There were no differences between the LD and MMR groups on the rhyme task in terms of their mean performance, whereas the NA group scored higher than both of them. A similar pattern was observed when the groups were compared on the percentage of children who were correct on no more than two of the four trials, which would reflect a chance level of performance. Only 24 percent of the NA group made no more than two correct choices, whereas 52 percent of the LD group and 73 percent of the MMR group performed at or below a chance level. Chi-square analyses contrasting adjacent groups, using the number of children falling into these two categories, resulted in the same outcome as is seen on Table 1. The NA versus LD contrast was significant, $\chi^2(1, N = 76) = 5.79, p < .02$, but the LD versus MMR was not, $p > .10$.

The last secondary analyses were conducted with the two oddity tasks. Looking at the mean performance data in Table 1, it can readily be seen that the standard oddity task was much easier than the oddity variations task for all three groups; NA (88% versus 58%), LD (77% versus 46%) and MMR (62% versus 43%). Contrasting the groups on the number of children performing at or below chance (less than or equal to 3 correct) versus those performing above chance (> 3 correct) on the oddity variation task, resulted in the same pattern of group differences; the NA group had proportionally fewer children scoring at or below chance (.12) compared to the LD group (.33), χ^2 (1, N = 76) = 4.89, $p < .03$, while a similar contrast for the LD (.33) and MMR (.27) groups was not significant, $\chi^2(1, N=49) < 1.0, p > .10$.

Relative Difficulty of the Tasks

A final comparison of these three groups of young children was made by ranking the eight tasks in terms of their relative difficulty and then examining the ordering of the tasks across groups. In order to put all the tasks on a common measure, children's scores were converted into a percentage correct measure and means were obtained for each group. For taxonomic generation, taxonomic information, and word meaning, the highest score obtained in the entire sample was used as the estimate of the highest possible score for that task. This approach was taken, that is, using the highest score over all the sample, so that as in the other tasks, the same denominator would be used for all children in all groups. The highest possible score was used for converting picture recall and picture pointing tasks, that is, scores of 8 and 12, respectively. The total number of trials, 4, 10, and 9 was used for the picture rhyme, oddity variation and standard oddity tasks. In addition, percent chance performance (e.g., 1 out of 3, or .33 for the oddity task and 2 out of 4, or .50 for the rhyme task) was subtracted from the total percent correct for the standard oddity task and picture rhyme task, respectively. This procedure was used because guessing or response bias behaviors (i.e., common in MMR children) might have allowed children to obtain several correct responses on the identification tasks, but not for the generating tasks. Subtracting percent chance performance resulted in a more reasonable measure of task difficulty for ranking both identification and generating tasks together.

Table 3. Ordering of the Eight Tasks in Terms of Percentage Correct Responses for the Three Educational Groups in Study 1

NA		*LD*		*MMR*	
Picture Pointing	56	Picture Pointing	44	Standard Oddity	29
Standard Oddity	55	Standard Oddity	44	Picture Recall	26
Picture Recall	47	Picture Recall	37	Picture Pointing	21
Word Meaning	40	Word Meaning	20	Word Meaning	10
Taxonomic Info.	38	Taxonomic Info.	13	Oddity Variation	10
Taxonomic Gen.	35	Oddity Variation	13	Taxonomic Info.	2
Picture Rhyme	29	Taxonomic Gen.	12	Taxonomic Gen.	2
Oddity Variation	25	Picture Rhyme	11	Picture Rhyme	0

The tasks and their rankings are shown in Table 3. Clearly, the relative difficulty of these eight tasks is (nearly) identical across the three groups. That is, the first four tasks, ranked as being less difficult, are the same for each educational group, as are the second four more difficult tasks. One noted difference is that the picture pointing task appears to be slightly more difficult for the MMR group, compared to the NA and LD group.

Summary

On the generating tasks, the NA group out-performed the LD group and the LD group out-performed the MMR group on all continuous and categorical measures with but two exceptions. On the word meaning task, similar numbers of children with LD and MMR failed to generate even a single scoreable response. In contrast, on the picture recall task, the LD showed a pattern of responding that was similar to the NA group where an initial error did not signal failure in the majority of children.

On the identification tasks, the relation among the three groups was not as consistent. The NA group showed a superior performance when compared to the LD group on all but one measure; there were similar numbers of children in both groups that made no error on the picture pointing task. As for the LD versus MMR comparisons, the LD group performed at a higher level than the MMR group with the exception of the picture rhyme task and the oddity variation task. Interestingly, these two tasks ranked as the most difficult tasks for the NA children, whereas the picture pointing task ranked as least difficult (see Table 3).

STUDY 2

Method

Participants

There were 31 children classified as having MMR, 31 classified as LD and 62 matched NA children. The mean chronological age for the MMR, LD and NA groups was 61 (range = 50–71), 62 (range = 48–71), and 62 (range = 48–71) respectively. The mean full scale IQ for the MMR group was 60 (range = 50–69) and for the LD group was 94 (range = 80–126). Seventy-one percent of the LD sample had full scale IQ scores > 85, 48 percent had full scale IQ scores > 90, and 26 percent had full scale IQ scores greater than or equal to 100.

The distribution of White/Hispanic, Black/non-Hispanic and White/non-Hispanic children in the MMR group was 13, 15, and three. The same distribution of race/ethnicity for the LD group was 21, four, and six. There were 19 males and 12 females in the MMR group and 25 males and six females in the LD group. Because NA children were matched to exceptional children on ethnicity and gender, it can be determined that there were 34 White/Hispanic, 19 Black/non-Hispanic and nine White/non-Hispanic children in the NA group, of which 44 were males and 18 were females.

Cognitive Battery and Instructions

This battery was administered in the same fashion as the previous battery, that is, one on one, tester and child for a single session. For all but the word task, meaningful colored pictures or letters were pasted onto 21.6 cm × 33.0 cm white posterboard cards that were then covered with clear contact paper. The word task was presented verbally. The tasks are described below in the same order as they appeared in the battery.

Picture recognition task. The children were pretrained to select both types of recurrences of a seen before picture; *exact recognition*, for example, same butterfly or same pen, or *same object-class recognition*, for example, different butterfly or different pen. The testers named each of the pictures in the eight picture set of to-be-remembered pictures twice; going twice through the entire set. Over four recognition test cards, each to-be-remembered picture was tested once with an exact recurrence and once with a same object-class recurrence.

Missing picture recall memory task. The children were asked to remember from two to eight pictures (levels 1 through 7) that the testers named once before presenting the same array with one picture missing. In place of the missing picture was a 8.3 × 10.2 cm rectangle within which a large black question mark was placed. The children were asked to recall the missing picture. There were two memory-test pairs at each level. The series was presented until the children failed to correctly recall the missing picture on both tests at a given level; this was the failure level.

Standard oddity task. This is the same task as was described in Study 1, that is, nine unique arrays of two identical and one different picture. A correction procedure was used on this first oddity task.

Letter-group oddity task. For this problem, the children were presented cards on which were displayed three groups of letters with the odd array having one letter that was different from the two same arrays. The letter-groups ranged from level 1, where there was no letter in common between the same and different arrays, for example, u versus u versus d, to level 2, where there was one letter in common between the same and different arrays, for examples, ld versus bd versus ld, through level 7 where, of the seven letters in each array, there were six letters in common and only one different letter, for example, fmlebnh versus fwlebnh versus fmlebnh. There were six unique letter arrays for each of the seven letter-group levels. The tester started with the level 1 oddity set, did not correct any incorrect choices, and presented the next level until the children made more than one error at any given level. This was called the failure level.

Dot matrix oddity task. There were same and different dot matrices. Each 3 × 3 in. matrix was composed of three rows of 1 in. squares (nine squares). Colored dots were placed within the 1 in. squares. For the four-year-old group, green dots were used and same and different matrices varied by two dots, that is, 3 versus 1 through 9 versus 7, for a total of seven cards. For the five-year-olds, orange dots were used and same and different matrices varied by only one dot, that is, 2 versus 1 through 8 versus 7 for a second seven card set. There was no correction and all seven cards were presented regardless of the children's accuracy.

Word meaning task. The children were asked what each of the following words, "sea," "orange," and "jack" meant. All three had multiple meanings. The testers probed until no (more) responses were forthcoming.

All of the children were tested in English except for one White/Hispanic child who was tested in Spanish, because he did not respond when tested in English. Responses in either English or Spanish were accepted. A tester who was fluent in both English and Spanish administered the battery in Spanish. Greater details for this study regarding sample, procedures and tasks can be found in Scott, Deuel, Claussen, & Sanchez, 1993.

Results

Primary Analyses

As in Study 1, the tasks were grouped into those that required the children to generate or produce responses and those that required only an identification response. The generation and identification tasks, and the mean performance associated with each, are presented in Table 4. There were only two generating tasks. These were the missing picture recall task and the word meaning task. The missing picture task was included in the generating group because although the response required was provided on the special memory card, it was one of several

Table 4. Means and SDs for the Performance of the Three Educational Groups on the Six Tasks in Study 2

	NA $N = 62$		*LD* $N = 31$		*MMR* $N = 31$
		Generating Tasks			
Missing Picture					
failure level	3.4 (1.5)	>	1.5 (0.8)	>	1.1 (0.4)
Word Meaning					
total score	2.0 (1.4)	>	0.9 (1.0)	=	0.7 (0.6)
		Identification Tasks			
Picture Recognition					
# correct/8 (exact)	7.4 (1.0)	>	5.7 (2.2)	>	4.0 (2.3)
# correct/8 (object-class)	6.3 (1.3)	>	5.1 (2.0)	>	4.0 (2.0)
Standard Oddity					
# correct/9	8.6 (0.9)	>	7.3 (2.7)	>	5.9 (2.6)
Letter-Group Oddity					
failure level	2.9 (1.4)	>	2.2 (1.2)	>	1.4 (0.8)
Dot Matrix Oddity					
# correct/7	5.0 (1.8)	>	3.8 (2.2)	>	2.2 (1.6)

that had to be stored in memory and then recalled when it was deemed absent from the test array. Like the recall task in Study 1, response on this task seemed to require a significant contribution from the children, that is, remember, survey stored information, identify and name missing picture. Clearly more than simple identification of pictures provided at the time of the response was required. The picture recognition, standard oddity, letter-group oddity, and dot oddity tasks were identification tasks.

A MANOVA of groups was computed with performance on the generating and identification tasks serving as the dependent measures. The mean total scores on the identification tasks for the NA, LD and MMR groups were 30.2, 24.2, and 17.5, while total mean scores for these three groups on the generating tasks were only 5.5, 2.5, and 1.8. As might be expected, the overall MANOVA was found to be significant, $F(4, 240) = 33.65$, $p < .001$. Follow-up univariate F-tests were also significant for both identification and generating measures, Fs $(2, 121) > 48.18$, ps $< .001$.

Generating tasks. For the generating tasks, the overall MANOVA was significant, $F(4, 240) = 22.67, p < .001$, as were the follow-up univariate F-tests for each of the two tasks, Fs$(2, 121) > 17.85$, ps $< .001$. On the missing picture task, both contrasts were significant, ps $< .03$, with the NA children performing better than the LD children, and the LD children performing better than the MMR children. As expected based on the means shown in Table 4, only the NA versus LD contrast was significant on the word meaning task, $p < .001$. The LD and MMR children performed at a similar, low level.

Identification tasks. When the identification tasks were examined, it was seen that the overall MANOVA was significant, $F(10, 234) = 10.85$, $p < .001$, as were all the follow-up univariate tests, $Fs(2, 121) > 16.59$, $ps < .001$. The 10 planned contrasts, two for each measure, were all also significant, $ps < .04$. The NA group performed at a higher level than the LD group and the LD group performed at a higher level than the MMR group on both measures associated with the picture recognition task, as well as on the three oddity tasks.

Secondary Analyses

Generating tasks. The small mean differences between the two exceptional groups on the missing picture task, although significant, cannot obscure the fact that this recall task was very difficult for both groups of exceptional children. Both, on average, were unable to correctly recall the missing picture when all they had to remember was two pictures. They could not pass, if you will, the first level of difficulty. The NA group, on the other hand, on average could remember and tell which one of three pictures was missing at level 2, but not which one of four to-be-remembered pictures was missing (level 3). For only a minority of NA children (35%) did the first error signal failure, while the first error signaled failure for the majority of the LD (74%) and nearly all the MMR children (90%). Using the number of children who failed at the same level that they committed their first error versus the number who failed at a higher level, chi-square analyses revealed that the NA versus LD contrast was significant, $\chi^2(1, N = 93) = 12.40$, $p < .001$, but the LD versus MMR comparison was not, $\chi^2(1, N = 62) = 2.76$, $p > .09$. Clearly, the LD and MMR groups are more like each other on this task and perform more poorly than the NA group.

On the word meaning task, we examined the percentage of children who were unable to generate a single acceptable definition to any of the three words. Just as for the total score measure, a higher percentage of NA (87%) than LD (55%) or MMR (58%) children were able to generate at least one definition. When the groups were contrasted on the number of children who generated no definitions versus one or more definitions, the NA versus LD contrast was significant, $\chi^2(1, N = 93) = 11.91$, $p < .001$ but the LD versus MMR contrast was not, $\chi^2(1, N = 62) < 1.0$, $p > .78$. On this generating task, as well as for the missing picture task, the two exceptional groups perform similarly and more poorly than the matched NA group.

Identification tasks. We further examined the picture recognition task to see if there were other measures that might shed additional light on the performance differences among the three educational groups. We first looked at the number of errors committed on this task. There were four distractors, not seen-before pictures, on each of the four recognition test cards. The LD and MMR groups made many more incorrect responses ($M = 7.1$ and 5.3, respectively) than did the NA group ($M = 1.7$). When these error data were analyzed using an ANOVA, the performance differences were associated with a significant effect of groups, $F(2, 121) = 20.03$, $p < .001$. Paired contrasts showed that, as might be expected, the NA versus LD comparison was reliable, $p < .001$, while the LD versus MMR comparison was not, $p > .12$.

One final look at this task led us to examine the pattern of difficulty over the two types of recognitions. It was expected that it would be easier to recognize pictures that were exactly like those seen before than to recognize pictures that were the same kind of object but were perceptually different. In order to examine this possibility, the children's scores were sorted into number correct out of eight exact recognitions and number correct out of eight same object-class recognitions. The latter was subtracted from the former and a chi-square analysis was conducted on the number of children whose difference score was greater than zero (higher exact recognition score) and those whose difference score was less than or equal to zero (higher same-object class score or no difference). While the majority of NA children (74%) achieved higher scores on the exact recognition task, most LD and MMR children (58%) had the same or a higher score on the same object-class recognitions. The different pattern between the NA and LD groups was reliable, $\chi^2(1, N = 93) = 9.27$, $p < .01$, while the same number of children with LD and MMR fell into each category (13 higher exact and 18 no difference or higher same object-class in both exceptional groups), eliminating any further analyses.

The oddity tasks were also of differential difficulty. Looking at the mean performance data in Table 4, it can readily be seen that the standard oddity task was much easier than the dot matrix oddity problems for all three groups: NA (96% versus 71%), LD (81% versus 54%) and MMR (66% versus 31%). Only the MMR group, however, showed an average performance (31%) that was very close to a chance level on the dot matrix task (33%). Chi-square comparisons of the number of children who performed at or below chance versus the number of the children who performed above chance showed that the proportion of children from the NA group who performed at or below chance (.15) was similar to the proportion of children from the LD group who performed at or below chance (.26), $\chi^2(1, N = 93) = 1.76$, $p > .10$, but the MMR group (.52) had a greater proportion of children performing at chance than did the LD group, $\chi^2(1, N = 62) = 4.35$, $p < .04$.

A similar contrast of the three groups was conducted based on their performance on the letter-group oddity task. The majority of children in the MMR group (74%) failed at level 1, which required children to identify the odd letter given two identical and one different letter. In contrast, the majority of the LD (71%) and NA (90%) were successful at level 1. Chi-square comparisons of the number of children who failed at level 1 versus the number of children who failed above level 1 showed that the proportion of children from the NA group who failed at level 1 (.10) was significantly less than the proportion of LD students (.29) who failed at this level, $\chi^2(1, N = 93) = 5.72$, $p < .02$, and the proportion of LD students who failed at level

Table 5. Ordering of the Six Tasks in Terms of Percentage Correct Responses for the Three Educational Groups in Study 2

NA		*LD*		*MMR*	
Standard Oddity	63	Standard Oddity	48	Standard Oddity	32
Picture Recognition	47	Picture Recognition	37	Picture Recognition	26
Missing Picture	43	Dot Oddity	21	Missing Picture	14
Dot Oddity	38	Missing Picture	19	Word Meaning	11
Word Meaning	34	Word Meaning	16	Dot Oddity	−2
Letter Oddity	8	Letter Oddity	−1	Letter Oddity	−14

1 was, in turn, significantly less than the proportion of MMR children who failed at level 1 (.74), $\chi^2(1, N = 62) = 12.66, p < .001$.

Relative Difficulty of the Tasks

To examine the relative difficulty of the tasks for each of the groups, each measure was again converted into a percentage correct score and averaged for each group. For the missing picture and letter-group oddity tasks, we used the highest level that could be achieved (7) to convert the scores. For the word meaning task, we used the highest total score achieved by a student which was 6. For the dot oddity tasks and standard oddity, scores were divided by the total number of cards, 7 and 9, respectively. Again, the percentage associated with chance performance was subtracted from the total percent correct scores for the oddity tasks (.33). When these conversions were completed, the mean percentages scores for each task were ranked separately for each of the three groups. This contrast is shown in Table 5.

For each group, the patterns of task difficulty were similar; standard oddity and picture recognition were ranked as being the easiest tasks, whereas word meaning and letter oddity were ranked as being more difficult. As was found in Study 1, the relative difficulty of the tasks is nearly identical across the three educational groups.

Summary

For all but one comparison associated with a generating task, the NA > LD > MMR pattern was dominant. Children with LD and MMR performed at similar levels on the word meaning task, which was particularly difficult for the NA children. Once again, the pattern for the identification tasks was less consistent, following the NA > LD > MMR pattern for the primary analyses but not for the secondary analyses. Secondary analyses revealed that the LD and MMR groups did not differ in terms of (1) the number of errors made on the recognition task and (2) the percentage of children scoring higher on the exact picture recognitions compared to object-class recognitions. However, the NA and LD groups did not differ in terms of the percentage of their samples falling to a chance level of performance on the dot matrix oddity problems, a task of moderate difficulty.

STUDY 3

In this study (Deuel, 1997), there were a few procedural differences from the previous two studies. In addition to matching exceptional and NA children on race/ethnicity, gender, and age, testing language (for the White/Hispanic group) was used as a matching variable. Also, age was matched within grade, such as, prekindergarten or kindergarten. Children were presented a brief picture task before the screening test in order to determine which of two languages (English or Spanish) was to be used to administer the test. The children were presented a battery of items, not as a set of items being evaluated as potential test items, but as items already selected for inclusion in the second version of the screening test. Because some tasks in the screening test were the same as those previously evaluated in Study 1 or 2 with some minor modifications, secondary analyses were only conducted on the new cognitive tasks.

Methods

Participants

In this sample there were 74 exceptional children and 74 NA matches. Seventeen of the exceptional children were classified as MMR and 57 as LD. Of these exceptional children, 16 were four-year-olds, 45 were five-year-olds and 13 were six-year-olds. Forty-eight of the exceptional children were in prekindergarten and 26 in kindergarten. The NA matched group, of course, had the same grade and age distribution. The mean chronological age was 65 for all three groups; ranges = 52–79 (MMR), 52–78 (LD) and 51–80 (NA).

The MMR group had a mean full scale IQ of 64 (range = 50–69) and the LD a mean full scale IQ of 101 (range = 80–146). In the LD sample, 82 percent had an IQ score of at least 85 and 49 percent had an IQ score of at least 100. Fifty-five of the 74 exceptional children (45 LD and 10 MMR) were male, 19 (12 LD and seven MMR) were female. The same distribution applied to the matched NA group. The race/ethnicity distribution for the LD group was five Black/non-Hispanic, 48 White/Hispanic, three White/non-Hispanic and one Other. This distribution for the MMR group was eight Black/non-Hispanic, and nine White/Hispanic. Totals for the NA group were 13 Black/non-Hispanic, 57 White/Hispanic, three White/non-Hispanic and one Other.

Cognitive Battery and Instructions

As in Studies 1 and 2, children were seen individually by one of several testers for a single session. For all but the word meaning task, colored pictures or dots were photocopied onto 35.6 (cm) × 21.6 (cm) white paper and a complete set of stimuli was placed into a black legal size binder. The screening test was made up of 10 tasks; three old tasks (previously described), and seven new tasks. All of the tasks are described below, however, in the order in which they appeared in the screening test.

Relative size task (new). This new task consisted of six pages on each of which appeared a small, medium and large picture, for example, dinosaur. The medium size picture was 1.5 times the size of the small picture and the large picture was 1.5 times the size of the medium size picture. The children were asked to point to the biggest, for example, flower, or the littlest, for example, dinosaur.

Picture pointing task (old). This is the same as was described in Study 1. The children's pointing sequences were scored 3, 2, 1 or 0 and the dependent measure, quality score, was the sum of the scores over the four arrays.

Phonological awareness task (new). This new task also consisted of six pages. On each were two items whose labels began with a different sound, for example, *d*oor and *b*ook. The testers named each of the pictures and then asked the children, for example, to point to the one that begins with "duh, that starts with duh." The children were pretrained with a single example.

Standard oddity task (old). This task was the same as described in Studies 1 and 2 except that in this battery there were only six pages of unique oddity problems. The children were corrected if necessary, on any of the first three problems.

Picture rhyming task (new). There were six pages of stimuli for this new task. On each were two pairs of pictures; one picture pair whose names rhymed and the other whose names did not rhyme. One pair appeared on the top of the page over a thick black line that bisected the page horizontally, and the other pair was below that black line. There was one set of six pages where the pictures rhymed in English, for example, man/fan, and another set where they rhymed in Spanish, for example, peso (dollar) versus queso (cheese). The English labels were one syllable in length and the Spanish names were two syllables. The children were asked to point to the pair whose names sounded the same. There was a single pretraining example for this task.

Picture sequencing task (new). For this new task, a horizontal array of colored dots or animals appeared on the top of the page with the last position in the array represented by an unfilled circle (i.e., dot sequence) or an underlined space (i.e., animal sequence) to indicate a missing item, for example, frog, frog, cow, frog, frog, cow, frog, frog, _______. Three choices were presented at the bottom of the page within a black box. One of the choices was the missing last item from the array, for example, cow. The children were asked to point to the missing picture, the one that comes next. The testers named all the items in each array, sometimes with the children spontaneously naming them along with the tester, and at the last one, the missing one, the tester gasped and said, "Something is missing. Which comes next (while pointing to the choice array)? Point to the one that is missing."

Oppositional concepts task (new). For this new task, one component of three oppositional concepts, that is, empty/full, top/bottom, inside/outside, was represented in a picture. Each of the six was shown to the child who was asked, for example, "Is the wagon empty or full?" The same probe was given once to the picture of an empty wagon and again to the picture of a full wagon. Conceptually appropriate probes were presented for the other two concepts.

Taxonomic generation task (old). This was a modified version of the same task described in Study 1. For this version, there were only two categories, such as, body parts and clothing. The testers named the exemplars and asked the children to name more, for example, body parts. A maximum of two responses for each of the two categories was imposed; so the maximum score attainable was 4. If the children merely pointed to a body part or piece of clothing, only 1/2 point was awarded rather than a full point.

Semantic information task (new). This was another new task which only used two pages. On one was an array of 12 cats and on the other, an array of fruit, such as, pineapple, watermelon, orange. There were two probes for each set of items. For the cat page, the children were first asked to name the items (cats) and then were asked, "What do they look like?" The testers gave one example, such as, "They have tails." Up to two responses were recorded and scored. For the second probe the children were asked to tell what cats do. Again an example was provided, such as, "They sometimes chase mice." Up to two responses were recorded and scored. The maximum number of points was 4. For the fruit page, probes were, "What can you do with fruit?" and "Where does fruit come from? Where go you get fruit?" No examples were provided for this second array. As before, two responses were scored. The maximum score was 4.

Word meaning task (new). This was a modified version of the word meaning task described in Study 1. Children were asked to tell the tester about an airplane. There were two specific probes, namely, "What does an airplane do?" and "What does an airplane look like?" Only the first two responses to each probe were scored. The maximum score was 4.

All of the children were tested in English except for 15 White/Hispanic children who, based on teacher nomination, tester/child discourse and performance on the language determination test, were tested in Spanish. One child was tested in both English and Spanish with instructions given in both languages. Responses in either English or Spanish were accepted. A tester who was fluent in both English and

Spanish administered the battery in Spanish. Greater details for this study regarding sample, procedures and tasks can be found in Deuel (1997).

Results

Primary Analyses

In this study there were three generating tasks and seven identification tasks. The means and standard deviations for each group are presented in Table 6. A MANOVA of groups with type of task as the two dependent measures, resulted in a significant overall effect, $F(4, 288) = 25.11, p < .001$, as well as significant univariate effects for both generating and identification tasks, $Fs(2, 145) > 46.87, ps < .001$.

Generating tasks. For the generating tasks, a significant overall MANOVA was obtained, $F(6, 286) = 14.52, p < .001$, as well as significant univariate tests for all three dependent measures, $Fs(2, 145) > 28.53, ps < .001$. Planned contrasts between

Table 6. Means and SDs for the Performance of the Three Educational Groups on the Five Tasks in Study 3

	NA N = 74		*LD* N = 57		*MMR* N = 17
	Generating Tasks				
Semantic Information total points	6.6 (1.5)	>	4.2 (2.7)	>	1.7 (2.5)
Word Meaning total points	3.1 (1.1)	>	1.9 (1.6)	>	0.7 (1.2)
Taxonomic Generation total points	3.5 (1.1)	>	2.3 (1.8)	>	0.5 (1.0)
	Identification Tasks				
Relative Size # correct/6	5.5 (1.0)	>	4.8 (1.5)	>	2.8 (1.2)
Phonological Awareness # correct/6	4.7 (1.3)	>	3.8 (1.4)	>	2.9 (1.4)
Oppositional Concepts # correct/6	5.4 (0.9)	>	4.4 (1.5)	>	2.4 (2.0)
Picture Sequence # correct/6	3.7 (1.6)	>	2.7 (1.5)	>	1.6 (1.0)
Picture Rhyme # correct/6	4.0 (1.6)	>	3.3 (1.4)	=	3.3 (1.2)
Standard Oddity # correct/6	5.1 (1.7)	>	3.6 (2.4)	>	2.7 (1.4)
Picture Pointing quality score	7.4 (2.6)	>	5.9 (3.3)	>	3.1 (3.1)

the NA and LD groups and the LD and MMR groups were all significant, all $ps < .01$.

Identification tasks. For the identification tasks, the overall MANOVA, $F(14, 278) = 8.71, p < .001$ and all the univariate follow-up tests, $Fs(2, 145) > 4.40, ps < .05$ were significant. Thirteen of the 14 planned contrasts were reliable, all $ps < .03$. Only the LD versus MMR contrast on the rhyme task was not significant, $p > .10$.

Secondary Analyses

Generating tasks. As previously reported in Studies 1 and 2, there were differences among the three educational groups in the number of children unable to generate a single scoreable response on generating tasks. The same was true in this study. For the semantic information task and the word meaning task, significantly more children with LD (11% and 32%, respectively) were unable to generate a single response compared to NA children (0% and 5%, respectively), both $\chi^2s(1, N = 131) > 8.00, ps < .01$. However, on these tasks, significantly more children with MMR (47% and 71%, respectively) were unable to generate a single scoreable response than children with LD, both $\chi^2s(1, N = 74) > 8.00, ps < .01$.

Identification tasks. For the identification tasks, there were differences in the numbers of children in each educational group performing at or below chance. For the picture sequence task, 94 percent of the children with MMR performed at or below chance, which was significantly more children than in the LD group (70%), $\chi^2(1, N = 74) = 4.08, p < .05$. The number of children in the LD group performing at or below chance, however, was greater than the number of NA children performing at or below chance (54%), $\chi^2(1, N = 131) = 7.69, p < .01$. The same pattern was found for the relative size task and the oppositional concepts task, with fewer of the NA children (11% and 5%, respectively) performing at or below chance compared to the children with LD (26% and 26%, respectively), both $\chi^2s(1, N = 131) > 5.00, ps < .05$, and fewer children with LD performing at or below chance compared to children with MMR (82% and 59%, respectively), both $\chi^2s(1, N = 74) > 6.00, ps < .05$.

For the phonological awareness task and the picture rhyme task, however, the pattern was different. Although fewer NA children performed at or below chance on these two tasks than children with LD, both $\chi^2(1, N = 131) > 5.00, ps > .05$, similar numbers of children with LD and children with MMR performed at or below chance on the phonological awareness and the picture rhyme tasks, both $\chi^2(1, N = 74) < 1.41, ps < .27$. For the phonological awareness task, 49 percent of the children with LD and 65 percent of the children with MMR performed at or below chance. Interestingly, for the picture rhyme task, there was a non-significant trend in the opposite direction, with fewer children with MMR (47%) performing at or below chance than children with LD (63%).

Table 7. Ordering of the Ten Tasks in Terms of Percentage Correct Responses for the Three Educational Groups in Study 3

NA		*LD*		*MMR*	
Taxonomic Gen.	86	Taxonomic Gen.	58	Picture Pointing	25
Semantic Info.	82	Semantic Info.	52	Semantic Info.	21
Word Meaning	77	Picture Pointing	49	Word Meaning	16
Picture Pointing	62	Word Meaning	47	Phonological Task	16
Relative Size	59	Relative Size	47	Relative Size	14
Standard Oddity	52	Standard Oddity	27	Taxonomic Gen.	13
Oppositional Task	40	Oppositional Task	23	Standard Oddity	11
Picture Sequence	29	Phonological Task	13	Picture Rhyme	5
Phonological Task	28	Picture Sequence	12	Picture Sequence	–7
Picture Rhyme	17	Picture Rhyme	5	Oppositional Task	–10

Relative Difficulty of the Tasks

To examine relative task difficulty, scores for each task were converted into percent correct measures (children's scores divided by the total possible number of points; see Table 6) and means were calculated for each educational group (minus percent chance performance). These data are presented in Table 7. Unlike Study 1 and Study 2, the rankings for task difficulty were more dissimilar across the three groups. Rankings for the NA children and the children with LD were somewhat similar, with the same tasks appearing in each half of the distribution. For these two groups, the picture rhyme and the phonological tasks were ranked as being particularly difficult. Yet, this was not the case for the MMR group, who had the most difficulty with the oppositional concepts task. In contrast to Study 1 and Study 2, the generating tasks (taxonomic generation, semantic information, and word meaning) were ranked as being less difficult for each educational group. This may, however, reflect a methodological difference across the studies because in Study 3, scores for each generating task were capped at either four or eight possible total points.

Summary

For all but one task, the predicted pattern of NA > LD > MMR was found. This pattern was also reflected in the secondary analyses for the new generating tasks, with more NA children generating a single scoreable response compared to children with LD, yet more children with LD generated a single response compared to children with MMR. For all of the identification tasks, fewer NA children performed at or below chance levels compared to children with LD. And for the picture sequence task, the relative size task, and the oppositional concepts task, fewer children with LD performed at or below chance levels compared to children with

MMR. However, for the picture rhyme task and the phonological awareness tasks, both requiring phonological processing skills, the number of children performing at or below chance levels did not differ in the LD and MMR groups. It should be noted that these two tasks were also ranked as the most difficult for the NA group.

GENERAL DISCUSSION

To investigate the cognitive abilities of LD and MMR children, we have presented data from three separate studies, encompassing 20 different cognitive tasks. Across each study, it was predicted that NA children would perform better than the children with LD, who would perform better than the children with MMR. For the primary analyses, the predicted pattern of NA > LD > MMR was observed for 16 out of the 20 tasks (80%). On all 20 tasks (100%), the NA children performed better than the LD children. The deviation from the predicted pattern occurred on only four of the 20 tasks on which the children with LD performed similarly to children with MMR. These results demonstrate that even on relatively simple cognitive tasks, young children classified as having MMR consistently perform at levels below that of young children classified as having LD. In turn, young children with LD consistently perform at lower mean levels than young NA children.

To better understand the cognitive abilities of children with LD and MMR, it is useful to examine those tasks on which the children with LD and MMR demonstrated similar performances. When examining primary analyses, these tasks included each rhyme task (Study 1 and 3), the oddity variations task (Study 1), and a word meaning task (Study 2). Secondary analyses also revealed several other instances of similar performance between LD and MMR children. These included the word meaning task (Study 1), the missing picture task (Study 2), and the phonological awareness task (Study 3). Examining these seven tasks, it was noted that three of the tasks involve the processing of phonological information and three of the tasks required a verbal response. Thus six of the seven tasks are language-based, seeming to support the notion that young children with LD have specific deficits in the language domain.

On the other hand, there were at least six other generating tasks that required a verbal response on which the children with LD performed better than the children with MMR. Moreover, if only children with LD exhibit specific deficits in language tasks, then they should perform similar to NA children on tasks involving more general cognitive processing such as memory and perception. Primary analyses, however, revealed that this was never the case. Deficits in general processing abilities such as metacognitive processing and memory strategies have been found in school-aged children with LD (Swanson & Cooney, 1996). Processing deficits of this nature are likely to influence performance on any cognitive task. Yet, these deficits are more subtle than those present in children with MMR, allowing children with LD to perform at a level between their NA and MMR peers. For young children with mild learning problems, children with LD and children with MMR appear to have general deficits across domains, yet differ in the level of such deficits.

What seems to affect the cognitive performance of children with LD is the level of task difficulty, or the task demands. That is, when the tasks were ranked as being difficult for the NA children, children with LD performed more similar to their MMR peers. For example, for the four tasks which deviated from the predicted pattern in the primary analyses, all four tasks were ranked either as being the most difficult task for the NA group, such as, oddity variation (Study 1) and rhyme (Study 3), or the second most difficult task for the NA group, such as word meaning (Study 2) and rhyme (Study 1). Conversely, when secondary analyses revealed that children with LD performed more like NA children, these tasks: picture pointing (Study 1), picture recall (Study 1), and dot oddity (Study 2) were ranked as being less difficult for the NA group.

Task demands therefore play an important role in the cognitive performance of LD children, with their performance being more similar to NA children on simple cognitive tasks and more like the performance of children with MMR on more difficult cognitive tasks. This pattern of results is consistent with an interactive theory of learning disabilities (Hagen, Barclay, & Schwethelm, 1982; Lipson & Wixson, 1986; Simmons & Kameenui, 1990). Within an interactive theory of learning disabilities, a learning disability is not assumed to be a stable trait but rather an interaction between the child's ability and the assessment context. Simmons and Kameenui (1990) hypothesized that task demands would influence the performance of children with LD. More specifically, they demonstrated that children with LD and NA children performed more similarly when they were provided with supportive vocabulary tasks (i.e., identification tasks) whereas less supportive vocabulary tasks (i.e., production tasks) resulted in differential performance for these two groups. However, in the present series of studies, there was no clear cut pattern indicating that the NA children and children with LD performed more similarly on identification tasks compared to generating tasks. Instead, regardless of task format, when the cognitive tasks were observed to be difficult for NA children (i.e., increased task demands), children with LD performed more poorly compared to NA children. Results from the present series of studies extends support for this theory across a wide range of cognitive tasks.

Thus, it appears that the performance of children with LD is influenced to a greater extent by the task demands, regardless of the specific task domain (i.e., language). However, an alternative hypothesis exists which might explain the cognitive performance of children with LD. Because samples of children with LD tend to represent the entire range of IQ scores, one might argue that the predicted pattern of results occurred so often because the higher functioning children with LD may have performed more like their NA peers, whereas the lower functioning children with LD performed more like their MMR peers. Attempts to identify young children with mild learning problems also indicated differential cognitive abilities of children with LD at different IQ levels. Recently, Scott, Fletcher and Deuel

(1998) found that classification accuracy for a cognitive screening test increased when children with LD with IQs equal to or greater than 115 were removed from the LD sample, suggesting that these higher IQ, LD children were performing more like their NA peers than were the LD children with lower tested IQ scores.

To examine this alternative hypothesis, an additional set of analyses was conducted. For each study, a total score was calculated for each child and the sample was divided into four different groups; (1) NA children, (2) children with LD with IQs greater than or equal to 100, (3) children with LD with IQs less than 100 and (4) children with MMR. Three separate oneway ANOVAs were conducted, one for each study, with total score as the dependent variable and group as the independent variable. In each analysis, there was an effect of group, with all *F*s > 37.00, all *p*s > .001. Duncan's comparisons revealed that, for each analysis, the NA children performed better than the children with LD with higher IQs, and the children with LD with lower IQs performed better than the children with MMR. Interestingly, in two of the three comparisons, the higher IQ, children with LD performed significantly better than the lower IQ, children with LD. Thus, the results from the present series of studies indicate that differences in cognitive performance between NA and children with LD are not solely related to intelligence.

This chapter provides the first comparison of cognitive abilities of four- and five-year-old children with MMR, children with LD, and NA children across a wide range of cognitive tasks. As expected, young children with MMR demonstrated generalized deficits across all cognitive tasks compared to NA children and on 80 percent of the cognitive tasks compared to children with LD. Contrary to expectations, however, young children with LD also demonstrated generalized deficits on all of the cognitive tasks compared to NA children. The performance of children with LD was influenced to a greater extent by the difficulty of the tasks, rather than the task domain, consistent with an interactive theory of learning disabilities.

The results are particularly important for the design of educational interventions for young children with LD or MMR. That is, children in each exceptional group appear to exhibit generalized cognitive deficits compared to NA children. So while special attention may be paid to the language deficits in young children with LD, these data indicate that children with LD will also benefit from enhanced instruction in other domains, such as perceptual learning and memory. Moreover, the data suggest that if cognitive tasks are simplified by providing more external support (i.e., pictures), children with LD may perform more similarly to NA children. Then, to improve the performance of children with LD, supports may be gradually subtracted within these same tasks, slowly increasing the level of task difficulty. Similarly, the use of more supportive cognitive tasks has been found to improve the performance of school-aged children with MMR (Bray, Fletcher, & Turner, 1997). Thus, the technique of providing extra external support and gradually reducing support may also benefit children with MMR. Future research will be necessary to investigate such possibilities.

ACKNOWLEDGMENT

We express our appreciation and gratitude to the teachers and administrators in the Dade County Public School System for facilitating this research. We also thank the children who participated and their parents who gave us their permission. This research was supported in part by NICHD Grant HD 22952 and by the Florida Diagnostic and Learning Resources System, a specialized university center funded through State General Revenue appropriations to provide multidisciplinary evaluation services in exceptional student education programs.

REFERENCES

Algozzine, K. M., Korinek, L., Morsink, C. V., & Algozzine, B. (1988). Who's on first, what's on second: Questioning in special education classrooms. *Journal of Classroom Interaction, 23*(1), 22–27.

Algozzine, B., Morsink, C. V., & Algozzine, K. M. (1988). What's happening in self-contained special education classrooms? *Exceptional Children, 55*, 259–265.

Berger, R. S., & Reid, D. K. (1989). Differences that make a difference: Comparisons of metacomponential functioning and knowledge base among groups of high and low IQ learning disabled, mildly mentally retarded, and normally achieving adults. *Journal of Learning Disabilities, 22*, 422–429.

Bray, N. W., Fletcher, K. L., & Turner, L. A. (1997). Cognitive competencies and strategy use in individuals with mild mental retardation. In W. E. McLean Jr. (Ed.), *Handbook of mental deficiency, psychological theory and research* (3rd ed.). Hillsdale, NJ: Lawrence Erlbaum.

Brown, A. L., & Palincsar, A. S. (1982). Inducing strategic learning from texts by means of informed self-control training. *Topics in Learning and Learning Disabilities, 2*, 1–18.

Deuel, L. S. (1997). *Evaluating the concurrent validity of a new screening test to detect mild cognitive impairments in young children*. Unpublished doctoral dissertation, University of Miami, Florida.

Finn, J. D., & Resnick, L. B. (1984). Issues in the instruction of mildly mentally retarded children. *Educational Researcher, 13*(3), 9–11.

Gottilieb, J., Alter, M., Gottilieb, B. W., & Wishner, J. (1994). Special education in urban America: It's not justifiable for many. *The Journal of Special Education, 27*, 453–465.

Gresham, F. M., MacMillan, D. L., & Bocian, K. M. (1996). Learning disabilities, low achievement, and mild mental retardation: More alike than different? *Journal of Learning Disabilities, 29*, 570–581.

Hagen, J. W., Barclay, C. R., & Schwethelm, B. (1982). Cognitive development of the learning-disabled child. In N. R. Ellis, (Ed.), *International review of research in mental retardation*. New York: Academic Press.

Hallahan, D. P., & Kauffman, J. M. (1976). *Learning disabilities versus emotional disturbance versus educable mental retardation. Introduction to learning disabilities*. NJ: Prentice Hall.

Hallahan, D. P., Keller, C. E., & Ball, D. W. (1986). A comparison of prevalence rate variability from state to state for each of the categories of special education. *Remedial and Special Education, 7*, 8–14.

Lipson, M. Y., & Wixson, K. K. (1986). Reading disability research: An interactionist perspective. *Review of Educational Research, 56*, 111–136.

MacMillan, D. L., Sipperstein, G. N., & Gresham, F. M. (1996). A challenge to the viability of mild mental retardation as a diagnostic category. *Exceptional Children, 62*, 356–371.

Neisworth, J. T., & Greer, J. G. (1975). Functional similarities of learning disability and mild retardation. *Exceptional Children, 42*, 17–21.

O'Sullivan, P. J., Marston, D., & Magnusson, D. (1987). Categorical special education teacher certification: Does it affect instruction of mildly handicapped pupils? *Remedial and Special Education*, *8*, 13–18.

Polloway, E. A., Epstein, M. H., Polloway, C. H., Patton, J. R., & Ball, D. W. (1986). Corrective reading program: An analysis of effectiveness with learning disabled and mentally retarded students. *Remedial and Special Education*, *7*, 41–47.

Polloway, E. A., Patton, J. R., Smith, T. E. C., & Buck, G. H. (1997). Mental retardation and learning disabilities: Conceptual and applied issues. *Journal of Learning Disabilities*, *30*, 297–308.

Scott, M. S., Deuel, L. S., Claussen, A. H., & Sanchez, M. (1993). Identifying young children with mild cognitive deficiencies. *Diagnostique*, *19*, 335–359.

Scott, M. S., Deuel, L. S., Urbano, R. C., Perou, R., Claussen, A. H., Scott, M. S., & Sanchez, M. (1996). Evaluating potential test components for a new cognitive screening test: A preliminary study. *Diagnostique*, *22*, 21–38.

Scott, M. S., Fletcher, K. L., & Deuel, L. L. (1998). The effects of intelligence on the identification of young children with learning disabilities. *Learning Disabilities: Research and Practice*, *13*, 81–88.

Scott, M. S., & Greenfield, D. B. (1992). A comparison of normally achieving, learning disabled and mildly retarded students on a taxonomic information task. *Learning Disabilities: Research and Practice*, *7*, 59–67.

Scott, M. S., Greenfield, D. B., & Partridge, M. F. (1991). Differentiating between two groups who fail in school: Performance of learning disabled and mildly retarded students on oddity problems. *Learning Disabilities: Research and Practice*, *6*(1), 3–11.

Scott, M. S., Greenfield, D. B., & Sterental, E. (1986). Abstract categorization as a predictor of learning disability classification. *Intelligence*, *10*, 377–387.

Scott, M. S., Perou, R., Greenfield, D. B., Partridge, M. F., & Swanson, L. J. (1993). A comparison of normally achieving, mildly retarded and learning disabled students on a perceptually based oddity task. *Journal of Developmental and Physical Disabilities*, *5*, 129–151.

Scott, M. S., Perou, R., Greenfield, D. B., & Swanson, L. J. (1993). Rhyming skills: Differentiating among mildly mentally retarded, learning disabled, and normally achieving students. *Learning Disabilities: Research and Practice*, *8*, 215–222.

Simmons, D. C., & Kameenui, E. J. (1988). Learning disabled and normal achievers' vocabulary knowledge: A quantitative and qualitative analysis. *National Reading Conference Yearbook*, *37*, 133–140.

Simmons, D. C., & Kameenui, E. J. (1990). The effects of task alternatives on vocabulary knowledge: A comparison of students with and without learning disabilities. *Journal of Learning Disabilities*, *23*, 291–297.

Slavin, R. E., Madden, N. A., Karweit, N. L., Dolan, L., Wasik, B. A., Shaw, A., Mainzer, K. L., & Haxby, B. (1991). Neverstreaming: Prevention and early intervention as an alternative to special education. *Journal of Learning Disabilities*, *24*, 373–378.

Swanson, H. L. (1989). The effects of central processing strategies on learning disabled, mildly retarded, average, and gifted children's elaborative encoding abilities. *Journal of Experimental Child Psychology*, *47*, 370–397.

Swanson, H. L. (1990). Executive processing differences between learning-disabled, mildly retarded, and normal achieving children. *Journal of Abnormal Child Psychology*, *18*, 549–563.

Swanson, H. L., Christie, L., & Rubadeau, R. J. (1993). The relationship between metacognition and analogical reasoning in mentally retarded, learning disabled, average, and gifted children. *Learning Disabilities: Research and Practice*, *8*, 70–81.

Swanson, H. L., & Cooney, J. B. (1996). Learning disabilities and memory. In D.K. Reid, W.P. Hresko, & H.L. Swanson, (Eds.), *Cognitive approaches to learning disabilities*. Austin, TX: PRO-ED.

Tu, S., Scott, M. S., Mason, C. A., & Urbano, R. C. (1997). Assessing cognitive similarities among young children of different ethnic/cultural backgrounds. Manuscript submitted for publication.

Wiss, C. A. (1986). A comparison of the performance of learning disabled and educable mentally handicapped children on a concept utilization task. *Canadian Journal of Exceptional Children, 2,* 84–89.

Wolman, C., van den Broek, P., & Lorch, R. F. (1997). Effects of causal structure on immediate and delayed story recall by children with mild mental retardation, children with learning disabilities, and children without disabilities. *The Journal of Special Education, 30,* 439–455.

Wood, T. A., Buckhalt, J. A., & Tomlin, J. G. (1988). A comparison of listening and reading performance with children in three educational placements. *Journal of Learning Disabilities, 21,* 493–496.

Ysseldyke, J. E., O'Sullivan, P. J., Thurlow, M. L., & Christenson, S. L. (1989). Qualitative differences in reading and math instruction received by handicapped students. *Remedial and Special Education, 10*(1), 14–20.

Ysseldyke, J. E., Thurlow, M. L., O'Sullivan, P., & Christenson, S. L. (1989). Teaching structures and tasks in reading instruction for students with mild handicaps. *Learning Disabilities Research, 4,* 78–86.

IN SEARCH OF A COMPREHENSIVE MODEL OF MATHEMATICAL WORD PROBLEM SOLVING:

IMPLICATIONS FOR THE DIAGNOSIS AND THE TREATMENT OF MATHEMATICAL WORD PROBLEM SOLVING DIFFICULTIES

Patrizio E. Tressoldi and Daniela Lucangeli

ABSTRACT

In this chapter we present a review and some of our data aimed at defining a comprehensive and economic model of the cognitive and metacognitive abilities involved in Mathematical Word Problems Solving. From the literature and the data obtained in our investigations we identified five main components: text comprehension, problem representation, problem categorization, planning of the solution and self-evaluation of the procedure. This model has been operationalized creating mathematical word problems (MWPs) with the possibility to have a measure of the efficiency of each of the five components (see text) and tested with students from the third to the seventh grade. Results obtained by the validation phase supported the

Advances in Learning and Behavioral Disabilities, Volume 13, pages 95–114.

ISBN: 0-7623-0429-4

model. From this base we devised an instrument to diagnose MWP difficulties which can give information on the efficiency of the five cognitive components. From this level of diagnosis it is now possible to carry out training programs to educate or treat MWP difficulties focusing on the components which result at a non optimal level.

Mathematical word problems (MWP) represent the mathematical activity where calculation abilities become applied to practical situations. Mathematical word problems are learned at school, but the calculations may be learned out of school where calculations are always connected to practical problems. If we can successfully discover the cognitive and metacognitive components of this activity, we may have more precise ideas on how to test, teach and train it.

With few exceptions, what emerges from the literature is a rich variety of investigations aimed at studying one or two components of those involved in the solution of MWP. What is lacking—perhaps because of the relatively small number of investigators interested in this area compared, for example to reading—are the descriptions of comprehensive MWP models, that is, models presenting all the necessary and sufficient components involved during this activity.

As may be expected, most previous literature has dealt with the first component, namely *text comprehension*. The semantic comprehension of the textual representation of the problem, the translation phase according to the terminology of Mayer, Larkin, and Kadane (1984), requires most of the cognitive processes necessary for the comprehension of every other text, such as argumentative or narrative, plus some special knowledge about the meaning of some mathematical terms, such as "altogether," "more than," or "less than."

For example Cummins (1991), demonstrated that the expression, "Mary has 5 more marbles than John," is interpreted as "Mary has 5 marbles," suggesting that children have at least tacit comprehension of part-whole relations, and what they acquire from instruction or from further familiarity with language is how certain verbal formats are associated with those relations. Low, Over, Doolan, and Michell (1994), confirmed the importance of text comprehension in training their students to detect necessary and sufficient information from algebraic word problems.

Problem representation is perhaps the second most frequently investigated component. Problem representation, that is, the construction of a mental model, is the phase where the information obtained through text comprehension is elaborated and transformed in a mental or graphical representation. According to Mayer (1981, 1992), information drawn from the text is connected (integrated) in a unified structure where the value of the different variables becomes related to each other and to the unknown data. This ability seems crucial or at least extremely important for guiding future choices for the problem solution. It is intuitive that an incorrect or a partial representation of the relation between the different variables and their values may heavily influence the solution plan and the choice of operation. There is a wide debate on the characteristics of this mental representation. Some authors argue that the problem is represented in a propositional format, others in pictorial format. Probably the format varies according to the type of problem and type of data, and doubtless is influenced by the expertise of the problem solvers (Nathan, Kintsch, & Young, 1992). However, there is a certain consensus on the fact that visual representation plays an important role in the organization of the information given in the text, and consequently on the comprehension of their relations favoring the ideation of the solution plan. (Antonietti, 1991; Hegarty, Mayer, & Monk, 1995; Kaufman, 1988; Lewis, 1989; Wicher, Weinstein, Yelich, & Brooks, 1978). Less frequently investigated is the component of *categorization*; that is, the capacity to recognize similarities and differences within the deep structure of different problems. For example, categorization includes the awareness that the problem is of the same type, even if in one case it is Pete who gives 4 marbles to Mary, and in another case, it is Mom who gives 4 marbles to Jimmy. This ability has been found in expert problem solvers (Hinsley, Hayes, & Simon, 1977; Larkin, McDermott, Simon, & Simon, 1980; Chi, Feltovich, & Glaser, 1981; Vanlehn, 1989) probably as a consequence of their experience with similar problems, and develops with increasing school experience. In fact, Morales, Shute, & Pellegrino (1985) observed that fifth and sixth graders sort a series of problems according to a schema theory of problem representation and solution, whereas third graders sort the problems according to their surface description. Swanson, Cooney, and Brock (1993) found that in third and fourth graders, problem classification added a separate contribution to problem solution with respect to other variables, such as reading comprehension and text recall. Rudnitsky, Etheredge, Freeman, and Gilbert (1995) demonstrated that this ability may be trained in order to facilitate the recovery of the inner structure of different typologies of addition and subtraction word problems by a method called structure-plus-writing. Third and fourth-grade students trained with this method outperformed controls not only at the end of the training but also at a follow up.

Planning the solution is a fourth ability generally recognized as necessary in every MWP requiring at least two steps in order to arrive at the solution. For example, consider the problem, "Tom has 4 marbles more than John. John has 2 marbles less than Mary who has 7 marbles. How many marbles do the children have overall?" It is quite obvious that, apart from the comprehension of the problem, it is necessary to be able to choose the correct order of the three required arithmetic calculations, in order to solve the problem.

In the literature, there are few studies of these cognitive components, although Fasotti (1993) has done some interesting investigations studying brain-damaged patients with frontal lobe impairment.

We considered three *metacognitive* components involved in MWPs that may be easily operationalized: estimation (approximate) of the result, self-evaluation of the procedure, and self-evaluation of the calculation. To estimate the solution may be considered a metacognitive ability to the extent that it involves a recall of past personal experiences with number calculations and with similar problems. Self-evaluation is the ability to monitor one's own performance considering one's own skills in solving MWPs in general, as well as the particular type of problem at hand. In some cases this self-evaluation is a sort of self-efficacy evaluation related to MWP ability. For example, Pajares and Kranzler (1995), and Kranzler and Pajares (1997) found that self-efficacy beliefs about problem-solving ability play a crucial role on performance.

COMPREHENSIVE MODELS

It is interesting to note that authors who propose comprehensive models—that is, models that take into account all the cognitive and metacognitive components thought to be involved in the solution of MWPs—are often interested in studying how to help normal or learning disabled children (see Jitendra & Ping Xin, 1997; Rivera, Smith, Goodwin, & Bryant, 1998 for reviews). The reason is quite obvious, given that in applied and special educational psychology it is necessary to devise training programs that may encompass all known resources in order to realize the best conditions to achieve the goals.

One of the more interesting examples is the model of Montague and her colleagues (Montague & Bos, 1986; Montague, 1992; Montague, Applegate, & Marquard, 1993). These authors demonstrated that learning disabled children improved their performance after training comprising strategies such as, read to understand, paraphrase, visualize, hypothesize a plan to solve the problem, estimate, compute the calculations, and check the procedure and the calculation. A similar approach is followed by different authors, such as Case, Harris, and Graham (1992); Miller and Mercer (1993); and for interesting proposals to implement their model using hypermedia technologies, see Babbitt (1993), Babbitt and Miller (1996), Mastropieri, Scruggs, and Shiah (1997).

Although these models are very interesting and produced interesting results, we considered it necessary to develop a validated model as a base. With a validated model, it is possible to diagnose with more precision the beginning level of subjects with MWP difficulties and devise training programs more focused on deficiencies in the components of MWP.

OUR MODEL

We decided to choose the six components (apart from the solution phase) of MWP that received the strongest empirical support: text comprehension, problem representation, problem categorization, result estimation, planning, and self-evaluation. We divided this latter component into self-evaluation of the procedure and self-evaluation of the calculation, for a total of seven components. The complete report of the validation phase is presented in Lucangeli, Tressoldi, and Cendron (1998); here we summarize the essential information.

Materials

For each grade, from the third to the fifth grades, ten pairs of word problems, and eight pairs for the sixth and the seventh grades, matched for their deep structure, were chosen from the students' textbooks and accepted after agreement with mathematics teachers.

For each grade, the battery of problems represented a range of MWPs commonly taught at that level. We were not interested in testing specific types of problems, for example following the Riley, Greeno, and Heller (1983) classification, but in devising a battery to validate a model valid for the common problems faced by students at that grade. For example, in the third grade the problems required students only to apply addition, subtraction, simple multiplication, and some knowledge of the relationship between meters and kilometers. In the seventh grade, some problems required knowledge of geometry, such as how to solve the perimeter or the area of triangles and the ability to use all the arithmetic calculations, fractions, and proportions. All problems required at least three steps and two different arithmetic calculations for the solution.

The 10 Standard Problems were transcribed on a single sheet of paper. For each of the other 10 Partitioned Problems, four answers were prepared for each of the problem solving components chosen for the present investigation: text comprehension, problem representation, problem categorization, result estimation, solution plan, procedure self-evaluation, calculation self-evaluation. Particular attention was paid to not provide suggestions on the calculations necessary for the solution.

Example of a Mathematical Word Problem for the Fourth Grade

(Reprinted from Lucangeli et al. 1998, pp. 261–264. Reprinted by permission.)

Standard Version:

I bought 6 notebooks at $2.00 each. Then I bought 2 pens at $1.00 each and one album at $3.50. Before paying the stationer gave me a discount of 8% on my total. How much did I spend?

Partioned Version:

Julia buys 4 notebooks at $3.00 each. Then she buys a ruler at $1.50 and an eraser at $1.70. At the end the stationer gave her a discount of 10% on the total she paid. How much does Julia spend?

COMPREHENSION:
Choose the sentence with the information more important for the solution:
___ The discount increased the total price Julia had to pay. (incorrect)
___ Julia should buy notebooks at a lower price. (irrelevant)
___ The discount lowered the price to pay. (correct)
___ The books cost more than the other things. (partially correct)

Figure 1.

REPRESENTATION

Choose among the pictures the one which correctly represents the problem.

CLASSIFICATION

Which of the following problems could you solve in the same way as the problem you are working with?

- Julia completes many notebooks each month. How many notebooks does she complete in one school year?
- Mary wishes to buy a ball which costs $15.00 to give to her friend Pat. On that day there was a general discount of 5%, so Mary bought 2 series of figures which cost $1.50 each. How much did Mary spend overall?
- Yesterday Mat bought some notebooks, which cost 10% more than last week when they cost $1.20 each. If he also bought a pen for $1.50, how much did he spend?
- Anthony buys 4 notebooks for $1.30 each and 2 erasers for $0.80 each. How much does he spend?

SOLUTION PLAN

Show how you would solve the problem, ordering the sequences and numbering them from 1 to 3.

____ I add the price of the eraser and of the ruler.
____ I take away the discount from the total to pay.
____ I find the total price of the notebooks.

EXECUTION

Solve the problem.

EVALUATION OF THE PROCEDURE

Indicate how certain you are of having correctly executed your solution plan:

_____I'm completely certain that I have correctly solved it.
_____I'm uncertain that I solved it correctly.
_____I may have done it incorrectly.
_____I'm certain that I have done it incorrectly.

Scoring

For the first four components the four choices represent different degrees of accuracy:

- correct answer (rated with four points);
- partial answer (rated with three points);
- incorrect answer (rated with two points);
- irrelevant answer (rated with one point);

We chose to rate the irrelevant choice lower than the incorrect choice, because we consider it more serious to refer to information not related to the problem goal than to fail to comprehend its deep structure.

The solution plan was evaluated according to the number of steps ordered correctly (minimum zero, maximum according to the steps indicated in the problem).

The solution was also rated along a four level scale:

- Correct solution (four points);
- Correct procedure but calculation errors (three points);
- Partial solution (two points);
- Incorrect solution (one point).

The two evaluation components were rated as follows:

- Three points in the case of an agreement between evaluation (certain of a correct solution or certain of a wrong solution) and solution (three-four points or one-two points, respectively);
- Two points in the case of the choice "I am unsure I solved it correctly" and "I may have done it incorrectly";
- One point in case of mismatch between evaluation and solution;
- Omissions were rated zero points.

It is evident that the score is higher as the subject is able to correctly monitor his/her performance. We tested a total of 366 students.

RESULTS

For each class, Cronbach's *alpha* and the Guttman split-half coefficient were calculated in order to verify the reliability of the problem battery. Cronbach's *alpha* ranged from .80 to .90 with a mean of .84, while the Guttman split-half ranged from .69 to .83 with a mean of .74. To have a measure of the concurrent validity, we

Table 1. Mean, Standard Deviation, Correlation and Effect Size (d) of the Solution Score for the Two Type of Problems, for Each Grade

	Standard Problems *Mean (s.d.)*	*Partitioned Problems* *Mean (s.d.)*	*R*	*Effect Size*
3rd grade	2.33 (.81)	2.14 (.70) +	.80*	24
4th grade	2.96 (.70)	2.91 (.78)	.75*	.06
5th grade	2.08 (.88)	1.93 (.95) +	.81*	.16
6th grade	2.13 (.76)	2.32 (.82) +	.65*	–.23
7th grade	2.45 (.94)	2.28 (.95) +	.55*	.18
Grand Mean	2.42 (.86)	2.33 (.9) +	.73*	.10

Notes: * = $r = p < .05$; + = $t = p < .05$

From Lucangeli et al. (1998), p. 265. Reprinted by permission.

compared the mean obtained at the solution of the two types of problems, those solved after a series of response choices, and those solved using traditional procedures.

In Table 1 we report the means of the scores obtained in the solution of all the problems (maximum score for each problem = 4), their standard deviations, the correlation and effect size of the two types of problems for each class.

DISCUSSION

All the correlation coefficients are very high and statistically significant, confirming that the two versions of the problems share a significant percentage of variance. Furthermore, the differences between the two versions were always small. We can then assume that during the solution of the Partitioned Problems, subjects utilize the same cognitive mechanisms employed in the solution of the Standard Problems.

Common Variance Between the Solution and the Cognitive Components

We then analyzed the data using a hierarchical multiple regression, taking the scores of the seven cognitive variables as independent variables and the score of the solution as an dependent variable ordered as follows: text comprehension, problem representation, problem categorization, result estimate, solution plan, procedure self-evaluation, calculation self-evaluation.

The mean and standard deviation (in parenthesis) of R^2 increment obtained from the six samples of subjects, for each variable, was: Comprehension, .28 (.17); Representation, .10 (.09); Categorization, .08 (.04); Estimate, .02 (.02); Solution Plan, .09 (.07); Procedure Self-Evaluation, .06 (.02); Calculation Self- Evaluation, .002 (.001). From these results we found that result estimation and calculation self-evaluation did not add a significant increment of variance. For the subsequent validations we then used a model with only five cognitive components, text comprehension, problem representation, problem categorization, solution plan and procedure self-evaluation.

To control the stability of this reduced model, for each grade we calculated the mean and the standard deviation of R^2 obtained with the hierarchical multiple regression analysis after 100 resamplings using a bootstrap procedure (Péladeau & Lacouture, 1993). These results are presented in Table 2.

Path Analysis

In order to test the mutual relationship among the variables of the model, we tested the goodness of fit of different relationships maintaining the comprehension as the first variable and the solution as the last, using the EQS program (Bentler 1995). The model which gives the best fit indices is the model presented in Figure 2, where comprehension influences directly the representation, the categorization

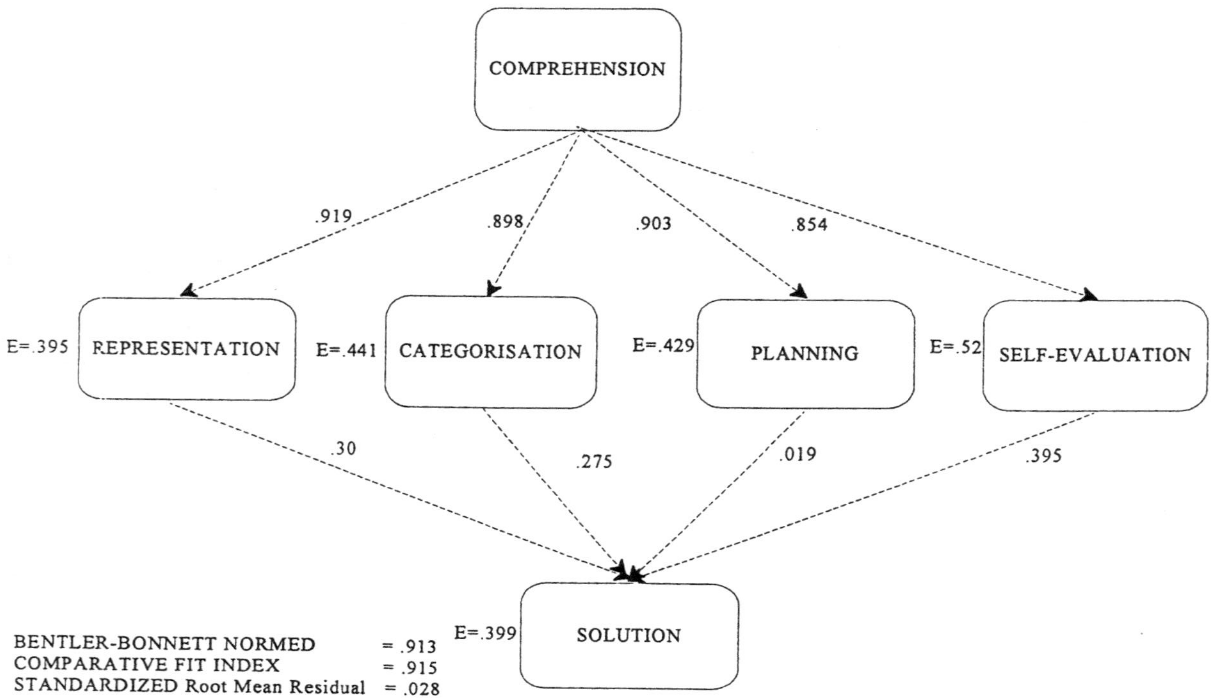

(Numbers along the arrows represents standardized coefficients; E, represent errors residuals)

Figure 2. (Reprinted from Lucangeli et al. (1998), p. 267. Reprinted by permission.)

Table 2. Mean and Standard Deviation of Multiple Correlation R^2 after 100 Bootstrap Resampling, for Each Grade

	Partitioned Problems		*Standard Problems*	
	Mean	*S.D.*	*Mean*	*S.D.*
3rd grade	.68	.06	.49	.09
4th grade	.81	.03	.55	.10
5th grade	.83	.05	.55	.08
6th grade	.68	.06	.43	.10
7th grade	.50	.08	.30	.07

Source: Reprinted from Lucangeli et al. (1998), p. 266. Reprinted by permission.

and the planning of the solution without postulating a mutual relationship among these variables.

Discriminant Validity

To control the discriminant validity of the variables retained in the regression model, we tested the degree of discrimination of different levels of solution efficiency. We divided the subjects into three categories according to their solution score in the Partitioned Problems. The three categories corresponded respectively to the first quartile (bad solvers), to the two interquartiles (medium solvers) and the fourth quartile (good solvers).

In Table 3 we report the rounded mean of percentage of categories prediction for all grades, obtained with a discriminant analysis using the Jackknife method (Huberty 1994), using the five cognitive components retained in the model as dependent variables.

Table 3. Prediction Percentages of the Three Problem Solver Categories Obtained with a Discriminant Analysis Using the Jacknife Method: Means of the Five Grades

Ability Category	*Bad Solvers Prediction*	*Medium Solvers Prediction*	*Good Solvers Prediction*
Bad solvers	**77.2**	32.8	
Medium solvers	9.5	**76.5**	14
Good solvers		27.2	**72.8**

Source: Reprinted from Lucangeli et al. (1998), p. 268. Reprinted by permission.

DISCUSSION

The percentages of the hits are not particularly impressive even if they are always substantially superior to the chance of 33 percent, using the control for the maximum chance criterion (Huberty 1984). However, the discriminant validity of the five variables receives support from the fact that the cases not predicted in the expected category fall only in the adjacent categories. Obviously, more refinements are needed in the choice of the problems within the battery to improve the discrimination among the three categories of problem solvers.

THE BATTERY

After the validation phase, the next step was to reduce the number of partitioned problems to a more manageable quantity so to devise a practical battery for the evaluation of the efficiency of the five components of MWP ability of students with learning disabilities. For each grade, we used a discriminant analysis to select the three problems for the third grade and the four problems for the other grades, sufficient to discriminate the three categories of problem solvers as indicated in the validation phase. We used as independent variables the total score of each problem (summing up the score obtained in each component), and as dependent variable the categories of problem solvers. At the end, we obtained a battery, MWPB, Mathematical Word Problem Battery (Lucangeli, Tressoldi, and Cendron, 1998) for the evaluation of five cognitive components of the MWP ability from the third to the seventh grade.

APPLICATIONS

As anticipated, the aim of the battery construction was to have an instrument that after the diagnosis of the efficiency of some of the main components of the MWP ability should serve to plan a more focused treatment to ameliorate only those components resulting at an insufficient level. Next, we describe as example an application and the obtained results after treatment, with two cases.

Erika

Erika is attending the fourth grade. She is of normal intelligence (IQ = 94), without problems in reading accuracy and comprehension, or in mathematical calculation. However, from the previous grade, she manifests a particular difficulty in the solution of MWPs. She has normal relationships with her peers, but scores within a significant range for Attention Deficit Hyperactivity Disorder (ADHD) problems on a behavioral scale (a revised version of the Conner's Teacher Rating Scale according to DSM-IV criteria). Her scores at the MWPB confirm her

Table 4. Erika's and Giovanni's Initial Profile at the MWPB

Name: Erika; Grade: 4th; Date: 5/96

	Percentile				
	10	*20*	*30*	*40*	*> 40*
Comprehension		*			
Representation		*			
Categorization			*		
Planning			*		
Self-evaluation					*
Solution	*				

Name: Giovanni; Grade: 5th; Date: 10/96

	Percentile				
	10	*20*	*30*	*40*	*> 40*
Comprehension	*				
Representation				*	
Categorization	*				
Planning		*			
Self-evaluation					*
Solution	*				

difficulties in the solution of MWPs. Furthermore, she scores at a low level in the Comprehension and Representation components (see Table 4) .

Giovanni

Giovanni is in the fifth grade. His IQ is within the normal range (105). He presents some difficulties in calculation (his score on a standardized test is equivalent to the 10th percentile) and in word problem solving. He does not have particular difficulties in reading and spelling. His scholastic motivation is sufficient, and he does not manifest particular emotional and relational difficulties. Table 4 reports the results obtained on the MWPB.

Treatment

For Erika a special teacher planned a one-to-one treatment plan one hour per week for four months, intended to promote her abilities to detect and comprehend the relevant information from the text of the math problems and to represent their mutual relationship. The training followed the suggestions presented in the book *Mathematics and Metacognition* (Cornoldi, Caponi, Falco, Focchiatti, Lucangeli, & Todeschini, 1995) and other sources (see examples in the Appendix). For

Table 5. Erika's and Giovanni's Scores at the MWPB Retest

Name: Erika; Grade: 4th; Date: 10/96

	Percentile				
	10	*20*	*30*	*40*	*> 40*
Comprehension					*
Representation					*
Categorization				*	
Planning					*
Self-evaluation					*
Solution				*	

Name: Giovanni; Grade 5th; Date: 2/97

	Percentile				
	10	*20*	*30*	*40*	*> 40*
Comprehension					*
Representation				*	
Categorization		*			
Planning		*			
Self-evaluation					*
Solution	*				

Giovanni, a special teacher planned a one-to-one treatment centered on promoting the comprehension, categorization and planning components of MWPs and arithmetic procedures.

At the end of the training period, Erika's scores at the MWPB retest demonstrated a substantial improvement in the two target components and in the solution, whereas Giovanni obtained a better score in the comprehension component, a mild improvement in categorization (from less than the 10th to the 20th percentile), but no substantial improvement on planning and solution (see Table 5).

CONCLUSION

In this chapter, we offered a hint on how a comprehensive model of MWP components may be operationalized, tested and transformed as a practical instrument of evaluation. Data obtained from this evaluation may serve as a base to devise treatments focused on those components that result at a non-optimal level. By this approach, we think it is possible to tailor educational and therapeutic resources for the specific needs of each student.

The examples of application of the MWPB we have presented serve only as a suggestion of the practical benefits this battery may offer to the teacher or to the clinician. The possibility to observe the level of efficiency of five important components of the MWP ability may be important information, first, to know more precisely why that subject has difficulties in solving MWPs and, second, what should be the goals of the treatment. What to do to improve the efficiency of the cognitive and metacognitive components which result at a nonsatisfactory level is an open and empirical question. Jitendra and Ping Xin (1997), and Rivera and colleagues (1998) offer a review of different approaches aimed at improving MWP solving ability. Our paper does not give indications on hòw to treat it, apart from the suggestion of a treatment based on a metacognitive approach. What we see as the main contribution of this model is the possibility that treatments may be personalized, and must consider all the components we have considered in our model, because each one adds a distinct contribution to MWP ability.

APPENDIX

Examples of the training units drawn from the Cornoldi and colleagues (1995) book, *Mathematics and Metacognition*.

General Guidelines:

Every activity is usually proposed in such a way that the student may become aware of:

- the task and its givens;
- how the task is made by the student himself or by other students and through which mental functions;
- what kind of strategies to use, how to learn to find them out (to formulate them) and how to check the application.

Goal: To Recognize the Relation between Text Comprehension and Problem Solving

The program presents different units to practice the abilities involved in the comprehension of the problem text.

In particular these units guide the children:

To Reflect on the Problem Data

The exercises are based on the selection of the relevant data and on the recognition of the relation between the data. The main steps are:

- analysis of the question of the problem to understand the request;
- selection of the relevant data;
- transcription of the relevant data;
- elaboration of a possible schema that summarizes the relationship between the data.

To Recognize the Text Structure and to Change It through a New Formulation

The exercises are based on texts not well lexically structured. To understand the text it is necessary to change the order of the words to obtain a new formulation.

For example:
"How many balls Bill has if now he lost 3 of the 11 balls he had yesterday?"
(how many balls does Bill have now if yesterday he lost 3 of his 11 balls?)

Children are guided to reflect on the role of the structure of the text and they become practiced to prepare good text structures of mathematical word problem solving. Furthermore, they practice to utilize the typical structure of the text to formulate new problems.

To Reflect upon the Question and on its Meaning for the Solution

The exercises are based on different steps:

a) To recognize if problems could be solved when the text does not contain the question.
b) To recognize possible questions for the same problem. For example the children has to formulate all the possible questions regarding the text "Bill has 6 toys less than Paul. Paul has 14 toys"
   How many toys Bill has less than Paul? ______________________
   How many. . . . . ______________________
c) To formulate possible texts knowing the question. For example:
   How much money the children have together? ______________________
   ____
   ____
   How much the father spent to buy the toys to his two children? ________
   ____
   ____

To be Able to Monitor Problem Comprehension

The children are guided to monitor the comprehension recognizing what is necessary to check:

- the comprehension of the relevant data;
- the comprehension of the questions;
- the relation among the data.

Goal: To Represent the Problem

The program presents different units to practice the abilities involved in the representation of the problem. In particular, these units guide the children:

To Recognize that a Representation of the Problem Summarizes the Main Information of the Problem

The children are guided to realize that it is possible to imagine the situation presented in the text in a unique way.

The children are invited to discuss together the purpose of these representations and to recognize their utility in summarizing the main information.

To Recognize Different Forms of Representation and their Goals

The exercises are divided in different parts:

1. Children are invited to produce different types of representations of a problem;
2. Children are guided to reflect upon the advantages and the disadvantages of these different representations;
3. Children have to choose the more efficient representation for different problems.

For example: Louise has 5 shirts and 4 pairs of pants. How many combinations of shirts and pants can Louise choose?

A garden of 3.6 hectometer^2, has 50% of trees, the 20% of flowers, the rest of grass. Calculate the area of each part of the garden.

Goal: To Plan the Steps Necessary to Obtain the Solution

The program presents different units to practice the abilities involved in the planning of the solution.

In particular, these units guide the children:

To Recognize that Planning Means an Ordered Sequence of Actions Toward the Solution

The children are invited to play with Tangram presented in Figure 3.

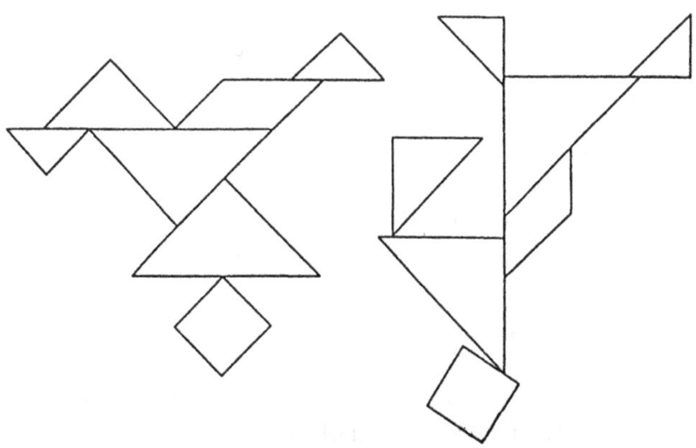

Figure 3.

Instruction: Form figures like those presented in the left column. You must use only the numbers of the tangram's pieces indicated in the first row. Write "impossible" when you think it is impossible to form the figure requested.

After the exercise, the children are invited to reflect and to describe the steps used to solve the task. The same approach is used with mathematical tasks. The children are guided to train themselves in planning mathematical word problems.

To Find the "Point of Approach": How to Find the First Step

The children are invited to discuss the situations required to find the first step.

For example, given a crossword puzzle, the subjects need to find the first answer to start with. It is necessary for the following answers. Every answer depends on the previous one.

To Recognize that there May be More Than One Correct Way to Solve Problems

The children are invited to find all the possible plans to solve the same word problem. They have to discuss together which would be the best plan. They must decide, considering the following criteria:

1. to verify the intrinsic coherence of the steps involved in the plan;
2. to obtain a plan based on a minimum numbers of steps, excluding the useless steps;
3. to choose the plan involving the simplest and more efficient arithmetical procedures.

Goal: To Monitor the Execution and Evaluate the Result of the Task

The program presents some units to learn monitoring the different phases involved in the solution of mathematical word problems. In particular, children are trained:

1. to recognize the importance of monitoring in performing some tasks.
2. to discuss together about the benefits they may obtain monitoring the text comprehension, the representation of the problems, the planning of solution and the execution of calculation.
3. and to learn how to use monitoring strategies for each of the abilities necessary to arrive at the solution. This means strategies to use self control procedures and to check the accuracy of every operation.

Evaluation:

- to be able to evaluate one's performance in order to verify the accuracy of the adopted procedure in the execution of the task;
- to be able to use the final result to find the error in the solution process;

- to learn how to check the heuristics of probability if the final result is not available;
- to learn to compare the performance with other people;
- to recognize the importance of the evaluation of performance with other people;
- to learn to evaluate the performance using the monitoring processes.

REFERENCES

Antonietti, A. (1991). Why does mental visualization facilitate problem solving? In R. H. Logie & M. Denis (Eds.), *Mental images in human cognition*. (pp. 221–227). Amsterdam: Elsevier.

Babbitt, B. (1993). Hypermedia: Making the mathematics connections. *Intervention in School and Clinic, 28*, 294–301.

Babbitt, B., & Miller, S. P. (1996). Using Hypermedia to improve the mathematical problem-solving skills of students with learning disabilities. *Journal of Learning Disabilities, 29*(4), 391–412.

Bentler, P. M. (1995). *EQS structural equations program manual*. Encino, CA: Multivariate Software Inc.

Case, L. P., Harris, K. R., & Graham, S. (1992). Improving the mathematical problem-solving skills of students with learning disabilities: self-regulated strategy development. *The Journal of Special Education, 26*, 1–19.

Chi, M. T. H., Feltovich, P. J., & Glaser, R. (1981). Categorization and representation of physics problems by expert and novices. *Cognitive Science, 5*, 121–152.

Cornoldi, C., Caponi, B., Falco, G., Focchiatti, R., Lucangeli, D., & Todeschini, M. (1995). *Matematica e metacognizione* (Mathematics and metacognition). Trento. Italy: Edizioni Erikson.

Cummins, D. D. (1991). Children's interpretations of arithmetic word problem. *Cognition and Instruction, 8, 3*, 261–289.

Fasotti, L. (1993). *Arithmetic word problem solving after frontal lobe damage. A cognitive neuropsychological approach*. Amsterdam: Swets & Zeitlinger.

Hegarty, M., Mayer, R. E., & Monk, C. A. (1995). Comprehension of arithmetic word problems: A comparison of successful and unsuccessful problem solvers. *Journal of Educational Psychology, 87*(1), 18–32.

Hinsley, D., Hayes, J. R., & Simon, H. (1977). From words to equation: meaning and representation in algebra word problems. In P. A. Carpenter & M. A. Just (Eds.), *Cognitive processes in comprehension*. (pp. 89–106). Hillsdale: Lawrence Erlbaum.

Huberty, C.J. (1984). Issues in the use and development of discriminant analysis. *Psychological Bulletin, 95*, 156–171.

Huberty, C. J. (1994). *Applied discriminant analysis*. Wiley: New York.

Jitendra, A., & Ping Xin, Y. (1997). Mathematical word-problem-solving instruction for students at risk for math failure: a research synthesis. *The Journal of Special Education, 30, 4*, 412–438.

Kaufman, G. (1988). Mental imagery and problem solving. In M. Denis, J. Engelkamp, & J. T. E. Richardson (Eds)., *Cognitive and neuropsychological approaches to mental imagery*. (pp. 231–240). Boston: Nijkoff.

Kranzler, J., & Pajares, F. (1997). An exploratory factor analysis of the Mathematics Self-Efficacy Scale-Revised. *Measurement and Evaluation in Counseling and Development, 29, 4*, 215–228.

Larkin, J. H., McDermott, J., Simon, D. P., & Simon, H. A. (1980). Expert and novice performance in solving physics problems. *Science, 208*, 1335–1342.Lewis, A. B. (1989). Training students to represent arithmetic word problems. *Journal of Educational Psychology, 81*, 521–531.

Low, R., Over, R., Doolan, L., & Michell, S. (1994). Solution of algebraic word problems following training in identifying necessary and sufficient information within problems. *American Journal of Psychology, 107*, 423–439.

Lucangeli, D., Tressoldi, P. E., & Cendron, M. (1998). Cognitive and metacognitive abilities involved in the solution of mathematical word problems: Validation of a comprehensive model. *Contemporary Educational Psychology, 23*, 257–275.

Lucangeli, D., Tressoldi, P. E., & Cendron, M. (1998). *SPM. Soluzione Problemi di Matematica*. Trento, Italy: Edizioni Erickson.

Mastropieri, M., Scruggs, T. E., & Shiah, R. (1997). Can computers teach problem-solving strategies to student with mild mental retardation? *Remedial and Special Education, 3*, 157–165.

Mayer, R. E. (1981). Frequency norms and structural analysis of algebra story problems. *Journal of Educational Psychology, 74*, 199–216.

Mayer, R. E. (1992). *Thinking, problem solving, cognition*. New York: Freeman.

Mayer, R. E., Larkin, J. H., & Kadane, J. (1984). A cognitive analysis of mathematical problem solving ability. In R. Sternberg (Ed.), *Advances in the Psychology of Human Intelligence*. (pp. 231–273). Hillsdale, NJ: Lawrence Erlbaum.

Miller, S. P., & Mercer, C. D. (1993). Using a graduate word problem sequence to promote problem-solving skills. *Learning Disability Research & Practice, 8*, 169–174.

Montague, M. (1992). The effects of cognitive and metacognitive strategy instruction on the mathematical problem solving of middle school students with learning disabilities. *Journal of Learning Disabilities, 25*(4), 230–248.

Montague, M., Applegate, B., & Marquard, K. (1993). Cognitive strategies instruction and mathematical problem-solving performance of students with learning disabilities. *Learning Disabilities Research & Practice, 8*, 223–232.

Montague, M., & Bos, C. S. (1986). The effect of cognitive strategy training on verbal math problem solving performance of learning disabled adolescents. *Journal of Learning Disabilities, 19*(1), 26–33.

Morales, R. V., Shute, V. J., & Pellegrino, J. W. (1985). Development differences in understanding and solving simple mathematics word problems. *Cognition and Instruction, 2*, 41–57.

Nathan, M. J., Kintsch, W., & Young, E. (1992). A theory of algebra word problem comprehension and its implications for the design of learning environments. *Cognition and Instruction, 4*, 329–390.

Pajares, F., & Kranzler, J. (1995). Self-efficacy beliefs and general mental ability in mathematical problem-solving. *Contemporary Educational Psychology, 20*(4), 426–443.

Péladeau, N., & Lacouture, Y. (1993). SIMSTAT: Bootstrap computer simulation and statistical program for IBM personal computer. *Behavior Research Method, Instruments, & Computers, 25*(3), 410–413.Riley, M. S., Greeno, J. G., & Heller, J. J. (1983). Developments of children's problem solving ability in arithmetic. In H. P. Ginsburg (Ed.), *The development of mathematical thinking*. (pp. 153–196). New York: Academic Press.

Rivera, D. P., Smith, R. G., Goodwin, M. W., & Bryant B. R. (1998). Mathematical word problem solving: A synthesis of intervention research for students with learning disabilities. *Advances in learning and behavioral disabilities* (vol. 12, pp. 245–285). Greenwich, CT: JAI Press.

Rudnitsky, A., Etheredge, S., Freeman, S. J., & Gilbert, T. (1995). Learning to solve addition and subtraction word problems through a structure-plus-writing approach. *Journal of Research in Mathematics Education, 26*(5), 467–486.

Swanson, H. L., Cooney, J. B., & Brock, S. (1993). The influence of working memory and classification ability on children's word problem solution. *Journal of Experimental Child Psychology, 3*, 374–395.

Vanlehn, K. (1989). Problem solving and cognitive skill acquisition. In M. Posner (Ed.), *Foundations of cognitive science* (pp. 527–579). Cambridge, MA: MIT Press.

Wicher, F. W., Weinstein, C. E., Yelich, C. A., & Brooks, J. D. (1978). Problem reformulation training and visualization training with insight problems. *Journal of Educational Psychology, 70*, 372–377.

THE ROLE OF WORKING MEMORY AND METACOGNITION IN READING COMPREHENSION DIFFICULTIES

Francesca Pazzaglia, Rossana De Beni, and Lucia Cacciò

ABSTRACT

This chapter presents an overview of the authors' work on children and adults who have comprehension difficulties. In the first part, several studies supporting the existence of a relationship between reading comprehension, metacognition and working memory (WM) are reviewed. In the second part, the relationships between WM and metacognition, and their relevance in reading comprehension are investigated in greater detail, examining groups of good and poor comprehenders of different ages (13, 14, 16 years old). Working memory ability was evaluated by using a revised Italian version of the listening span test (Daneman & Carpenter, 1980), and metacognitive proficiency was evaluated by a metacognitive test (Pazzaglia, De Beni, & Cristante, 1994) on four metacognitive areas: knowledge about (1) task, (2) strategies,

Advances in Learning and Behavioral Disabilities, Volume 13, pages 115–134.

ISBN: 0-7623-0429-4

(3) text sensitivity, and (4) control. Correlation and regression analyses support the existence of a relationship between working memory and metacognitive variables, stronger when areas of text sensitivity and control are considered.

This paper is primarily an overview of our work on children and adults who have comprehension difficulties, though we outline other theories, and discuss their relation to our work. In the first part, several studies supporting the existence of a relationship between reading comprehension, metacognition and working memory (WM) are reviewed. In the second part, the relationships between WM and metacognition and their relevance in reading comprehension are investigated in greater detail.

Many studies on comprehension difficulties (for a review see Cornoldi & Oakhill, 1996; De Beni & Pazzaglia, 1995; Garner, 1987; Yuill & Oakhill, 1991) have pointed to a series of cognitive variables as discriminators of good and poor comprehenders, e.g. decoding, general and lexical knowledge, syntactic ability (Norman, Kemper, & Kynette, 1992; Penning & Raphael, 1991), working memory efficiency (Yuill, Oakhill, & Parkin, 1989); ability to activate adequate schema of knowledge and change the wrong ones (Blachowicz, 1984); ability to make inferences (Yuill & Oakhill, 1988), and to organize the material just read (Golinkoff, 1976; Ryan, 1981). Differences between good and poor comprehenders were also found in a number of metacognitive variables involved in reading: knowledge of reading goals and of reading strategies, text sensitivity, and comprehension monitoring (Brown, Armbruster, & Baker; 1986; Garner, 1987; Garner & Kraus, 1981–1982).

These studies show clearly that reading comprehension is a complex ability that requires several specific cognitive components; some of them are likely to be central and to involve a number of attentional resources as well as a general executive function (Baddeley, 1990; Moscovitch & Umiltà, 1991). Given the complexity of the task, it is not surprising that research comparing good and poor comprehenders has found a high variety of deficits. On the other hand, analysis of the profiles of single poor comprehenders showed that they differed widely and did not have the same deficits (see for example, Cacciò, De Beni, & Pazzaglia, 1996; Cornoldi, De Beni, & Pazzaglia, 1996; Palladino, De Beni, & Cornoldi, 1995). Such evidence suggests that there are different types of poor comprehenders who may be affected selectively either by WM problems, or by metacognitive deficits, or by more general semantic processing deficits involving oral language as well, or, finally, by any combination of two or more deficits. From a clinical viewpoint, it is important to make an accurate analysis of the abilities of poor comprehenders in order to intervene correctly in each case. This approach focused more on the study of single cases, but is complementary to a comparison between groups of good and poor comprehenders, which would allow us to highlight the variables which may normally be involved in a reading comprehension task.

In this chapter, we focus on the following two variables: elaboration processes, referred to as working memory efficiency, and a high order variable, which comprises metacognitive knowledge and monitoring activity during reading. We do not wish to minimize the influence of other areas, but our research focused on these areas.

WORKING MEMORY

Working memory is a system for temporary storage and processing of information. It is involved in the execution of a range of cognitive tasks such as learning, reasoning and reading comprehension (e.g. Baddeley, 1986). According to Baddeley (1992), working memory can be divided into different subsystems: the central executive, involved in attention-demanding activities not specifically related to information modality, and the articulatory loop and the visuo-spatial sketchpad, which are devoted to maintaining and processing auditory-articulatory and visuo-spatial information, respectively.

The existence of a relationship between working memory and reading comprehension has been supported by several studies (Daneman & Carpenter, 1980; Masson & Miller, 1983; Yuill, Oakhill, & Parkin, 1989). Daneman and Carpenter (1980) found significant correlations between reading comprehension and two working memory tests: the reading and the listening span tests. They then found that high reading span were better than low reading span subjects in interpreting the meaning of ambiguous words when they were a long way away from the portion of text necessary to disambiguate them (Daneman & Carpenter, 1983). Since then, a large number of studies have shown positive correlations between listening and reading span tests and reading comprehension tasks (Masson & Miller, 1983; Baddeley, Logie, Nimmo-Smith, & Brereton, 1985; Dixon, Lefevre, & Twilley, 1988; Ehrlich, Brébion, & Tardieu, 1994). From a meta-analysis performed by Daneman & Merikle (1996) on seventy-seven studies, reading and listening span tests turned out to be good predictors of comprehension in all but two studies.

In a study carried out by two of us (De Beni & Pazzaglia, 1995), we intended to verify, within the framework of Baddeley's working memory model, which component of WM was the most important in reading comprehension. The following tests were administered to two groups of poor and good comprehenders:

- A revised Italian version of the listening span test (Daneman & Carpenter, 1980), to assess verbal working memory efficiency with semantically relevant material. Subjects were presented with 4 sets, each containing 5 groups of 2, 3, 4, 5, and 6 sentences. Half the sentences were true and half were false. In each trial the subject listened to a group of sentences and answered "true" or "false" to each sentence. At the end of each group, subjects recalled in order the last word in each sentence;

- The digit working memory span test (Yuill, Oakhill, & Parkin, 1989) to assess verbal working memory efficiency when a complex semantic process was not required. Subjects were required to read sets of 2, 3, 4, 5, and 6 strings of digits. At the end of each set, subjects recalled in order the last digit in each string;
- Three tests which required random generation of letters at different rates (one letter every half, one and two seconds), (see Baddeley, 1966), to assess central executive functioning;
- The Figure Intersection Test by Pascual-Leone and Ijaz, a completely non-verbal test with visuo-spatial material that is thought to involve a more general working memory component (Pascual-Leone & Ijaz, 1989).

Comparison between groups showed that poor comprehenders did less well on the listening span and WM digit span tests, the Figure Intersection Test, and the random generation letters task (at the rate of one letter per second) than good comprehenders. Analysis showed significant correlations between the listening span and WM digit span tests, both supposed to depend strongly on articulatory loop functioning. Very low, not significant correlations were found between the other variables. Similar results were found for older groups of good and poor comprehenders aged 14 and 16 (Cacciò, DeBeni, & Pazzaglia, 1996). The two groups differed for all variables.

Taken together, our results support Baddeley's multicomponential model of working memory, suggesting the existence of a central-executive component assessed by random generation tests and separated from the two slave domain-specific (verbal and visuo-spatial) subsystems. Poor comprehenders' difficulties were not specifically linked to any one of these components, but seemed to involve them all, with poor performance in processing and storing both visuo-spatial and verbal materials. Our results are not consistent with Daneman and Carpenter's (1980, 1983) "semantic elaboration" hypothesis. They suggested that processing and storage compete for the limited capacity in working memory and that less-skilled comprehenders would devote more resources to semantic processing, thus saving fewer resources for the memory test. This hypothesis would predict that working memory measures correlate with reading only when they require the processing of sentences, but has difficulty in explaining why poor comprehenders do worse in working memory tests (such as the digit working memory test) which do not require processing of linguistic material (see also Daneman & Tardif, 1987; Engle, Cantor & Carullo, 1992) . Yuill, Oakhill, and Parkin (1989), with their "general processing" hypothesis, claimed that poor comprehenders' difficulty is not specific to semantic-processing tasks, but may also be found with numerical and visuo-spatial materials, as supported by our data. This last explanation would suggest the influence of a more general, superordinate factor on performance.

The relationship between the listening span test and reading comprehension raises questions about which processes required in the listening span test are mainly involved in comprehension. Indeed, such a relationship can be explained in many different ways. Some studies (Hamm & Hasher, 1992; Hartman & Hasher, 1991; May, Kane, Hasher, Multhaup & Valenti, 1996) suggested that both working memory and comprehension deficits may be due to poor inhibitory mechanisms, that is the difficulty in inhibiting information irrelevant to the goals of the reading task (Gernsbacher, 1990; Gernsbacher, 1993; Gernsbacher, Varner, & Faust, 1990; Hasher & Zacks, 1988; Meiran, 1996).

In some recent investigations (Borella, 1998; De Beni, Palladino, Pazzaglia, & Cornoldi, 1998; De Beni & Pazzaglia, 1997; Zambianchi, 1996), we examined the implications of a suggested relationship between inhibitory mechanisms, working memory and comprehension by studying groups of good and poor comprehenders of different ages. We analyzed samples of primary school (Zambianchi, 1996), secondary school (De Beni & Pazzaglia, 1997), undergraduate students (De Beni & Pazzaglia, 1997), and old people aged from 65 to 75 (Borella, 1998). We thought that, if a deficit in inhibiting irrelevant information affected performance in the listening span test, an important index was the number of intrusions made during the task. Intrusions were non-final words incorrectly recalled during execution of the listening span task. In fact, the task required the whole sentence to be processed, and then all the words in the sentence except the last one had been put aside. In other words, during the test, inhibitory processes were required in order to reduce accessibility of non-final words and prevent their recall. If this inhibitory mechanism is not working well during the listening span test, the subject has far too much information available, both relevant and irrelevant, thus leading to an overload of the working memory system. The result of this will be poorer memory of final words together with a greater number of intrusions, i.e. of recalled non-final words.

Our studies demonstrated that poor comprehenders retained a higher number of intrusions than good comprehenders for all age levels considered. The same difference was also found in a new test, which was constructed for the purpose in order to emphasize the role of intrusions. It required the last words in strings of words to be remembered (De Beni, Palladino, Pazzaglia, & Cornoldi, 1998). Participants were asked to detect animal-words in the strings and then inhibit them in order to recall only the last words. The results again showed a higher number of intrusions for poor comprehenders, particularly noticeable with the animal words. Our results support the hypothesis that in working memory tasks poor comprehenders maintain irrelevant information at a level of activation that overburdens the system and produces interference.

Discussion

The results described above, on the one hand, make suggestions about the implication of WM in reading comprehension, but on the other, they raise important questions. In fact, our studies on groups of poor and good comprehenders of different ages demonstrated the existence of a general processing deficit, which involves different aspects of working memory. The studies on inhibition processing suggest that a more basic deficit in inhibiting irrelevant information could explain poor performance in the listening span and other WM tests. It remains to be checked whether the same deficient inhibitory mechanism could also explain performance in other WM tests, such as the digit span test and the random production of letters. For, both in the digit span test and in the random letter generation task, performance could be impaired by the difficulty in suppressing digits (or letters) just read (or pronounced). The latter hypothesis requires further experimental demonstration.

METACOGNITION

The literature on reading comprehension and metacognitive ability strongly supported the existence of a relationship between them (see Garner, 1987, for a review): Poor comprehenders were found to have less adequate knowledge about reading (Myers & Paris, 1978; Pazzaglia, Cornoldi, & De Beni, 1995) and less efficient mechanisms for controlling the reading process. They are also less aware of the importance of giving meaning to text and are more focused on decoding than on comprehension (Baker & Brown, 1984). Moreover, they often do not realize when they have not understood (Garner & Reis, 1981), are less able to evaluate the complexity of a text, and detect its characteristics, such as structure or its anomalies, than are good comprehenders (August, Flavell, & Clift, 1984; Brown, Armbruster, & Baker, 1986; Canney & Winograd, 1979; Garner, 1980; 1981). They rarely use reading strategies (Brown, Armbruster, & Baker, 1986) and they cannot adjust the strategy to the task (Palincsar & Brown, 1987).

Myers and Paris (1978) found in second- and sixth- graders that younger children have less adequate knowledge about person, task, and strategy than older ones. Similar results were found by Forrest and Waller (1980) with subjects of different ages and reading abilities. Kirby and Moore (1987) found that poor readers knew little about the characteristics of a good reader, the different times required to read stories of different lengths, the importance of sentence order in a story, the use of imagery during reading, and the relationship between success in reading and arithmetic. Paris and Myers (1981) asked fourth-grade good and poor readers to evaluate the efficacy of several study strategies and found that poor readers had lower metacognitive knowledge. Garner and Kraus (1981–82) asked seventh-graders at two reading levels questions about reading. Differences between good and poor readers emerged in interview responses as well as in an error detection task proposed two weeks later.

These results support the idea that younger children and poor readers have, on the whole, lower metacognitive knowledge about reading than older children and good readers. However, they also raised some questions. The literature presents a series of models of unitary, sometimes interrelated, components of metacognitive knowledge, but the interconnection between the different components is still unclear. According to Brown and collaborators (1986), metacomprehension concerns both metacognitive knowledge and control. Knowledge is thought to include: task (knowledge of reading purposes), strategies, text, and individual differences.

One piece of knowledge about task, which begins to develop early on from the second grade (Myers & Paris, 1978), is that the main purpose of reading is to reach good text comprehension. After this, the reader becomes aware that there are different goals in reading and that each goal needs specific and efficient strategies. Knowledge about strategies can tap both reading and studying. For example, Myers and Paris (1978) found that only older children thought about the possibility of using a dictionary or asking someone when they had comprehension problems. Similarly, Garner and Reis (1981) found that poor comprehenders, unlike good ones, did not adopt the re-reading strategy when they had failed to comprehend a part of the text they were reading. Knowledge about text has also been defined as "text sensitivity" and has been mainly associated with control processes in reading (e.g., Brown, Armbruster, & Baker, 1986). It allows evaluation of the difficulty and importance both of an entire text and of its single parts and enables the reader to detect inconsistencies. This last task is also related to metacognitive control, an on-line process which "informs" the reader when comprehension is failing. Paris and collaborators (Paris, Lipson, & Wixon, 1983; Jacobs & Paris, 1987) distinguished between *declarative, procedural* and *conditional* knowledge:

> *Declarative* and *procedural* knowledge (or knowing *that* and knowing *how)* are crucial in forming strategies, but alone are not sufficient to ensure that children read strategically. They only emphasize the knowledge and skills required for performance and do not address the conditions under which one might wish to select or execute actions. Because strategic behavior involves intentionality and self-control, any analysis that ignores learners' motivation is incomplete (Jacobs & Paris, 1987, pp. 302–3).

The same authors also introduce *conditional knowledge,* that includes knowing *when* and *why* to apply various strategies.

Italian studies on metacognition and reading comprehension take here as their theoretical reference Brown's metacognitive model (Brown, Armbruster, & Baker, 1986) and Paris's distinction between declarative, procedural (see also Flavell, 1981), and conditional knowledge. Our purpose was as follows:

1. To investigate the distinction, within the more general concept of metacognition, between control and knowledge, according to Brown' s multicomponential metacognitive model. This issue was examined by administering a metacognitive questionnaire to a large sample of children from third to eighth grade (see Pazzaglia, De Beni, & Cristante, 1994);
2. To demonstrate that the developmental trend of monitoring differed from that of metacognitive knowledge and that the two areas have a special relationship with reading comprehension (see De Beni & Pazzaglia, 1997).

Furthermore, we investigated the relationship between metacognition and reading comprehension by comparing the metacognitive performance of groups of good and poor comprehenders, tested for their reasoning ability and decoding (Borella, 1998; Cacciò, De Beni, & Pazzaglia, 1996; De Beni, Palladino, & Pazzaglia, 1995; Pazzaglia, Cornoldi, & De Beni, 1995).

The metacognitive questionnaire (Pazzaglia, De Beni, & Cristante, 1994) includes 32 multiple choice questions regarding knowledge about: (a) reading purposes, (b) reading strategies, (c) monitoring of comprehension, and (d) text sensitivity. Analysis of psychometric properties (see Pazzaglia, De Beni, & Cristante, 1994; Pazzaglia, Cornoldi, & De Beni, 1995) supported its internal consistency (Cronbach's *alpha* = .78).

The area of reading purposes (items 1–8) analyzed knowledge about task. The child is asked to state the main purpose of reading, what a person must attend to during reading, what different goals different people may have (a child, a doctor, an adult) when reading different sources, and, finally, to recognize that reading is a form of communication. Examples are reported below.

The main purpose in reading is (choose one of the following alternatives):

a. to pronounce all the words correctly
b. to understand the meaning
e. to read speedily without errors

During reading it is more important:

a. to read aloud and clearly
b. to extract meaning from the text
e. to read speedily and correctly

A person is reading a newspaper. His purpose is: (Choose one of the following alternatives)

a. to become an expert on scientific topics
b. to know what is going on in the world
e. to enjoy oneself

Item 1, 3 and 7

The other area in which knowledge is tested is strategies (questions 17–24): in order to succeed, the child must choose alternatives related to the fact that the approach to a text may be different and must be changed according to the reading purpose. Furthermore, the child is asked to say what he or she does when the requirement is to skim through a text or to find a single specific piece of information, or to read specific sources (a telephone directory, a story, a school book, etc.), or when he or she has comprehension difficulties. Two further questions examine children's awareness of the function of re-reading a text. Examples are reported below.

Read a text twice (choose one of the following alternatives):

a. It might help you to understand the difficult parts
b. it is very boring and you will never do it
c. it takes too long
d. it is always very useful

You have to find only one piece of information in a text. It is more useful:

a. to read paying attention to each word
b. to reread the text many times and repeat it
c. to skim the text searching for information
d. to read aloud and clearly

There are many reading strategies: i.e., skimming, selective and analytic reading, rereading.

Choose the most useful strategies in order to execute the following tasks:

- study for a class test
- read a novel
- prepare a chapter in your history book for a test
- read a comic book
- paraphrase a poem
- check the railway time-table to find out when to leave Rome for Florence

Items 20, 22 and 23

The monitoring questions (items 9–16) list a series of sentences with a variety of semantic, syntactic, and spelling mistakes that the child is invited to detect. For example:

The following sentences have something wrong. Find it, underline and correct it.

- During the night the fishermen lighted a fire **with** the beach to warm themselves.
- Many people were waiting at the station, but **the** was late.
- Catia gave me an umbrella because the day was sunny and I might have **got** wet.
- The day I visited you I **mt** your brother John.

From Items 9, 10, 11.

The sensitivity questions (25–32) require the child to read a series of texts and assign different importance to parts, define their literary genre, and compare their relative difficulty.

Read the following passage and put the underlined sentences in order of importance (give number 1 to the most important sentence, 2 to the second, 3 to the third):

- It was a sunny day of April and I was slowly going home.
- <u>The air was fresh, but not cold, and the colors were brilliant under a clear sky.</u>
- <u>All at once I heard a meow.</u>
- I approached and I saw two little cats.
- <u>The cats were curled up, their eyes were closed, one was black and the other grey.</u>
- I realized that they had been abandoned and immediately decided to take them home.

Item 25.

Our goal was to determine whether the questionnaire effectively evaluated knowledge about reading purposes and strategies, text sensitivity and control. A factor analysis performed on all the items of the questionnaire yielded four factors. Results were in agreement with our predictions and support the existence of different categories of metacognitive knowledge and control activity as hypothesized by Brown, Armbruster, & Baker, (1986):

1. Knowledge about text. We found that items requiring identification of the differences between easy and difficult texts, important elements versus trivia, and textual structure have high loading under factor 1. Also, all items requiring detection of textual anomalies load under the same factor, regardless of the fact that anomalies were syntactic, semantic or of spelling.
2. Knowledge about task. We found a distinction between knowledge that the primary goal of reading is to understand the content (items 1 and 3 under factor 3) and awareness about the array of reading tasks and reading purposes (items 5–7 under factor 2).
3. Knowledge about strategies. Three items requiring "declarative" and "procedural" knowledge about strategies (see Jacobs & Paris, 1987) have high loading under factor 4. Otherwise, when items required "conditional" knowledge of strategies (i.e. items 22, 23), namely, choosing the most efficient strategy for reading purposes, they loaded under factor 1, which was characterized by an active attitude toward the reading task.

The same distinction between active and on-line aspects of comprehension on the one hand, and declarative and procedural knowledge about reading purposes and strategies on the other was found when analyzing the developmental trend of these metacognitive abilities (De Beni & Pazzaglia, 1997). Children aged from eight to 13 exhibited the following developmental trends: items about control and text sensitivity (which turned out to have high saturation under factor 1) showed a continuous positive trend. In a subsequent study (Cacciò, De Beni, & Pazzaglia, 1996), it appeared that abilities of control and text sensitivity continued to develop in secondary school and in undergraduate students. Both knowledge about goals and strategies exhibit a different developmental trend, with dramatic improvements for knowledge about goals (one from 8 to 9, and the other from 11 to 12), and improvements from 8 to 9, 9 to 10, and 11 to 12 for knowledge of strategies.

Comparisons between subjects with three different levels of reading (poor, medium, good) again supported the distinction between text sensitivity and control on the one hand, and knowledge about purposes and strategies on the other. When eighth to 10th graders were taken together in the analysis, it was found that all three levels of readers differed in monitoring and text sensitivity, whereas good readers performed better than medium and poor ones only in knowledge of strategies and task. From 11th to 13th grades the pattern was the same as before as regards monitoring and text sensitivity, except that there were no differences between medium and good comprehenders in that performance was perfectly matched in knowledge of strategies and task: poor readers performed worse than either good or medium comprehenders.

Our final goal was to test whether groups of good and poor comprehenders, tested for their reasoning ability and decoding, also differed in metacognitive abilities, and whether distinct metacognitive areas were better for discriminating between good and poor comprehenders (Cacciò, De Beni, & Pazzaglia, 1996; De Beni, Palladino, & Pazzaglia, 1995; Pazzaglia, Cornoldi, & De Beni, 1995). We examined good and poor comprehenders of different ages: aged 13 (De Beni, Palladino, & Pazzaglia, 1995; Pazzaglia, Cornoldi, & De Beni, 1995), aged 14, 16 (Cacciò, De Beni, & Pazzaglia, 1996), aged 65–75 (Borella, 1998). Results support the existence of a strong relationship between metacognition and reading comprehension, regardless of general reasoning ability. For all ages considered, poor comprehenders performed worse than good ones. In particular, the two groups of good and poor comprehenders aged 13 differed in all areas of knowledge about task and strategies, control and text sensitivity (Pazzaglia, Cornoldi, & De Beni, 1995), whereas a subsample selected by more rigid criteria in comprehension differed in all the metacognitive abilities, except for knowledge about task (De Beni, Palladino, & Pazzaglia, 1995). As regards the older participants, secondary students were tested only in monitoring and text sensitivity subtests and old people performed monitoring, text sensitivity and knowledge of strategies subtests. With these samples (which were not tested for decoding) we found that poor comprehenders did worse than good ones both in control and text sensitivity.

Discussion

According to the numerous data in specialized literature, our results support the hypothesis that metacognitive variables are deeply involved in reading comprehension and that metacognitive deficits are often associated with comprehension difficulties. The use of a questionnaire composed of different areas allowed to us to check the validity of a multicomponential model of metacomprehension and to verify selectively the importance of distinct metacognitive abilities in reading comprehension. Our major results concern a strong differentiation between on-line aspects of metacognition (detection of anomalies, individuation of important indices from the text, judgement on text importance and difficulty) and declarative/procedural knowledge about text and strategies. These metacognitive variables have different psychometric properties (see factor analysis results), peculiar developmental trend and different power at different ages in discriminating subjects with different proficiency in reading comprehension. When selected cases of poor comprehenders were tested (checked for reasoning ability and, sometimes, decoding), significant differences were found between poor comprehenders and average readers. Poor comprehenders aged 13, 14, 16, and poor elderly comprehenders do less well in knowledge of strategies, text sensitivity, monitoring, and, though not for all samples, in knowledge about task.

RELATIONSHIP BETWEEN WORKING MEMORY AND METACOGNITION IN READING COMPREHENSION

Research concerning the implications of working memory and metacognition in reading comprehension has indicated that these abilities do play a role in comprehension. The third part of this paper is concerned with the possible relationship between WM and metacognitive ability. In other words, we intended to verify whether low performance in one area is due to a deficit in the other. The theoretical point is this: if these two abilities are independent of each other, do they work together in reading comprehension; or if they are not independent, does poor performance of poor comprehenders in one ability depend on the other? A possible suggestion is that the difficulty in detecting incongruencies in the text, that is, an ability of metacognitive control and text sensitivity, may depend on an elaboration deficit, as on working memory problems. Our data collected from the same groups of good and poor comprehenders of different ages in both the listening span test and in our metacognitive questionnaire allowed us to analyze the relationship between the two variables and their specific influence on reading comprehension.

Data in the literature on reading comprehension suggest that monitoring activity during reading could be influenced by memory. For example, Vosniadou, Pearson, and Rogers (1988) claimed that the difficulty in detecting inconsistencies in written texts may derive from a difficulty in remembering logically inconsistent propositions. In fact, when subjects are forced to remember them, their difficulty in detecting inconsistencies decreases. Wimmer (1979) also found that children's difficulties in detecting empirical inconsistencies depended on their ability to remember the inconsistent premise. Other research highlighted the importance of working memory variables. For instance, Yuill and Oakhill (1989) found that poor comprehenders were significantly worse than good comprehenders at detecting inconsistencies when the inconsistencies were spread out in a text rather than when they were adjacent. Similar results were also obtained by Ackerman (1984a; 1984b) and Zabrucky and Ratner (1986). In the study of Yuill, Oakhill, and Parkin (1989) (see Oakhill & Yuill, 1996 for a review), good and poor comprehenders aged nine- to 10-years old were used as participants. Subjects were asked to read some passages alone at their own pace and underline any problems they encountered. In this case, the internal inconsistencies within the text were contradictory statements that could either be found in adjacent sentences or separated by several sentences. Data analysis showed an interaction between the distance and the skill variables: the less skilled comprehenders were more affected by the distance manipulation than were the skilled ones. Yuill and Oakhill claimed that processing limitations could be implied in the difficulties of poor comprehenders in integrating information within the text, in order to make inferences, and in understanding text structure.

Whitney, Ritchie and Clark (1991) also highlighted the influence of processing variables in detecting text coherence. In a recent study, Swanson and Alexander (1997) examined how cognitive processes interrelate as well as predict learning-disabled readers' comprehension performance. In their study metacognitive abilities were also considered. Results support the relationship between working memory and metacognition, showing significant correlation between a metacognitive questionnaire adapted by Paris, Cross and Lipson (1984) and the sentence span adapted by Daneman and Carpenter (1980). The metacognitive questionnaire evaluated a wide range of metacognitive knowledge, such elements as reading goals and strategies. By contrast, no relationship was found between the sentence span and an inconsistencies detection task. These results were obtained for both learning-disabled and skilled readers. Furthermore, a factor analysis computed on all the variables considered in the research (phonological, orthographic, semantic, metacognitive, and working memory measures) showed that metacognitive knowledge and working memory variables (sentence span and visual matrix text) loaded on the same component (component 3), which was interpreted as measuring metacognition-working memory span. The same factor analysis revealed the existence of a factor (factor 1) under which loaded the majority of working memory measures, along with higher (metacognition) and lower order (phonemic deletion, orthographic choice, semantic choice) tasks. This outcome is consistent with the assumption that a working memory system underlies many higher and lower order processes.

VERBAL WORKING MEMORY AND METACOGNITION

Several findings support the idea that the ability to store and process information may influence the ability to detect text inconsistencies and text coherence. Furthermore, other findings (see Swanson & Alexander, 1997) supported the existence of a relationship between a more general metacognitive competence and working memory measures. Our purpose was to verify the relationship between verbal working memory and metacognition, and to distinguish between the different components of the wider concept of metacognition, as stressed in our previous research: text sensitivity and control, on the one hand, and knowledge about reading task and strategy, on the other. In particular we suggested:

1. The existence of a relationship between WM and metacognition, in that processing ability influences metacognitive variables;
2. That this influence is selective, in the sense that it mainly involves on-line aspects of metacognitive variables (control and text sensitivity) as compared to metacognitive knowledge about task and strategies. In fact the abilities to detect text's incongruencies, to decide the literal genre, to take into account the titles or other textual indices in order to improve comprehension, to evaluate the importance of the difficulty of some parts of a text, normally

required to maintain in memory large parts of the previously read information and, at the same time, to continue to process the following text. In our hypothesis these activities require strong working memory demands.

Another important question was raised by the listening span test. As we have already seen, this is a complex test that requires the subject to store the final words of a series of sentences and, at the same time, to process them semantically. In our version participants were asked to judge the semantic value of each sentence (true/false task), before recalling all the last words. Thus, there may be an inverse relationship between control and performance in the listening span test, or, in other words, that monitoring ability in detecting semantic anomalies may influence performance in the listening span test.

In the present study on the relationship between working memory and metacognitive abilities, groups of good and poor comprehenders of different ages (13, 14, 16 years old) were examined.

Participants

Younger Sample (13 years old)

Forty children aged 13 took part in this study (see De Beni, Palladino, & Pazzaglia, 1995). The participants were assigned to two groups of good and poor comprehenders, each composed of 20 participants.. The two groups of good and poor comprehenders were screened from a sample of 589 children attending schools with different sociocultural backgrounds in north-eastern Italy. (For criteria used in screening, see De Beni, Palladino, & Pazzaglia, 1995; Cornoldi, De Beni, & Pazzaglia, 1996; Pazzaglia, Cornoldi, and De Beni, 1995). Poor comprehenders were characterized by good logical abilities as evaluated by the arithmetic, visuo-spatial and verbal fluency subscales of the Primary Mental Abilities intelligence test (Thurstone & Thurstone, 1941); normal or good linguistic ability tested by a syllable division task and a search-task for hidden words; sufficient performance in two speed and accuracy reading tests (Cornoldi, Colpo, & MT Group, 1981); seriously inadequate reading comprehension, as measured by two standardized reading comprehension tests (Cornoldi, Colpo, & MT Group, 1981; Cornoldi, Rizzo, & Pra Baldi, 1991), which consisted in the presentation of a one-page text followed by multiple-choice questions. Good comprehenders were matched for sex, age, school, grade, logical and linguistic ability. By contrast, performance in comprehension tests was adequate.

Older Sample (14–16 years old)

Sixty-two secondary school students (49 aged 14 and 13 aged 16) took part in the study. Thirty-one were screened from a sample of 398 students, and were classed as poor reading comprehenders on the basis of the following criteria:

1. Poor reading comprehension: scores were lower than −1 standard deviation from the mean in a reading comprehension test (MT-advanced comprehension test by Cornoldi, Rizzo, & Pra Baldi, 1991) based on the presentation of seven texts and of 90 multiple-choice questions;
2. Normal cognitive abilities and average school proficiency: teachers were asked to evaluate general ability and global school proficiency of their students. Students who were said to have general cognitive deficits and low school proficiency were dropped.

The control group was matched for sex, age, grade, but had a good level of comprehension (scores above 1 standard deviation from the mean in the comprehension test).

Materials

The following materials were used:

1. An Italian version of the listening span test (Daneman & Carpenter, 1980) for evaluation of verbal working memory. This test requires memorization of the last word of each of a series of sentences which had to be processed semantically.
2. The metacognitive questionnaire by Pazzaglia, De Beni, & Cristante, (1994). With the older sample, only text sensitivity and control subtests were used.

Results

Younger Sample

Pearson's correlation analysis between metacognitive and WM variables revealed significant correlations with text sensitivity, control and knowledge about strategies with several indices of the listening span test (LST).

1. Span (LST) with: control ($r = .47, p < .005$), text sensitivity ($r = .40, p = .01$), strategies ($r = .42, p < .01$).
2. Number of words recalled (LST) with control ($r = .49$, $p = .001$), text sensitivity ($r = .37, p < .05$), strategies ($r = .34, p <. 05$).
3. Number of errors in giving true/false judgements in sentences of LST with: control in metacognitive test ($r = -.59, p < .001$), text sensitivity ($r = -.45$, $p < .005$).

Older Sample

Correlation analyses performed on metacognitive and WM scores of older participants revealed significant correlations between:

1. Span (LST) with: control ($r = .43$, $p < .001$), text sensitivity ($r = .50$, $p < .001$).
2. Number of words recalled (LST) with control ($r = .56$, $p < .001$), text sensitivity ($r = .59$, $p < .001$).
3. Number of errors in giving true/false judgements in sentences of LST with: control in metacognitive test ($r = -.48$, $p < .001$); text sensitivity ($r = -.31$, $p < .01$).

Two multiple regression analyses, stepwise method, (i.e., one for each sample), were performed having as dependent variable scores in the comprehension test, and as independent variables: listening span test (span, number of words recalled and errors) and metacognitive areas (knowledge about goals, strategies, control and text sensitivity for the younger sample; text sensitivity and control for the older one). The following variables entered in the regression equation in the sample of younger subjects: number of words recalled (beta = .53). The following variables entered in the regression equation for the sample of older subjects: text sensitivity (beta = .37), errors (beta = –.27), number of words recalled (beta = .36).

These results only partially agree with our hypothesis. In fact, the sample of younger subjects suggests that WM variables contributed unique variance to comprehension. A different pattern was evidenced with the older sample. In this case, text sensitivity, errors, and number of recalled words accounted for different percentages of variance.

A second interesting result was the significant correlation between control and errors. This result suggests that control ability could influence the performance in the listening span test. In order to analyze this issue better, a multiple regression analysis, stepwise method, was performed having as dependent variable the number of errors in the listening span test, and as independent variables the listening span, number of words recalled, goals, strategies, text sensitivity, control and reading comprehension. The variables control and listening span were in the equation (beta values were respectively –.44 and –.31) when younger subjects were considered. The following variables entered in the regression equation: control (beta = –.28), reading comprehension (beta = –.38), when the older subjects were considered.

Discussion

Correlation analyses support the existence of a relationship between WM and metacognition, even if it is not immediately evident which components of LST and of the metacognitive questionnaire are particularly responsible for such a relationship. For younger participants it is restricted to three out of four metacognitive variables, and for older ones it involves both text sensitivity and control. We suggested that metacognitive on-line abilities had a selective relationship with the working memory task. Results from the sample of younger students only partially confirmed our hypothesis. A point in favor is that knowledge about text has very low correlations with all WM variables. From factor analysis on items of the metacognitive questionnaire, items on knowledge about task were clearly distinct from the others, presenting high saturations in two separate factors, both devoted to different kinds of declarative knowledge about task. On the other hand, items about control (8 out of 8), text sensitivity (5 out of 8) and strategies (2 out of 8) presented saturations > .35 under the same factor 1, thus showing common characteristics. This result was interpreted in terms of a common, on-line characteristic which unifies control and text sensitivity items, but also items on strategies when they investigated conditional knowledge. This same on-line characteristic could explain the significant correlations of LST with control, text sensitivity and knowledge of strategies. On this point further investigation is needed.

A second problem is that the correlational paradigm does not permit identification of the direction of the relationship. Can good metacognitive abilities help performance in LST, or, by contrast, does an efficient working memory system allow better performance in typical text sensitivity or control tasks? Results on regression analyses, having as dependent variable the number of errors in LST, seem to suggest that the ability to detect inconsistencies in text and a general processing ability are involved in the task of giving true/false judgements in the sentences of listening span.

ACKNOWLEDGMENT

The authors thank Cesare Cornoldi for his suggestions on an earlier version of this chapter, and Nicoletta Whitteridge, who corrected the English.

REFERENCES

Ackerman, B. P. (1984a). The effects of storage and processing complexity on comprehension repair in children and adults. *Journal of Experimental Child Psychology, 37*, 303–334.

Ackerman, B. P. (1984b). Storage and processing constraints on integration story information in children and adults. *Journal of Experimental Child Psychology, 38*, 64–92.

August, D. L., Flavell, J. H., & Clift, R. (1984). Comparison of comprehension monitoring of skilled and less skilled readers. *Reading Research Quarterly, 20*, 39–53.

Baddeley, A. D. (1966). The capacity for generating information by randomization. *Quarterly Journal of Experimental Psychology, 18*, 119–129.

Baddeley, A. (1986). *Working Memory*. (Oxford Psychology series No. 11). Oxford: Clarendon Press.

Baddeley, A. (1990). *Human memory: Theory and practice*. Hillsdale, NJ: Erlbaum.

Baddeley, A. D. (1992). Is working memory working? The fifteenth Bartlett lecture. *Quarterly Journal of Experimental Psychology, 1*, 1–31.

Baddeley, A., Logie, R., Nimmo-Smith, J., & Brereton, R. (1985). Components of fluent reading. *Journal of Memory and Language, 24*, 119–131.

Baker, L., & Brown, A. L. (1984). Metacognition skills of reading. In D. Pearson, R. Barr, M. Kamil, & P. Monsenthal (Eds.), *Handbook of reading research*, New York: Longman.

Blachowicz, C. L. Z. (1984). Reading and remembering. *Visible Language, 18*, 4, 391–403.

Borella, E. (1998). *Memoria di lavoro e metacompresione in soggetti anziani* [Working memory and metacomprehension in aged people] Unpublished master's thesis, University of Padua, Italy.

Brown, A. L., Armbruster, B. B., & Baker, L. (1986). The role of metacognition in reading and studying. In J. Orasanu (Ed.), *Reading comprehension: From research to practice* (pp. 49–75). Hillsdale, NJ: Erlbaum.

Cacciò, L., De Beni, R., & Pazzaglia, F. (1996). Analisi di alcune variabili implicate nelle difficoltà di comprensione della lettura: confronto tra due metodi in una ricerca su soggetti adulti. In P. Boscolo, F. Cristante, A. Dellantonio, & S. Soresi (Eds.), *Aspetti quantitativi e qualitativi nella ricerca psicologica* (pp. 81–90), Padova, Italia: Il Poligrafo.

Canney, G., & Winograd, P. (1979). *Schemata for reading comprehension performance*. Tech. Report, 120, Urbana: University of Illinois, Center for the Study of Reading.

Cornoldi, C., & Colpo, G., & MT Group (1981). *La verifica dell'apprendimento della lettura. Prove MT* [Checking reading learning: MT tests]. Firenze, Italia: Organizzazioni Speciali.

Cornoldi, C., De Beni, R., & Pazzaglia, F. (1996). Profiles of reading comprehension difficulties: An analysis of single cases. In C. Cornoldi & J. Oakhill (Eds.), *Reading comprehension difficulties: Processes and intervention* (pp. 113–136). Mahwah, NJ: Erlbaum.

Cornoldi, C., & Oakhill, J. (1996). *Reading comprehension difficulties: Processes and intervention*. Mahwah, NJ: Erlbaum.

Cornoldi, C., Rizzo, A., & Pra Baldi, A, (1991). Prove avanzate MT di comprensione nella lettura [Advanced MT reading comprehension tests]. Firenze, Italia: Organizzazioni Speciali.

Daneman, M., & Carpenter, P. A. (1980). Individual differences in working memory and reading. *Journal of Verbal Learning and Verbal Behaviour, 19*, 450–466.

Daneman, M., & Carpenter, P. A. (1983). Individual differences in integrating information between and within sentences. *Journal of Experimental Psychology: Learning, Memory and Cognition, 9*, 561–583.

Daneman, M., & Merikle, P. M. (1996). Working memory and language comprehension: A meta-analysis. *Psychonomic Bulletin & Review, 3*, 422–433.

Daneman, M., & Tardif, T. (1987). Working memory and reading skill reexamined. In M. Coltheart (Ed.), *Attention and performance, XII: The Psychology of reading* (pp. 491–508). Hillsdale, NJ: Erlbaum.

De Beni, R., Palladino, P., & Pazzaglia, F. (1995). Influenza della memoria di lavoro e delle abilità metacognitive e sintattiche nella difficoltà specifica di comprensione della lettura [Working memory and metacognitive and syntactic abilities implied in specific reading comprehension disabilities], *Giornale Italiano di Psicologia, 22*, 615–640.

De Beni, R., Palladino, P., & Pazzaglia, F. (1997, October). *Standardizzazione di una prova per la valutazione della memoria di lavoro verbale su un campione di studenti di scuola media* [Standardization of a test for the evaluation of verbal working memory on a sample of primary school students]. Paper presented at the meeting of the AIRIPA Congress, Milano, Italy.

De Beni, R. Palladino, P., Pazzaglia, F., & Cornoldi, C. (1998). Increases in intrusion errors and working memory deficit of poor comprehenders, *The Quarterly Journal of Experimental Psychology, 51A*, 305–320.

De Beni, R., & Pazzaglia, F. (1995). *La comprensione del testo: Modelli teorici e programmi di intervento* [Text comprehension: Theory and intervention]. Torino, Italia: Utet.

De Beni, R., & Pazzaglia, F. (1997). Sviluppo di alcune abilità metacognitive implicate nella comprensione della lettura [Development of some metacognitive abilities implied in text comprehension]. *Età evolutiva, 58*, 67–78.

Dixon, P., Lefevre, J., & Twilley, L. C. (1988). Word knowledge and working memory as predictors of reading skill. *Journal of Educational Psychology, 80*, 465–472.

Ehrlich, M. F., Brébion J., & Tardieu, H. (1994). Working memory capacity and reading comprehension in young and older adults. *Psychological Research, 56*, 110–115.

Engle, R. W., Cantor, J., & Carullo, J. J. (1992). Individual differences in working memory and comprehension: A test of four hypotheses. *Journal of Experimental Psychology: Learning, Memory and Cognition, 18*, 972–992.

Flavell, J. H. (1981). Cognitive monitoring. In W.P. Dickson (Ed.), *Children's oral communication skills* (pp. 35–60). New York: Academic Press.

Forrest, D. L., & Waller, T. G. (1980, April). *What do children know about their reading and study skills?* Paper presented at the annual meeting of the American Educational Research Association, Boston.

Garner, R. (1980). Monitoring of understanding: An investigation of good and poor readers' awareness of induced miscomprehension of text. *Journal of Reading Behavior, 12*, 55–64.

Garner, R. (1981). Monitoring of passage inconsistency among poor comprehenders: A preliminary test of the "piecemeal processing" explanation. *Journal of Educational Research, 74*, 159–162.

Garner, R. (1987). *Metacognition and reading comprehension*. Norwood, NJ: Ablex.

Garner, R., & Kraus, C. (1981–82). Good and poor comprehenders differences in knowing and regulating reading behaviors. *Educational Research Quarterly, 6*, 5–12.

Garner, R., & Reis, R. (1981). Monitoring and resolving comprehension obstacles: An investigation of spontaneous text lookbacks among upper-grade good and poor comprehenders. *Reading Research Quarterly, 18*, 439–447.

Gernsbacher, M. A. (1990). *Language comprehension as structure building*. Hillsdale, NJ: Erlbaum.

Gernsbacher, M. A. (1993). Less skilled readers have less efficient suppression mechanisms. *Psychological Science, 4*, 294–298.

Gernsbacher, M. A, Varner, K. R., & Faust, M. E. (1990). Investigating differences in general comprehension skill. *Journal of Experimental Psychology: Learning, Memory and Cognition, 16*, 430–445.

Golinkoff, R. (1976). A comparison of reading comprehension in good and poor comprehenders. *Reading Research Quarterly, 11*, 623–659.

Hamm, V. P., & Hasher, L. (1992). Age and the availability of inferences. *Psychology and Aging, 7*, 56–64.

Hartmann, M., & Hasher, L. (1991). Aging and suppression: Memory for previously relevant information. *Psychology and Aging, 6*, 587–594.

Hasher, L., & Zacks, R. (1988). Working memory, comprehension, and aging: A review and a new view. In G. H. Bower (Ed.), *The psychology of learning and motivation: Advances in research and theory* (vol. 22, pp. 193–225), San Diego, CA: Academic Press.

Jacobs, J. E., & Paris, S. G. (1987). Children's metacognition about reading: Issues in definition, measurement, and instruction. *Educational Psychologist, 22*, 3–4, 225–278.

Kirby, J. R., & Moore, P. J. (1987). Metacognitive awareness about reading and its relation to reading ability. *Journal of Psychoeducational Assessment, 5*, 119–137.

Masson, M. E. J., & Miller, J. A. (1983). Working memory and individual differences in comprehension and memory of text. *Journal of Educational Psychology, 75*, 314–318.

May, C. P., Kane, M. J., Hasher, L., Multhaup, K., & Valenti, M. (1996). *Working memory span task: Capacity or proactive interference?* Paper presented at the Cognitive Aging Conference, Atlanta.

Meiran, N. (1996). Is reading ability related to activation dumping speed? Evidence from immediate repetition priming. *Memory & Cognition, 24*, 41–59.

Moscovitch, M., & Umiltà, C. (1991). Conscious and nonconscious aspects of memory: A neuropsychological framework of modules and central system. In R. G. Lister & H. G. Weingartner (Eds.), *Perspectives on cognitive neuroscience* (pp. 229–266). Oxford: Oxford University Press.

Myers, M., & Paris, S. G. (1978). Children's metacognitive knowledge about reading. *Journal of Educational Psychology, 70*, 680–690.

Norman, S., Kemper, S., & Kynette, D. (1992). Adults' reading comprehension: Effect of syntactic complexity and working memory. *Journal of Gerontology: Psychological Sciences, 4*, 258–265.

Oakhill, J., & Yuill, N. (1996). Higher order factors in comprehension disability: Processes and remediation. In C. Cornoldi & J. Oakhill (Eds.), *Reading comprehension difficulties: Processes and intervention* (pp. 69–92). Mahwah, NJ: Erlbaum.

Palincsar, A. S., & Brown, D. A. (1987). Enhancing instructional time through attention to metacognition. *Journal of Learning Disabilities, 20*, 66–75.

Palladino, P., De Beni, R., & Cornoldi, C. (1995). L'evoluzione di difficoltà specifiche di comprensione del testo: uno studio longitudinale [The time course of specific reading comprehension difficulties: A longitudinal study]. *Archivio di Psicologia, Neurologia e Psichiatria, 5–6*, 548–564.

Paris, S. G., Cross, D. R., & Lipson, M. Y. (1984). Informed strategies for learning: A program to improve children's reading awareness and comprehension. *Journal of Educational Psychology, 76*, 1239–1252.

Paris, S. G., Lipson, M. Y., & Wixon, K. K. (1983). Becoming a strategic reader. *Contemporary Educational Psychology, 8*, 293–316.

Paris, S. G., & Myers, M. (1981). Comprehension monitoring, memory, and study strategies of good and poor readers. *Journal of Reading Behavior, 13*, 5–22.

Pascual-Leone, J., & Ijaz, H. (1989). Mental capacity testing as a form of intellectual-development assessment. In R. Samud, S. Jong, J. Pascual-Leone, & J. Lewis (Eds.) *Assessment and placement of minority students* (pp. 143–171). Toronto: Hogrefe.

Pazzaglia, F., Cornoldi, C., & De Beni, R. (1995). Knowledge about reading and self-evaluation in reading disabled children. In T. Scruggs & M. Mastropieri (Eds.), *Advances in learning and behavioral disabilities* (vol. 9, pp. 91–117). Greenwich, CT: JAI.

Pazzaglia, F., De Beni, R., & Cristante, F. (1994). Prova di metacomprensione [Metacomprehension test]. Firenze, Italia: Organizzazioni Speciali.

Penning, M. J., & Raphael, T. E. (1991). The impact of language ability and text variables on sixth-grade students' comprehension. *Applied Psycholinguistics, 12*, 397–417.

Ryan, E. B. (1981). Identifying and remediating failures in reading comprehension: Toward an instructional approach for poor comprehenders. In T. G. Walker & G. E. MacKinnon (Eds.), *Reading research: Advances in theory and practice* (vol. 3, pp. 9–50). New York: Academic Press.

Swanson, L., & Alexander (1997). Cognitive processes as predictors of word recognition and reading comprehension in learning-disabled and skilled readers: Revisiting the specificity hypothesis. *Journal of Educational Psychology, 89*, 128–158.

Thurstone, N. L., & Thurstone, T. G. (1941). Factorial studies of intelligence. *Psychometric Monographs, 2*.

Vosniadou, S. P., Pearson, D., & Rogers, Y. (1988). What causes children's failures to detect inconsistencies in text? Representation versus comparison difficulties. *Journal of Educational Psychology, 80*, 27–39.

Whitney, P., Ritchie, B. G., & Clark, M. B. (1991). Working memory capacity and the use of elaborative inferences in text comprehension. *Discourse Processes, 14*, 133–145.

Wimmer, H. (1979). Processing of script deviations by young children. *Discourse Processes, 2*, 301–310.

Yuill, N., & Oakhill, J. (1988). Understanding of anaphoric relation in skilled and less skilled comprehenders. *British Journal of Psychology, 79*, 173–176.

Yuill, N., & Oakhill, J. (1991). *Children's problems in text comprehension: An experimental investigation.* Cambridge: Cambridge University Press.

Yuill, N. M., Oakhill, J. V., & Parkin, A. J. (1989). Working memory, comprehension ability and the resolution of text anomaly. *British Journal of Psychology, 80*, 351–361.

Zabrucky, K., & Ratner, H. (1986). Children's comprehension monitoring and recall of inconsistent stories. *Child Development, 57*, 1401, 1418.

Zambianchi, E. (1996). *Memoria di lavoro e comprensione del testo in bambini di scuola elementare* [Working memory and reading comprehension in primary school children]. Unpublished specialization thesis, University of Padua, Italy.

ATTENTION DEFICIT HYPERACTIVITY DISORDER AND THE EFFICACY OF STIMULANT MEDICATION:
A META-ANALYSIS

Teresa Meade Crenshaw, Kenneth A. Kavale, Steven R. Forness, and Ronald E. Reeve

ABSTRACT

In this meta-analysis, we synthesize findings from 115 studies published between 1985 and 1995 investigating the efficacy of stimulant medication for students with attention-deficit/hyperactivity disorder (ADHD). In addition to reviewing medication effects on the core features of ADHD (impulsivity, attention, and activity), the impact of stimulant medication on three important correlates of ADHD was also reviewed. These correlates were academic achievement, social/peer relations, and aggressive/noncompliant behavior. Several additional variables were also reviewed, such as the effect of low versus high dosages of stimulant medication on behavioral and academic outcomes, differences related to study designs, adolescent outcomes, out-

Advances in Learning and Behavioral Disabilities, Volume 13, pages 135–165.

ISBN: 0-7623-0429-4

comes of students with ADHD and mental disability, and longer-term treatment results. Overall results indicated positive effects for stimulant medication on behavioral variables, with the largest effect found for the core components of ADHD. Academic outcome variables did not show as robust an effect as behavioral variables, but demonstrated better results when measured with classroom-type measures as opposed to academic achievement tests.

Beginning in the 1970s, significant ideological and moral attacks were directed at the use of stimulant medication to treat hyperactivity. The tenor of these dissents can be gleaned from their titles: "Drug-Pushing in the Schools: The Professionals" (Hentoff, 1972), "Pills for Classroom Peace" (Ladd, 1970), "The Educator as Pusher: Drug Control in the Classroom" (Rappoport & Repo, 1971), and "The Myth of the Hyperactive Child and Other Means of Child Control" (Schrag & Divoky, 1975). Additionally, drug intervention was criticized as focusing on symptom removal rather than cure (e.g., Sroufe & Stewart, 1973) and their use to control classroom behavior was assumed a subversion of "what should be our educational ideals" (Grinspoon & Singer, 1973, p. 544).

The opposing view was expressed primarily by medical personnel who believed stimulant medication was the most efficacious treatment for hyperactivity (e.g., American Academy of Pediatrics, 1975; Eisenberg, 1972; Wender, 1971). The empirical evidence brought to bear on the question of efficacy generally resulted in equivocal conclusions (e.g., Adelman & Compas, 1977; Barkley, 1977; Lambert, Windmiller, Sandoval, & Moore, 1976; Sprague & Sleator, 1973; Whalen & Henker, 1976). To bring closure to the question, Kavale (1982) conducted a meta-analysis on the extant empirical literature. Although across 135 studies the synthesized findings were generally positive, the controversy surrounding the use of stimulant medication was not completely resolved. Some 15 years later, the controversy remains, and the debate has expanded to include new issues. The purpose of this chapter is to address both the old and new issues surrounding the efficacy of stimulant medication in the treatment of childhood disorders.

ATTENTION-DEFICIT/HYPERACTIVITY DISORDER

Nomenclature

Kavale (1982) investigated the question of drug effectiveness for students classified as hyperactive. Presently the preferred terminology is "attention-deficit/hyperactivity disorder" (ADHD) and the new terminology suggests the possibility of a slightly different population being served. The disorder is marked by developmentally inappropriate levels of inattention, impulsivity, and hyperactivity (American Psychiatric Association [APA], 1994). The three primary features produce a variety of problems including academic difficulties as well as disruption of classroom activities (Rostain, 1991). The prevalence estimates of 3 percent to 5 percent for school-age students suggests the possibility of the typical classroom having at least one student with ADHD (DuPaul & Stoner, 1994).

The ADHD concept has been identified by many different names and labels. The foundation for all nomenclature was the assumption that brain injury and subsequent behavioral deficits were linked (Carlson & Rapport, 1989), and, at times, emphasized brain injury with terminology that included minimal brain damage, minimal brain dysfunction, and minimal cerebral dysfunction (APA, 1980). The shift in emphasis to the behavioral phenomenon of hyperactivity was seen in terminology such as hyperkinetic reaction of childhood, hyperkinetic syndrome, and hyperactive child syndrome (APA, 1980). Research and evaluation on the hyperactive child syndrome during the 1970s led to the decision to emphasize inattention and re-name the disorder "attention deficit disorder" that included a diagnosis with and without hyperactivity in the *Diagnostic and Statistical Manual of Mental Disorders—Third Edition* (DSM-III) (APA, 1980). The attention deficit disorder with hyperactivity was marked by developmentally inappropriate levels of inattention, hyperactivity, and impulsivity, while attention deficit disorder without hyperactivity was similar but with the absence of the overactivity component.

The DSM-III diagnostic procedures were an improvement over past methods (Henker & Whalen, 1989), but a revision (DSM-IIIR) changed the name to attention deficit hyperactivity disorder (ADHD). In DSM-IIIR, ADHD was described as a single syndrome not having the hyperactivity and no hyperactivity components (APA, 1987). In DSM-IV, three subtypes of ADHD were described and included: (a) ADHD, combined type, where both inattention and hyperactivity-impulsivity were significant features; (b) ADHD, predominately inattentive type; and (c) ADHD, predominately hyperactive-impulsive type (APA, 1994).

Correlates and Effects of ADHD

The ADHD syndrome is among the most common reasons for referral with its 3 percent to 5 percent prevalence estimate (Barkley, 1990). Males are more likely to be diagnosed with ADHD, with rates ranging from 4-to-1 to 9-to-1 (APA, 1994). Barkley (1990) reported five primary symptoms; three of the five include the DSM features of inattention, hyperactivity, and impulsivity or behavioral disinhibition (difficulty in regulating or inhibiting behavior). The two additional characteristics of ADHD are deficient rule-governed behavior (difficulties in responding to rules and instructions) and task performance variability. DuPaul and Stoner (1994) suggested that ADHD is a performance deficit, not a skill deficit, and the impact of the disorder is on the individual's ability to regulate behavior over a period of time. In addition, individuals with ADHD are described as being not as sensitive to or as motivated by reinforcements that may motivate individuals without ADHD (Busch, 1993).

The long- and short-term effects of ADHD are multiple and varied. Besides the five primary features, the three most frequent difficulties associated with ADHD are problems with peer relations, academic difficulties, and increased levels of aggression and noncompliance (DuPaul & Stoner, 1994). The presence of these difficulties have raised questions about whether ADHD is a distinct entity from behavior disorders (e.g., conduct disorder), and from learning disabilities (LD) because of the high comorbidity rates among the disorders as well as crossover features between the disorders. For example, the comorbidity between ADHD and externalizing disorders may be near 50 percent (Henker & Whalen, 1989). Estimates of comorbidity between ADHD and conduct disorder range from 30 percent to 50 percent, while the co-occurrence between oppositional defiant disorder (ODD) and ADHD is reported to range between 35 percent to 65 percent (Biederman, Newcorn, & Sprich, 1991). Comorbidity estimates range from 10 percent to 92 percent for LD and ADHD (Biederman, Newcorn, & Sprich, 1991).

The comorbidity relationships lead to issues about the validity of subtypes of ADHD. The most recognized subtype is ADHD without hyperactivity, often termed attention deficit disorder (ADD). The DSM-IV refers to this subtype as attention-deficit/hyperactivity disorder, predominately inattentive type (APA, 1994). In lieu of a subtype of ADHD, ADD has been suggested as a separate and distinct disorder (Lahey & Carlson, 1991). Another possible subtype includes the presence or absence of aggression (e.g., DuPaul & Stoner, 1994) that might be a specific subtype or a precursor to the development of a separate externalizing disorder.

STIMULANT MEDICATION

Research and Controversy

Bradley (1937) is often cited as the first to use stimulant medication (amphetamine sulfate) for children with behavior problems. Vigorous research on the use of stimulant medication began in the 1960s but over the intervening decades remains not only the most widely used treatment for ADHD, but also the most controversial (e.g., Frankenberger, Lozar, & Dallas, 1990; Stevenson & Wolraich, 1989; Wilens & Biederman, 1992). The controversy ranges from simple objections to using medication for treating behavior difficulties to specific concerns about the lack of research documenting long-term efficacy or improved academic functioning. There is also concern that stimulant medication may be viewed as a simple cure (e.g., Combrinck-Graham, 1987; Cowart, 1988; Pihl, 1980).

Multimodal Treatment

The expressed concerns over the use of stimulant medication led to the recommendation of a multimodal approach to the treatment of ADHD. The complexity of the disorder, with multiple symptoms and coexisting disorders, as well as the lack of unequivocal evidence about long-term improvement with stimulant medication, is the reason cited for suggesting more than one treatment modality (e.g., Anastopoulos, DuPaul, & Barkley, 1991; Busch, 1993; Pelham, 1993). The use of cognitive-behavior modification and social skills training is often recommended as additional treatments (e.g., Braswell & Bloomquist, 1991; Gomez & Cole, 1991; Gordon, Thomason, Cooper, & Ivers, 1991) even though the later two have not received positive evaluations (e.g., Abikoff, 1991; Braswell, 1993; Vinson, 1994).

The argument for multimodal treatment suggests that since stimulant medication is effective in the behavioral realm, behavior therapy might be more effective with social and academic difficulties (Murray, 1987). Within the context of behavior therapy, behavior modification reveals more positive results with ADHD symptoms than cognitive-behavioral intervention (Wells, 1986). Even though behavior modification and stimulant medication may demonstrate significant effect individually, stimulant medication enhances the effects of behavior modification, whereas the reverse is not true (Pelham, Carlson, Sams, Vallano, Dixon, & Hoza, 1993).

Multimodal treatments might be questioned since other interventions (e.g., behavior modification) require considerably more time and effort and do not demonstrate improvement over stimulant medication (e.g., Greenhill, 1992; Horn et al., 1991; Vinson, 1994). Although the use of multimodal treatments over the use of only stimulant medication does not appear supported in long-term studies (Schacher & Tannock, 1993), the suggestion remains that combined interventions are preferred because individual differences among children means some respond better to behavioral intervention or to medication or to a combination of both (Abramowitz, Eckstrand, O'Leary, & Dulcan, 1992; Hoza, Pelham, Sams, & Carlson, 1992). The question about the efficacy of multimodal treatment remains open.

Modes of Action

Even with the controversies surrounding its use, stimulant medication remains the most prevalent form of treatment as well as the most studied (DuPaul & Stoner, 1994; Henker & Whalen, 1989; Wolraich, Lindgren, Stromquist, Milich, Davis, & Watson, 1990). It is generally reported that the use of stimulant medication has increased substantially and at a steady rate during the past few decades (Wilens & Biederman, 1992). Although prevalence estimates may vary across school districts and geographic location (e.g., Frankenberger, Lozar, & Dallas, 1990; Safer & Krager, 1988), the rate of stimulant medication use appears to be about 2 percent (Barkley, 1990).

The stimulant medications currently prescribed for ADHD include methylphenidate (Ritalin), dextroamphetamine (Dexedrine), and pemoline (Cylert). The most usually recommended is methylphenidate which accounts for about 90 percent of stimulant medication prescribed (Greenhill, 1992). All three medications appear equally effective and are relatively safe (Safer, 1995). Although believed initially to have a paradoxical calming effect on hyperactive children, more recent research has demonstrated this not to be the case (e.g., Evans & Pelham, 1991; Henker & Whalen, 1989; Jacobvitz, Sroufe, Stewart, & Leffert, 1990). Methylphenidate has the same effect in individuals who are not hyperactive, exerting a "wake-up" effect on the central nervous system (Barkley, 1977).

Stimulant medication appears to work for preschool and school-age children as well as adults (Wilens & Biederman, 1992). The actual effects on the brain, however, are not known; the assumption is that stimulant medication affects the frontal lobes of the brain that help regulate attention, activity level, and emotionality (Nahlik, 1995). The efficacy of stimulant medication has been postulated to involve its ability to induce the release or increase the production of neurotransmitters (e.g., dopamine, norepinephrine), and subsequently block reuptake at the presynaptic terminal or inhibit action of monoamine oxidase (Solanto, 1984).

The question of dosing remains unanswered, with some suggestions for dosage based on weight of the individuals while other suggestions propose absolute dosing (Wilens & Biederman, 1992). Although there is some sentiment for target and maximum dosages (e.g., Sylvester, 1993), the effects of drugs are often idiosyncratic and therefore must be titrated individually (Schachar & Tannock, 1993), with no set maximum dose (Vinson, 1994). It has been argued that drug doses should be titrated specifically for learning improvements rather than behavioral enhancement. Sprague and Sleator (1977) were among the first to report that lower doses were needed for improvement in learning and attention, while higher doses resulted in improvement in behavior and social responses. Subsequent findings indicating that the rate of accuracy on classroom tasks to increase with increasing drug dosages (e.g., Rapport, DuPaul, Stoner, & Jones, 1986) led to the suggestion that a group linear dose-response curve across all target areas (including attention and behavior) is preferred (Douglas, Barr, Amin, O'Neill, & Britton, 1988; Hinshaw, 1991). Individual responses on behavior and academic measures have been found to not always follow the group linear dose-response curve, however, and thus suggest the need for individual titration (Hinshaw, Henker, Whalen, Erhardt, & Dunnington, 1989).

Side Effects

Generally, stimulant medication is reported to be safe with relatively few side effects (Safer, 1995). The most common side effects are decreased appetite and insomnia (Barkley, 1990). Additional side effects reported have been weight loss (probably due to decreased appetite), headache, stomachache, small increase in blood pressure, and elevation of heart rate (Greenhill, 1992). A behavioral rebound may also occur where the individual might increase the level of ADHD-type symptoms (e.g., irritability, increased talking, hyperactivity, non-compliance) over pre-medication levels as the majority of medication is eliminated (Greenhill, 1989). It has been suggested, however, that these mood-related effects might be due to

ADHD itself and not the medication (Barkley, McMurray, Edelbrock, & Robbins, 1990). Although it has been suggested that stimulant medication might exacerbate or unmask tics or Tourette's syndrome (e.g., Greenhill, 1992), recent research has questioned this assumption (e.g., Gadow, Sverd, Sprafkin, Nolan, & Ezor, 1995; Klein, 1995; Safer, 1995). Substance abuse risk does not appear to be increased with the use of stimulant medication (Safer, 1995).

The most prominent long-term concerns involve a slowing in height and weight gain. The slowing in height and weight appears to be relatively mild, however, with eventual adult height and weight at normal levels (Stevenson & Wolraich, 1989). Generally, most side effects are mild, often get better with time or reduced dosages, and are eliminated when medication use is discontinued (Barkley, DuPaul, & Costello, 1993).

Effects of Stimulant Medication

The effects of stimulant medication have been well studied. The most dramatic effects are on the core components of the disorder (i.e., hyperactivity, impulsivity, and inattention); about 75 percent of children diagnosed with ADHD demonstrate improvements in these areas after medication use (Barkley, 1977; Greenhill, 1992), with no response difference between males and females (Barkley, 1989). More recently, it has been reported that perceived "nonresponders" often demonstrate a positive response to either methylphenidate or dextroamphetamine when dose is increased (Elia, Borcherding, Rapoport, & Keysor, 1991), with one study reporting that all children made gains on at least some measures with increased dosage (Douglas, Barr, Amin, O'Neill, & Britton, 1988).

Although a majority of studies report the basic components of ADHD to improve with stimulant medication, the individuals receiving medication may not move into the average (i.e., "normal") range. For example, one investigation reported that the behaviors of children with ADHD were normalized on motor activity measures, and were improved, but not in the average range, on measures of impulsivity and inattentiveness (Abikoff & Gittelman, 1985). Other studies suggest stimulant medication does normalize behavior for many individuals with ADHD, particularly with respect to the core components of ADHD (Rapport, Denney, DuPaul, & Gardner, 1994). A variety of other effects of stimulant medication have also been studied, including peer relationships, social behavior, aggressiveness, and academic achievement. The findings with such variables are mixed, with some studies showing short-term improvement but not long-term gains. A recurring concern and criticism of stimulant medication use is the lack of data supporting significant long-term outcomes in important areas such as education and behavior, because students treated with stimulant medication often do not differ significantly from non-treated students at follow-up (e.g., Barkley & Cunningham, 1978; Hechtman, 1985, 1989; Ialongo et al., 1993).

Some studies report no academic gains resulting from stimulant treatment (Barkley, 1977), while others suggest that academic effects are not yet clear (Gadow, 1983; Wilens & Biederman, 1992). Of central importance is criticism about the use of standardized achievement tests to measure academic gains; treatment studies are usually short term in nature (e.g., two months), and standardized achievement tests may not contain enough items at each grade level to be sensitive to modest academic gains (e.g., Barkley & Cunningham, 1978; Douglas, Barr, O'Neill, & Britton, 1986; Pelham, Bender, Caddell, Booth, & Moorer, 1985). More sensitive measures (e.g., daily assignments, classroom tests, number of items attempted) have shown positive findings, leading to speculation that academic gains are, in fact, present (Balthazor, Wagner, & Pelham, 1991; Carlson & Bunner, 1993; Douglas, Barr, O'Neill, & Britton, 1986; Elia, Welsh, Gullotta, & Rapoport, 1993; Evans & Pelham, 1991; Swanson, Cantwell, Lerner, McBurnett, & Hanna, 1991; Tannock, Schachar, Carr, & Logan, 1989). In addition, Kavale's (1982) meta-analysis reported academic improvement for students treated with stimulant medication, although the effects were much smaller than behavioral effects. Other factors to consider when evaluating academic findings, in addition to the difficulties associated with achievement tests, include looking at the length of treatment, noncompliance factors, dosage factors, and individual differences (Forness & Kavale, 1988).

The findings related to peer relationships are also mixed (Pelham et al., 1990), although, in general, improved social interactions are observed (Barkley, 1990). Although students may show a decrease in negative social behaviors (e.g., disruptiveness, aggression, noncompliance), it is unclear whether prosocial behaviors (e.g., sharing) are also increased (Allen, Safer, & Covi, 1975; Buhrmester, Whalen, Henker, MacDonald, & Hinshaw, 1992; Hinshaw, 1991). It has also been suggested, however, that the prosocial behavior of children with ADHD and comparison children do not differ prior to medication use (Hinshaw, Henker, Whalen, Erhardt, & Dunnington, 1989). A similar concern exists with respect to the demonstration of long-term gains; ADHD adolescents who were treated with stimulants in childhood did not differ from non-treated ADHD adolescents on measures of social or emotional problems (Hechtman, 1985).

Different populations may respond differently to stimulant medication. For example, children with different ADHD subtypes or those with comorbid conditions may respond differently (Forness, Swanson, Cantwell, Youpa, & Hanna, 1992). One investigation attempted to determine if methylphenidate works differently with aggressive and nonaggressive children with findings indicating that most component areas respond similarly (e.g., levels of attention), with perhaps a reduced activity level noted for nonaggressive (but not aggressive) children with ADHD (Matier, Halperin, Sharma, Newcorn, & Sathaye, 1992). In addition, there is some evidence that individuals with internalizing disorders and comorbid ADHD do not respond as well to methylphenidate as those without an accompanying internalizing disorder (DuPaul, Barkley, & McMurray, 1994).

Effectiveness of Stimulant Medication

The effectiveness of stimulant medication for ADHD is still subject to debate. The extensive literature investigating the efficacy of stimulant medication has not resulted in closure about the question. In many respects, empirical findings have proven less manifest than ideological and ethical positions regarding the use of stimulant medication. To move beyond the single study and to make empirical findings more meaningful, a literature review is an important aid in integrating knowledge and clarifying the current status of research (Cooper, 1982).

A popular methodology for conducting literature reviews is meta-analysis, the analysis of analyses (Glass, 1976). Quantitative methods of research synthesis (i.e., meta-analysis) were developed to overcome the perceived theoretical and pragmatic difficulties associated with traditional methods of summarizing research (Cooper & Rosenthal, 1980; Jackson, 1980). The methods of meta-analysis have been described (e.g., Glass, McGaw, & Smith, 1981; Rosenthal, 1984; Wolf, 1986) and have become accepted as a means of summarizing statistically a research domain (Wachter & Straf, 1990). The techniques of meta-analysis have witnessed a number of technical advances (e.g., Cooper & Hedges, 1993; Hedges & Olkin, 1985) that have served to enhance the objectivity, verifiability, and replicability of the meta-analytic review process (Hunt, 1997; Kavale, 1984).

Three meta-analyses were published during the 1980s focusing on the efficacy of stimulant medication in treating hyperactivity. Kavale (1982) presented perhaps the most comprehensive overview when 135 studies were reviewed across three outcome categories: behavioral, cognitive, and physiological. A moderately large treatment effect was reported for the overall effectiveness of stimulant medication, and Kavale thus concluded that stimulant medication was an effective treatment for hyperactivity. The largest effects were found in the behavioral area (e.g., activity-level concentration), with positive but generally less robust effects reported for the cognitive domain (e.g., IQ scores, reading scores). Thurber and Walker (1983) reviewed 20 studies and reported a mean effect size that was described as relatively small. The area with the most positive effect was attention variables. Lastly, Ottenbacher and Cooper (1983) reviewed 61 studies, and the largest effect was found on behavioral/social measures, while academic measures demonstrated the smallest effect. Ottenbacher and Cooper reported that drug treatment produced significant effects, although they reported a large placebo effect as well. None of the three reviews found significant differences in efficacy among the most popular stimulant drugs. In an attempt to reconcile the diverse findings from the three meta-analyses, Swanson (1993) examined the behavior/attention ratings and academic ratings across the three studies, and found that all three meta-analyses reported significantly larger behavior/attention effects than academic achievement effects. Swanson also noted that even though each analysis proposed to review the literature through 1980, the overlap among references was low. It was further noted that they addressed different questions and did not have the same criteria for study inclusion.

The previous meta-analyses were conducted during the 1980s. With stimulant medication being the "most prevalent and most controversial therapeutic modality in child psychopathology" (Henker & Whalen, 1989, p. 221) as well as the most investigated (Barkley, 1990), the need for an updated quantitative synthesis is evident. Additionally, advances in ways of measuring behavior and academic gains suggested the need to review the later literature in this area (Stoner, Carey, Ikeda, & Shinn, 1994). In addition, factors such as different subtypes of ADHD and comorbidity with other disorders may be better addressed by integrating research that has identified these components. Comparative studies are also important to integrate in order to determine the efficacy of stimulants as compared to other treatments. Finally, replication studies are an often neglected aspect of the research process and possess the potential for validating findings as well as reconciling conflicting findings.

METHODOLOGY

Methods of Meta-analysis

The present investigation reviewed empirical research studies investigating stimulant drug efficacy published between the years 1981 and 1995 using the methods of meta-analysis. As a research methodology, meta-analysis parallels primary research activities and includes the following elements:

1. *Problem Formulation*: Meta-analysis typically attempts to explore comprehensive questions. In the present case, the effectiveness of stimulant medication in treating ADHD is the focus. Outcome variables included behavioral and academic effects of stimulant drugs for school-aged children and adolescents. Additionally, current issues of concern, such as behavioral and academic outcomes under low versus high medication dosages as well as academic outcomes assessed by standardized achievement tests versus more sensitive measures, were also addressed.
2. *Sampling*: The goal of meta-analysis is to be both representative and inclusive by incorporating a majority of the research in the domain under consideration. A sampling framework was developed using the following data bases: PsychLit, ERIC, and MEDLINE with multiple keywords entered (e.g., ADHD, methylphenidate/Ritalin, psychostimulant/stimulant). The years searched were 1981 to 1995 inclusive since the previous meta-analyses were completed in studies published through 1980, but no meta-analysis was located since that time.

The search sought only published journal articles, primarily because they are plentiful and typically undergo a peer review process that enhances quality. In order to allow for comparisons and continuation of Kavale's (1982) meta-analysis, inclusion criteria remained basically the same. The following inclusion criteria were used: (a) studies had to be published in journals dated 1981 to 1995, (b) studies had to use samples between the ages of five and 18, (c) a primary diagnosis was ADHD, ADD, or hyperactivity, (d) the study had to include a comparison/control group, (e) the findings had to be reported in a form appropriate for meta-analysis, and (f) the study had to measure the efficacy of stimulant medication on behavioral or academic outcomes. The literature search yielded 115 studies (two studies were reported in one article) that met all study criteria. Although many more studies were located, they did not meet specific criteria, most usually because of the lack of adequate statistical information or unsuitable outcome measures. (A list of the studies included in this meta-analysis is available from the first author.)

3. *Study Classification*: The initial step in meta-analysis is to organize study information for analysis. A recording form was constructed to uniformly code study information about subject data, treatment details, outcome variables, and design components. Multiple variables were coded when available to permit more discrete comparisons for answering specific questions (e.g., parent versus teacher checklist outcomes). The reliability of study coding was assessed by calculating inter-rater agreement on 15 percent of the obtained studies (18 of 115). Percent of agreement was calculated by dividing the number of agreements by the number of agreements and disagreements combined with the resulting number multiplied by 100. The average percent of agreement for the 18 studies coded was 94 percent (range was 85% to 100%).

4. *Data Analysis*: The primary statistic in meta-analysis is the effect size (ES) that is a standardized index of effect magnitude for the dependent variable under study. To assess the efficacy of stimulant medication intervention, the ES is defined by

$$ES = \frac{M_T - M_C}{SD_C}$$

where $M_T =$ mean (average) score of drug treated group on an outcome measure,
$M_C =$ mean (average) score of control (comparison) group in an outcome measure, and
$SD_C =$ standard deviation of the control (comparison) group.

The present meta-analysis combined individual ES from studies into a single overall ES estimate for either behavioral and academic outcomes using the "study effect size meta-analysis" (Hunter & Schmidt, 1990) that averages individual ES into one ES per study. With a single ES per study, problems associated with possible statistical dependency resulting from having multiple ES from a single study are avoided (Mostert, 1996). Within the behavioral realm, separate ES were calculated for the following areas: ADHD behavior (attention, activity, and impulsivity), positive social behavior, and aggressive/noncompliant behavior. For the academic category, ES for achievement tests and classroom measures were calculated separately.

5. *Effect Size Interpretation*: An ES may be interpreted like a z-score and interpreted to show the level of improvement attributed to stimulant medication treatment. For example, in studies investigating the effects of stimulant medication, an ES of +1.00 indicates an one standard deviation superiority for the treatment group, which means that 84 percent of drug-treated subjects were better off than untreated (control) subjects. On average, the effects of drug intervention would move treated subjects to the 84th percentile where they would demonstrate a 34 percentile rank gain on a behavioral or academic outcome measure compared to untreated subjects who remain at the 50th percentile.

STIMULANT MEDICATION AND ADHD

Demographic Information

The 115 studies included about 3,300 subjects whose average age was 9.4 years and average IQ was 99.2. Across the 115 studies, 91 percent included samples of children with average ages between 5 and 12, with 9 percent including students with an average age between 13 and 18. In terms of IQ, an average range (90 to 110) was reported in 81 percent of studies while six studies included samples with IQ levels below 70. For diagnostic category, 70 studies included a classification of ADD, 33 a classification of ADHD, two studies included both ADD and ADHD, and 10 studies described subjects as "hyperactive." The DSM-III and DSM-IIIR were the diagnostic criteria used in 85 studies, while the remaining studies used less specific classification criteria. For example, the basis for sample inclusion might be checklist or interview data, physician statement, or a prior diagnosis of hyperactivity.

Comorbid diagnoses, and their relationship to outcome measures, although important variables, were difficult to determine. Many studies reported that a portion of the study population had at least one comorbid diagnosis, but results were not generally reported separately in order to allow for overall comparisons of "pure" ADHD groups versus nonpure groups. Further confounding the problem, many studies did not report information concerning comorbid diagnoses or suggested that comorbid diagnoses were probably present but did not address them further, suggesting that the included sample could not be considered a pure ADHD group. The most common comorbid diagnoses were conduct disorder ($n = 36$), oppositional defiant disorder ($n = 31$), and learning disability ($n = 25$) while 63 studies reported no comorbid diagnoses. In addition, the presence of hyperactivity is an important variable, but only one study was conducted with a sample diagnosed ADD without hyperactivity; other studies either mixed hyperactive and nonhyperactive groups, used groups of students with hyperactivity only, or did not report on the presence or absence of hyperactivity.

Further description of the study samples included in this meta-analysis found 48 percent of studies that reported gender ratios included only male subjects, while 52 percent included both male and female; no study included female students only. In the studies with both genders, however, males outnumbered females by a ratio of 4.5 to 1, which is in accord with ADHD prevalence estimates (APA, 1994). Socioeconomic status (SES) was not reported in a majority of studies (85 out of 115), and, when reported, it varied from estimates based on Hollingshead indexes to income level to simple qualitative descriptions (e.g., "low to middle"); SES appeared to be in the low- to upper-middle-class range. Race was also often not reported (84 of the 115 studies), but when reported, 24 studies included two or more races, 6 included Caucasians only, and 1 study included only an African-American sample. Sample selection procedures also varied, with over half of the studies either reporting insufficient information about sampling techniques or utilizing samples from multiple sources (e.g., newspaper advertisements and school referrals). The average sample size across studies was 28.59.

Medication information coded included type of stimulant medication, dosage, and duration of treatment. Methylphenidate was by far the most studied stimulant, with 103 studies using it. Ten studies used dextroamphetamine, and two studies used pemoline. More than one stimulant was used in some studies, either because of adverse reactions to one stimulant or to compare stimulants efficacy. Eighty-four studies used the same dosages for all subjects, while the others either titrated

Table 1. Methods of Measurement for Academic and Behavioral Outcomes

Measures	*Number of Studies Using Measures*
Academic	
Achievement tests	8
Assignment accuracy	25
Percentage assignment complete	20
Test/quiz scores	1
Curriculum-based measures	1
Grades	1
Other	7
Behavioral	
Observations	43
Parent checklists	43
Teacher checklists	67
Compliance ratings	1
Peer ratings	1
Lab measures	44
Other	23

dosages for optimal results or used already prescribed medication dosages for subjects. In addition, 37 studies reported the effects of high versus low dosages on outcome variables. Most studies were classified as short term (less than 12 weeks), with 12 studies lasting longer (six of these 12 studies lasted at least 12 weeks). The average treatment duration across all studies was 5.7 weeks.

Study design characteristics were also coded. Eighty-three studies utilized a crossover design, double blind procedures, and placebo control. Of these 83 studies, nine did not report whether subject assignment was random. Concurrent treatment variables were rarely addressed, but 29 studies did report some sort of concurrent treatment (e.g., summer treatment program, tutoring, behavior modification). Outcome variables included both behavioral and academic outcomes in 31 studies, while 78 studies reported only behavioral outcomes, and five studies reported only academic outcomes. Table 1 shows the methods used to assess academic and behavioral outcomes.

EFFICACY OF STIMULANT MEDICATION

Overall Effects

The average subject receiving stimulant medication exhibited an average ES ($\overline{ES}$) of .673 with a standard deviation (SD) of .512 and standard error (SE) of .042. The .673 SD superiority for the average drug-treated subject indicated that drug intervention moves the average ADHD subject from the 50th to the 75th percentile. This 25 percentile rank gain on outcome assessments suggests that a subject taking stimulant medication would be expected to be better off than 75 percent of subjects not taking stimulant medication. The diverse assortment of outcome assessments that covers such a broad spectrum makes a single index of drug effects difficult to interpret except in the most general sense. For this reason, the focus of this investigation shifted to drug effects in the behavioral and academic realms.

Behavioral Effects of Stimulant Medication

Across 110 studies, the $\overline{ES}$ for behavior was .743 with an SD of .549 and SE of .052. Behavioral outcomes exhibited positive changes as a result of drug treatment indicating that the average subject would be better off than approximately 77 percent of comparison subjects. Assessments of behavior change show the average drug-treated subject would improve by about 27 percentile ranks on outcome measures.

The behavioral outcome category included three different components that were each calculated separately and are shown in Table 2.

Seventeen studies provided measures of positive social behavior (e.g., peer interactions, social skills, and popularity measures); the $\overline{ES}$ was .413, suggesting a moderate increase of 16 percentile ranks on positive social behavior for students

Table 2. Effects of Stimulant Medication on Behavior

Outcome	*Number of Effect Sizes*	*Mean Effect Size*	*Standard Deviation of Effect Size*
ADHD behavior	90	0.716	0.415
Positive social behavior	17	0.413	0.236
Aggressive/Noncompliant behavior	57	0.608	0.286

taking stimulant medication. Social behavior was most commonly evaluated with checklists and through observation. The outcome measures of conduct/aggression/noncompliance were generally measured by observations and checklists as well. A greater level of medication effect was found in the 57 studies measuring aggression/noncompliance, with an $\overline{ES}$ of .608 amounting to a 23 percentile rank gain. Thus, stimulant medication does appear to increase positive social behavior and decrease negative behaviors, with a significant effect on reducing negative behaviors ($t_{(72)} = 2.53, p < .05$).

Lastly, the core behavior components of ADHD were assessed. Ninety studies described outcome measures tapping attention, activity level, and impulsivity. This category yielded the largest behavioral $\overline{ES}$ (.716) indicating that the average drug-treated subject would be better off than 76 percent of non-treated subjects. Stimulant medication appears to have the greatest influence on the core components of ADHD as evidenced by significantly larger effects than found for both positive social behavior and aggressive/noncompliant behavior ($F_{(2,162)} = 6.03$, $p < .01$). ADHD characteristics were rated in a variety of ways, including checklists/rating scales (most usually completed by teachers or parents), laboratory measures (e.g., continuous performance test), and observations. The different methods for assessing ADHD behavior were further evaluated to determine whether some types of measures were more sensitive or gave different results than others with the findings shown in Table 3. ADHD behavior rated by checklists demonstrated the largest improvement, with an $\overline{ES}$ of .963. Teacher checklists demonstrated better results than parent checklists in showing positive effects for stimulant medication on ADHD behavior ($\overline{ES}$ = 1.059 for teachers versus .833 for parents). Observations

Table 3. ADHD Behavior Effect Sizes

Outcome Measures	*Number of Effect Sizes*	*Mean Effect Size*	*Standard Deviation of Effect Size*
Checklists	46	0.963	0.562
Teacher	36	1.059	0.576
Parent	18	0.833	0.742
Lab measures	40	0.522	0.570
Observations	32	0.547	0.513

and laboratory-type measures, although still indicating a positive medication response, revealed lower $\overline{ES}$ (observation $\overline{ES} = .547$; lab measure $\overline{ES} = .522$) When $\overline{ES}$s were compared, checklists revealed larger effects than either lab measures or observational techniques ($F_{(2,115)} = 8.05, p < .001$) while there was no difference in the way parents and teachers assessed outcomes on checklists ($t_{(52)} = 1.24, p < .20$).

Academic Effects of Stimulant Medication

Across 36 studies, the $\overline{ES}$ for academic performance was .460 with a SD of .399 and SE of .067. The average drug-treated subject would be better off than about 68 percent of subjects not receiving medication and gain approximately 18 percentile ranks on assessments of academic performance. Thus, stimulant medication appears to have a positive influence on school achievement. When compared to the effects on behavior ($\overline{ES} = .743$), however, stimulant medication appears to have a more modest effect on academic performance ($t_{(144)} = 2.98, p < .01$).

During the 1980s, there was increased use of classroom-type measures (e.g., percentage of work completed, accuracy on classroom assignments) to assess achievement. Table 4 shows the effects of stimulant medication on academic performance as measured by classroom-type assessments and more traditional standardized achievement tests.

The classroom-type measures produced an $\overline{ES}$ of .517 that translates into 20 percentile rank gain for the average drug-treated subject. When assessed with standardized achievement tests, the $\overline{ES}$ was .249 that translates into a 10 percentile rank gain for the average student receiving stimulant medication. When classroom measures of achievement are used, students on stimulant medication reveal more positive effects, but the difference from standardized achievement measures is not significant ($t_{(34)} = 1.76, p < .10$).

Comparative Effects of Stimulant Medication: Low versus High Dosages

The effect of low versus high dosages of methylphenidate was analyzed for both behavioral and academic outcomes. Because some studies used body weight (mg/kg) for dosages and others used fixed dosages (mg), the low and high dosages had to be defined using both methods. A low dosage was defined in one of the following two ways: (a) less than .5 mg/kg, or (b) less than or equal to 10 mg per dose. Conversely, a high dosage was defined as: (a) equal or greater than .5 mg/kg,

Table 4. Effects of Stimulant Medication on Academic Performance

Outcome	*Number of Effect Sizes*	*Mean Effect Size*	*Standard Deviation of Effect Size*
Classroom achievement measures	28	0.517	0.425
Standardized achievement tests	8	0.249	0.103

or (b) greater than 10 mg per dose. These are the dosage levels that were generally used across studies (e.g., 5, 10, 15, and 20 mg were compared; .3 mg/kg was compared with .6 mg/kg). Thirty-six studies compared varying dosages of methylphenidate on behavioral outcomes, while 17 studies compared dosages for academic outcomes (there were other studies that compared dosages but reported statistics for dosages combined). The $\overline{ES}$ for low and high dosages across behavioral and academic categories are shown in Table 5. A larger $\overline{ES}$ was demonstrated across all outcomes (i.e., behavior and academic), and the difference between low and high dosage for the behavior versus academic comparison was significant ($t_{(34)} = 2.16$, $p < .05$). This difference was most evident for ADHD behavior; the $\overline{ES}$ for low dosages of methylphenidate on ADHD behavior was .654 while the $\overline{ES}$ for high dosage was .924. The smallest difference was seen on positive social behavior (low dose $\overline{ES} = .318$ versus high dose $\overline{ES} = .342$). The academic functioning (classroom measures) $\overline{ES}$ was larger on higher dosages as well (.563 for high versus .446 for low).

Study Design

The question of whether a better study design influenced outcome was addressed by comparing $\overline{ES}$ for studies using double-blind, crossover, and placebo control features with pre-post designs, nontreated comparisons, and other comparison groups. The $\overline{ES}$ for the different designs are shown in Table 6. When comparing study designs, pre-post studies produced a larger $\overline{ES}$ (behavior $\overline{ES} = 1.265$; academic $\overline{ES} = .640$) than the better designed studies using double blind, crossover, and a placebo control (behavior $\overline{ES} = .748$; academic $\overline{ES} = .466$). Only three studies used a nontreated comparison group, so a separate ES was not calculated. Stimulant medication $\overline{ES}$ were still positive when compared with treatments other than a

Table 5. Low Versus High Dosages[a]

	Low	*High*
Outcome Measures	*Mean Effect Size*	*Mean Effect Size*
Behavior	.557 (.228)	.795 (.400)
ADHD behavior	.654 (.286)	.924 (.439)
Positive social behavior	.318 (.198)	.342 (.300)
Aggressive/noncompliant behavior	.442 (.196)	.596 (.223)
Academic	.434 (.264)	.546 (.374)
Classroom measures	.446 (.268)	.563 (.381)

Notes: [a]low = < .5 mg/kg or 10 mg or less
high = > .5 mg/kg or > 10 mg
Standard deviations are in parentheses

Table 6. Effect Sizes for Study Designs

	Behavior	Academic
Study Designs	*Mean Effect Size*	*Mean Effect Size*
Double-blind/placebo/crossover	.745 (.367)	.466 (.314)
Pre-post design	1.265 (1.022)	.640 (.687)
Other comparison groups	.303 (.327)	.165 (.212)
Other medication comparisons	.229 (.324)	n/a
Nonmedication comparisons	.437 (.319)	.165 (.212)

Note: Standard deviations are in parentheses

placebo (e.g., other medications, parent training). The $\overline{ES}$ were lower when compared with other drugs (behavior $\overline{ES}$ = .229). Larger $\overline{ES}$ were noted for comparisons with other nonmedication treatments (e.g., behavior modification, parent training), suggesting stimulant medication is more effective than these methods of treatment ($\overline{ES}$ = .437 for behavior).

In addition, one additional ES comparison was calculated. When coding studies, it was noted that when actual means and standard deviations were provided, all possible outcomes (positive, negative, significant, and nonsignificant) were often included, whereas studies reporting only *t*-tests or *F*-tests generally included only significant statistical information. Thus, studies reporting descriptive means and standard deviations were compared with studies reporting only inferential statistical test data. The studies reporting only inferential statistics demonstrated a larger behavior $\overline{ES}$ for stimulant medication ($\overline{ES}$ = .927) than those reporting actual means and standard deviations ($\overline{ES}$ = .712), perhaps suggesting caution in interpretation when means and standard deviations are not reported.

Comparing Stimulants

Since only two studies were located that used pemoline, methylphenidate was compared with pemoline and dextroamphetamine combined. The $\overline{ES}$ for methylphenidate in ameliorating the core components of ADHD was .743 (SD = .414) while an $\overline{ES}$ of .601 (SD = .366) was calculated for the other two stimulant medications; the difference was not significant.

Intelligence Levels

The current study did not exclude samples with IQ levels below 70, where six studies included such samples. The $\overline{ES}$ for these six studies were only slightly lower than the overall average, suggesting stimulant medication does have positive effects on behavior for subjects with both ADHD and mental disability. The behavior $\overline{ES}$

Table 7. Longer-term Treatment Effect Sizes[a]

Outcome Measures	*Number of Effect Sizes*	*Mean Effect Size*	*Standard Deviation of Effect Size*
Behavior	12	0.682	0.495
ADHD behavior	11	0.669	0.670
Academic[b]	6	0.289	0.103

Notes: [a]12 weeks or longer
[b]5 were standardized achievement tests

for these six studies was .649 (SD = .363), while the ADHD behavior $\overline{ES}$ was .609 (SD = .464).

Duration of Treatment

Treatment length was confounded by the fact that only three of the 12 studies that lasted 12 weeks or longer also used a double blind, placebo control, crossover design. This makes it difficult to interpret pre-post design studies on academic performance, because of the possibility that all students improve their academic skills during a period of 12 or more weeks. The $\overline{ES}$ for treatment duration are shown in Table 7 and are comparable with but slightly lower than behavior ES (.743).

Effects for Older Students

Although only nine studies included samples with an average age between 13 and 18, the ES was calculated on this subset in order to determine if effects were similar for adolescents to those of younger students. Only three of the nine studies included academic outcome measures, so an academic $\overline{ES}$ was not calculated. The $\overline{ES}$ for behavior displayed in Table 8 are comparable to the overall behavior ES (.743) reported with the effect for stimulant medication on ADHD behavior almost exactly the same.

Meta-Analytic Comparisons

The overall $\overline{ES}$ found in the present meta-analysis (.673) was similar to that found in the Kavale (1982) meta-analysis (.578). Although not strictly a replication,

Table 8. Behavior Effect Sizes for Adolescents

Outcome Measures	*Number of Effect Sizes*	*Mean Effect Size*	*Standard Deviation of Effect Size*
Behavior	9	0.620	0.278
ADHD behavior	7	0.712	0.228
Aggressive/noncompliant	7	0.569	0.230

confidence in the present findings may be enhanced by comparing the two meta-analyses on other common variables. These comparisons are displayed in Table 9.

Table 9 is remarkable for the similarities found for $\overline{ES}$ between the two meta-analyses in the areas of behavioral functioning, academic achievement, drug type, and study-design features. Among the 12 comparisons, only the $\overline{ES}$ for teacher ratings were significantly different ($t_{(91)} = 2.18, p < .05$). The consistency between findings suggests that general conclusions about the efficacy of stimulant medication may be validly drawn.

The major conclusion to be drawn suggests that stimulant medication is associated with a positive effect on behavior in general as well as on particular facets of ADHD evaluated with various assessment methods. It also appears that more modest gains are associated with academic performance; behavioral variables demonstrate a much stronger response to stimulant medication than academic variables. There also appears to be substantiation for methylphenidate (Ritalin) being the drug of choice. The best evidence was once again garnered from the more rigorous research designs. The comparability of findings for studies reported through 1980 to studies published after 1980 suggests a confidence in conclusions about the effectiveness of stimulant medication even though the samples may have changed slightly because of revised and clearer diagnostic criteria as well as changes in assessment resulting from better and more reliable instruments and an increased emphasis on behavioral observations (Barkley, 1990).

Table 9. Comparisons Between Meta-Analyses of 1982 and 1997

	Mean Effect Sizes	
Outcome	*1982*	*1997*
Behavior		
Global improvement	.804	.743
ADHD behavior	.814	.716
Conduct/Aggression/Noncompliance	.634	.608
Checklists	.886	.963
Parent ratings	.788	.833
Teacher ratings	.793	1.059
Academic		
School performance	.367	.460
Achievement test	.383	.249
Drug		
Methylphenidate	.634	.743
Dextroamphetamine/Pemoline	.563	.601
Design		
Placebo/Double-blind/Crossover	.562	.606
Pre-post	.628	.803

CONCLUSION

Behavior and Academic Effects

The present investigation synthesized empirical research published over a fifteen-year period examining the efficacy of stimulant medication in treating ADHD. It was an extension of the Kavale (1982) meta-analysis with the goal of updating that review as well as allowing for some additional comparisons (e.g., classroom academic measures versus standardized achievement tests). The reported effects were quite similar and demonstrated a positive effect on behavior. Although academic gains were also noted, stimulant medication produces a greater response on behavioral outcomes. The $\overline{ES}$ for behavior (.743) indicates that the average subject treated with stimulant medication would show a more positive response than 77 percent of subjects not receiving stimulant medication. The percentage of subjects showing a more positive response drops to 68 percent when academic performance is assessed. The comparable percentage of students treated with stimulant medication who would be better off in the Kavale (1982) meta-analysis in the behavior and academic realms is 79 percent and 65 percent, respectively. Thus, there is confidence in the expected magnitude of effect produced by stimulant medication treatment.

Effects for ADHD Correlates

Although overall effects in the behavior and academic areas were comparable in the two meta-analyses, it is also important to examine more narrowly defined variables evaluated in the current investigation. Stimulant medication produced its greatest effect on the core components of ADHD, namely overactivity, impulsivity, and inattention. This finding should not be surprising because these variables represent the defining features of the disorder for which stimulant medication is prescribed. There is concern, however, about other significant correlates often associated with ADHD, including poor academic achievement, aggressive/noncompliant behavior, and poor peer/social relations. If the core components of ADHD are ameliorated but one of all of these correlates remain, major difficulties above and beyond the behavioral elements associated with impulsivity, hyperactivity, and inattention may be created.

It is therefore important to note that stimulant medication does appear to also have positive effects on aggressive/noncompliant behavior as well as social behavior, although the magnitude of effect for these correlates were indeed smaller (particularly for the positive social behavior) than the effect found for ADHD behavior. That is, students prescribed stimulant medication demonstrated less negative, aggressive, and noncompliant behavior, albeit with smaller effects but near the level found for ADHD behaviors (more than half a standard deviation in both cases). More modest, albeit positive, increases in social behavior, which included measures of social skills and prosocial behavior, were also found. It is also noted that negative behaviors decreased more than positive behaviors increased, but this could be due to rates manifested for such behaviors before stimulant medication. Hinshaw, Henker, Whalen, Erhardt, & Dunnington (1989) suggested that rates of prosocial behavior may not be different for ADHD students versus comparison students before medication initiation. It could also be that negative behaviors are more frequent and noticeable, so that they are more likely to stand out as modified behavior after stimulant medication use. In any case, the data from this meta-analysis suggest an important decrease in negative and aggressive behavior as well as a moderate increase in positive social behaviors. The mechanism by which stimulant medication might exert such effects is unknown, but the theory that the impulsive, inattentive, and overactive features of ADHD could be the basis for other behavioral disorders involving aggressive or noncompliant behavior (e.g., conduct disorder) is a possibility needing further investigation (Loeber, 1990). That is, the core components of ADHD could directly or indirectly be causal factors in aggressive behavior, so that reducing such core components in turn reduced aggressiveness.

The third frequently observed correlate of ADHD, poor academic achievement, is another important feature. Although the current meta-analysis found an overall academic effect not much larger than that reported by Kavale (1982), this difference becomes more noticeable when findings for classroom measures and standardized achievement tests are separated. Criticism has been leveled against the use of achievement-test data in studies investigating stimulant medication because most studies are short term in nature, and achievement tests do not include enough items to be sensitive to academic change over a relatively short period, such as the average treatment duration of five to six weeks in the 115 studies reviewed here. It is possible, then, that stimulant medication does indeed enhance academic work over a period of five to six weeks, but that it is not measurable on standardized achievement tests. Classroom measures, such as percentage of work completed accurately or number of words read correctly in a given time, might more accurately reflect academic gains if present. Thus, when assessments use classroom-type measures, an ES of .517 was obtained, indicating that the average subject in the stimulant medication group scored more than one half a standard deviation better than the average child in the control/comparison group. This level of improvement is comparable to what might be expected for about six months of instruction.

Short-Term Versus Long-Term Results

Longer-term academic gains are difficult to assess because five of the six studies measuring academic outcomes over a period of 12 or more weeks included only standardized achievement-test data which produced lower effect sizes as noted. It is recognized, however, that short-term classroom academic measures should logically translate into achievement-test gains over the long term. These longer-term studies, however, may still not have been long enough; five of the six studies lasted only between 12 and 16 weeks, so that standardized achievement-test gains might still not be expected.

It is noted that follow-up studies that have compared students who previously received stimulant medication with those who did not take stimulant medication have reported virtually no differences between these two groups over the long term (Hechtman, 1985, 1989). Barkley (1990) suggested that long-term studies have serious methodological difficulties, and consequently, long-term effects of stimulant medication have not been clearly investigated. Nevertheless, there appears to be a research gap between important short-term academic gains in the classroom and the absence of evidence about academic gains over the long term.

An important consideration in this regard is whether students are, in fact, currently taking medication. Short-term studies typically include samples currently taking medication, while follow-up studies generally do not because students have usually stopped taking stimulant medication at the time of follow-up. The chronicity of ADHD may be an important factor here; although students may continue to demonstrate components of ADHD, the effects of discontinuing medication are unknown. It is possible that in order for gains to continue, whether behavioral or academic, the student must continue taking stimulant medication. This point produces much criticism and is a point of contention concerning continued use of stimulant medication. In addition to length of treatment, other important factors to consider when evaluating long-term efficacy are factors related to noncompliance and dosage (Forness & Kavale, 1988). Thus, a student with a stimulant medication dosage titrated for academic performance, treated for a longer period of time with good compliance and response, may demonstrate considerably different results than a student prescribed medication with no titration for dosage and with poor compliance. Although these factors are difficult to separate and assess in empirical studies, they are important to consider, nonetheless.

Factors Influencing the Efficacy of Stimulant Medication

Findings from the present meta-analysis also examined the ways outcome variables were measured. The most frequent measures to assess behavioral outcomes were teacher and parent checklists, laboratory measures, and observations. Checklists demonstrated the most positive effects, and teacher checklists revealed more positive effects than checklists completed by parents, although both were positive. The larger effect for teacher checklists may be due to several reasons. One is the fact that stimulant medication is often prescribed during the school day, and since effects are short-lived (i.e., three to four hours), parents may not see these same effect magnitudes unless students take medications in the evening or on weekends as well. Additionally, the core components of ADHD are usually more pronounced in a structured setting (e.g., school) so amelioration of such ADHD symptoms would probably also be more noticeable in such settings. The effects of stimulant medication on laboratory measures and observations were similar, with both lower than effects reported on checklists. This information is important in assessing stimulant medication effects on ADHD symptoms because it must be recognized that effects of stimulant medication may appear much higher when rated by checklists than by observations, for example.

In terms of the intelligence levels, the majority of studies examined did not include samples with mental disability. The present findings suggested, however, positive behavioral effects for stimulant medication for subjects with both ADHD and mental deficiency. Because the sample of studies was small (n = 6), few conclusions about stimulant medication and ADHD within this combined population are possible. Additionally, with one study reporting that this population may be at more risk of developing side effects (Handen, Feldman, Gosling, Breaux, & McAuliffe, 1991; Handen, Janosky, McAuliffe, Breaux, & Feldman, 1994), the need for further identifying sub-types of students who respond well to stimulant medication, or who may respond in different ways is demonstrated. Subgroups such as students with conduct disorder and ADHD, or learning disabilities and ADHD, as well as students diagnosed with ADHD with and without hyperactivity, are also important groups to investigate.

Another important group to investigate is adolescents (Biederman & Steingard, 1989). Study samples from the current review consisted primarily of children ages five to 12. The effects found for the nine studies that did provide data on adolescents (ages 13 to 18) were encouraging; the effects were comparable to the overall results across all studies. This is important because it was once thought that children outgrew ADHD at adolescence, and stimulant medication was therefore rarely prescribed. Across behavioral categories (i.e., overall behavior, noncompliant/aggressive behavior, and ADHD behavior) the magnitudes of effect suggested the average adolescent in the stimulant medication groups demonstrated behavior that is more than one half a standard deviation above, or better than, a comparison subject not taking stimulant medication.

Kavale (1982) reported no significant differences between efficacy rates for stimulant medications, with methylphenidate effectiveness ($\overline{ES}$ = .634) only slightly above that of dextroamphetamine ($\overline{ES}$ = .585) or pemoline ($\overline{ES}$ = .540). The present meta-analysis located relatively few studies that used dextroamphetamine or pemoline, but effectiveness rates remained comparable between methylphenidate ($\overline{ES}$ = .743) and dextroamphetamine and pemoline effectiveness rates combined ($\overline{ES}$ = .601). Methylphenidate thus continues to be the best researched and most prescribed medication.

Varying effects were noted when different study designs were compared. Studies utilizing double blind, crossover, and a placebo control produced effects close to effects reported overall for the meta-analysis. Studies with a pre-post design demonstrated larger effects that could be due in part to awareness (i.e., nonblind) of stimulant medication by participants and most likely by raters as well, so that positive expectancy levels might be higher. Lower effects were found when stimulant medication was compared with other drug treatments, suggesting that other medications beside stimulants also have some effectiveness on ADHD symptoms. Medications such as anti-depressants have been studied and are sometimes recommended for populations with multiple diagnoses (e.g., subjects diagnosed with depression and ADHD). The $\overline{ES}$ of .437 when comparing stimulant medication to other treatments (e.g., behavior modification and parent training) suggests stimulant medication possesses a larger effect on behavior than other treatments, even though these nonmedication comparison treatments often require considerable time and effort.

Although stimulant medication demonstrated better results than nonmedication comparison treatments, the use of these other treatments in conjunction with drugs is an area needing more research. The use of other treatment modalities in addition to stimulant medication was not specifically addressed here. Since it appears that the core components of ADHD are significantly reduced by stimulant medication and the correlates of ADHD (e.g., decreased academic functioning, poor peer relations, and increased aggression) are also positively affected but less so, additional treatments might best address these correlates of ADHD to achieve maximum efficacy. That is, since stimulant medication is effective for the majority of students in ameliorating the core components of ADHD, during the time these students are on medication may be preferred for addressing poor academics with intensive tutoring or addressing aggressive behavior with behavior modification techniques. It is possible that such a combination might be a more efficient and profitable use of multimodal techniques in lieu of addressing ADHD behaviors in multiple ways.

Lastly, it was found that higher dosages generally revealed better results across outcome measures. This finding corroborates research suggesting a group linear dose-response curve (Douglas, Barr, Amin, O'Neill, & Britton, 1988; Hinshaw, 1991). The idea of individual titration appears quite important, however, since not only do different students respond differently to the same dose, but that the same student might respond differently to the same dose across various response classes, such as academic versus hyperactivity variables (Forness, Swanson, Cantwell, Guthrie, & Sena, 1992). Thus, the dosage might need to be titrated to the area of primary concern; it is unknown presently how often doses are actually titrated for optimal results, but it represents an important consideration in stimulant medication use.

Cautions

There were several limitations in the present meta-analysis related primarily to the available study samples. These limitations included the inability to assess stimulant medication efficacy in such areas as male versus female samples and on comorbidity factors. This review located only one study that compared male and female students on stimulant medication and no studies that utilized a sample of females only. Thus, possible differences or similarities on outcome measures for boys versus girls could not be determined. In addition, although the role of comorbidity with other disorders and the subsequent impact of stimulant medication on outcome measures is at the forefront of ADHD research currently, the present review found, in general, mixed samples of ADHD with comorbid disorders. It was, therefore, not possible to tease out comorbidity factors to arrive at an adequate sample for investigating pure ADHD groups versus groups with ADHD plus conduct disorder, oppositional defiant disorder, or learning disability. This may be a prime area of investigation in future research. An additional limitation of the present meta-analysis is related to the paucity of research investigating actual long-term effects of stimulant medication. Although this review originally defined a long-term study as greater than six months, only one study met this requirement. Thus, long-term effectiveness rates for stimulant medication across behavioral and academic categories remain in need of more well-designed research studies.

In conclusion, this meta-analysis provides an update about the efficacy of stimulant medication in treating the behavioral and academic consequences of ADHD. The results continue to be positive for behavior variables and appear better than was once thought for academic variables. The large volume of research on ADHD is certainly positive since it allows for more narrow research questions to be formulated and investigated. Continued research concerning whether the positive findings for classroom-type measures translate into longer-term academic gains is needed. Important research directions for ADHD include several areas that were beyond the scope of this meta-analysis and include the impact of comorbidity with other disorders on outcomes, comparing ADHD with ADD and subsequent outcomes, long-term versus short-term gains, and the role of possible mitigating factors (e.g., family functioning, presence of other difficulties, use of multimodal treatments) that might increase or decrease the chances of longer positive gains (either directly or indirectly) from the use of stimulant medication.

REFERENCES

Abikoff, H. (1991). Cognitive training in ADHD children: Less to it than meets the eye. *Journal of Learning Disabilities, 24*, 205–209.

Abikoff, H., & Gittelman, R. (1985). The normalizing effects of methylphenidate on the classroom behavior of ADHD children. *Journal of Abnormal Child Psychology, 13*, 33–44.

Abramowitz, A. J., Eckstrand, D., O'Leary, S., & Dulcan, M. K. (1992). ADHD children's responses to stimulant medication and two intensities of a behavioral intervention. *Behavior Modification, 16*, 193–203.

Adelman, H. S., & Compas, B. E. (1977). Stimulant drugs and learning problems. *Journal of Special Education, 11*, 377–416.

Allen, R. P., Safer, D., & Covi, L. (1975). Effects of psychostimulants on aggression. *The Journal of Nervous and Mental Disease, 160*, 138–145.

American Academy of Pediatrics Council on Child Health. (1975). Medication for hyperkinetic children. *Pediatrics, 55*, 560–562.

American Psychiatric Association (APA). (1980). *Diagnostic and statistical manual of mental disorders* (3rd ed., rev.). Washington, DC: Author.

American Psychiatric Association (APA). (1987). *Diagnostic and statistical manual of mental disorders* (3rd ed., rev.). Washington, DC: Author.

American Psychiatric Association (APA). (1994). *Diagnostic and statistical manual of mental disorders* (4th ed., rev.). Washington, DC: Author.

Anastopoulos, A. D., DuPaul, G. J., & Barkley, R. A. (1991). Stimulant medication and parent training therapies for attention deficit-hyperactivity disorder. *Journal of Learning Disabilities, 24*, 210–218.

Balthazor, M. J., Wagner, R. K., & Pelham, W. E. (1991). The specificity of the effects of stimulant medication on classroom learning-related measures of cognitive processing for attention deficit disorder children. *Journal of Abnormal Child Psychology, 19*, 35–52.

Barkley, R. A. (1977). A review of stimulant drug research with hyperactive children. *Journal of Child Psychology and Psychiatry, 18*, 137–165.

Barkley, R. A. (1989). Hyperactive girls and boys: Stimulant drug effects on mother-child interactions. *Journal of Child Psychology and Psychiatry, 30*, 379–390.

Barkley, R. A. (1990). *Attention deficit hyperactivity disorder: A handbook for diagnosis and treatment.* New York: The Guilford Press.

Barkley, R. A., & Cunningham, C. E. (1978). Do stimulant drugs improve the academic performance of hyperkinetic children? *Clinical Pediatrics, 17*, 85–92.

Barkley, R. A., DuPaul, G. J., & Costello, A. (1993). Stimulants. In J.S. Werry & M.G. Aman (Eds.), *Practitioner's guide to psychoactive drugs for children and adolescents* (pp. 205–237). New York: Plenum Publishing Corporation.

Barkley, R. A., McMurray, M. B., Edelbrock, C. S., & Robbins, K. (1989). The response of aggressive and nonaggressive ADHD children to two doses of methylphenidate. *Journal of the American Academy of Child and Adolescent Psychiatry, 28*, 873–881.

Barkley, R. A., McMurray, M. B., Edelbrock, C. S., & Robbins, K. (1990). Side effects of methylphenidate in children with attention deficit hyperactivity disorder. A systemic, placebo-controlled evaluation. *Pediatrics, 86*, 184–192.

Biederman, J., Newcorn, J., & Sprich, S. (1991). Comorbidity of attention deficit hyperactivity disorder with conduct, depressive, anxiety, and other disorders. *American Journal of Psychiatry, 148*, 564–577.

Biederman, J., & Steingard, R. (1989). Attention-deficit hyperactivity disorder in adolescents. *Psychiatric Annals, 19*, 587–596.

Bradley, W. (1937). The behavior of children receiving benzedrine. *American Journal of Psychiatry, 94*, 577–585.

Braswell, L. (1993). Cognitive-behavioral groups for children manifesting ADHD and other disruptive behavior disorders. *Special Services in the Schools, 8*, 91–117.

Braswell, L., & Bloomquist, M. L. (1991). *Cognitive-behavioral therapy with ADHD children.* New York: The Guilford Press.

Buhrmester, D., Whalen, C. K., Henker, B., MacDonald, V., & Hinshaw, S. P. (1992). Prosocial behavior in hyperactive boys: Effects of stimulant medication and comparison with normal boys. *Journal of Abnormal Child Psychology, 20*, 103–121.

Busch, B. (1993). Attention deficits: Current concepts, controversies, management, and approaches to classroom instruction. *Annals of Dyslexia, 43*, 5–25.

Carlson, C. L., & Bunner, M. R. (1993). Effects of methylphenidate on the academic performance of children with attention-deficit hyperactivity disorder and learning disabilities. *School Psychology Review, 22*, 184–198.

Carlson, G. A., & Rapport, M. D. (1989). Diagnostic classification issues in attention-deficit hyperactivity disorder. *Psychiatric Annals, 19*, 576–583.

Combrinck-Graham, L. (1987). Commentary on drug treatment for behavioral control. *Clinical Pediatrics, 26*, 262–263.

Cooper, H., & Hedges, L. V. (1993). *The handbook of research synthesis*. New York: Russell Sage Foundation.

Cooper, H., & Rosenthal, R. (1980). Statistical versus traditional procedures for summarizing research findings. *Psychological Bulletin, 87*, 442–449.

Cooper, H. M. (1982). Scientific guidelines for conducting integrative research reviews. *Review of Educational Research, 52*, 291–302.

Cowart, V. S. (1988). The ritalin controversy: What's made this drug's opponents hyperactive? *Journal of the American Medical Association, 259*, 2521–2523.

Douglas, V. I., Barr, R. G., Amin, K., O'Neill, M. E., & Britton, B. G. (1988). Dosage effects and individual responsivity to methylphenidate in attention deficit disorder. *Journal of Child Psychology and Psychiatry, 29*, 453–475.

Douglas, V. I., Barr, R. G., O'Neill, M. E., & Britton, B. G. (1986). Short-term effects of methylphenidate on the cognitive learning and academic performance of children with attention deficit disorder in the laboratory and the classroom. *Journal of Child Psychology and Psychiatry, 27*, 191–211.

DuPaul, G. J., Barkley, R. A., & McMurray, M. B. (1994). Response of children with ADHD to methylphenidate: Interaction with internalizing symptoms. *Journal of the American Academy of Child and Adolescent Psychiatry, 33*, 894–903.

DuPaul, G. J., & Stoner, G. (1994). *ADHD in the schools: Assessment and intervention strategies*. New York: The Guilford Press.

Eisenberg, L. (1972). Symposium: Behavior modification by drugs III: The clinical use of stimulant drugs in children. *Pediatrics, 49*, 709–715.

Elia, J., Borcherding, B. G., Rapoport, J. L., & Keysor, C. S. (1991). Methylphenidate and dextroamphetamine treatments of hyperactivity: Are there true nonresponders? *Psychiatry Research, 36*, 141–155.

Elia, J., Welsh, P. A., Gullotta, C. S., & Rapoport, J. L. (1993). Classroom academic performance: Improvement with both methylphenidate and dextroamphetamine in ADHD boys. *Journal of Child Psychology and Psychiatry, 34*, 785–804.

Evans, S. W., & Pelham, W. E. (1991). Psychostimulant effects on academic and behavioral measures for ADHD junior high school students in a lecture format classroom. *Journal of Abnormal Child Psychology, 19*, 537–552.

Forness, S. R., & Kavale, K. A. (1988). Psychopharmacologic treatment: A note on classroom effects. *Journal of Learning Disabilities, 21*, 144–147.

Forness, S. R., Swanson, J. M., Cantwell, D. P., Guthrie, D., & Sena, R. (1992). Response to stimulant medication across six measures of school-related performance in children with ADHD and disruptive behavior. *Behavioral Disorders, 18*, 42–53.

Forness, S. R., Swanson, J. M., Cantwell, D. P., Youpa, D., & Hanna, G. L. (1992). Stimulant medication and reading performance: Follow-up on sustained dose in ADHD boys with and without conduct disorders. *Journal of Learning Disabilities, 25*, 115–123.

Frankenberger, W., Lozar, B., & Dallas, P. (1990). The use of stimulant medication to treat attention deficit hyperactivity disorder (ADHD) in elementary school children. *Developmental Disabilities Bulletin, 18*, 1–13.

Gadow, K. D. (1983). Effects of stimulant drugs on academic performance in hyperactive and learning disabled children. *Journal of Learning Disabilities, 16*, 290–299.

Gadow, K. D., Sverd, J., Sprafkin, J., Nolan, E. E., & Ezor, S. N. (1995). Efficacy of methylphenidate for attention-deficit hyperactivity disorder in children with tic disorder. *Archives of General Psychiatry, 52*, 444–455.

Glass, G. V. (1976). Primary, secondary, and meta-analysis of research. *Educational Researcher, 5*, 3–8.

Glass, G. V., McGaw, B., & Smith, M. L. (1981). *Meta-analysis in social research*. Beverly Hills, CA: SAGE Publications.

Gomez, K. M., & Cole, C. L. (1991). Attention deficit hyperactivity disorder: A review of treatment alternatives. *Elementary School Guidance and Counseling, 26*, 106–114.

Gordon, M., Thomason, D., Cooper, S., & Ivers, C. L. (1991). Nonmedical treatment of ADHD/hyperactivity: The attention training system. *Journal of School Psychology, 29*, 151–159.

Greenhill, L. L. (1989). Treatment issues in children with attention deficit hyperactivity disorder. *Psychiatric Annals, 19*, 604–613.

Greenhill, L. L. (1992). Pharmacologic treatment of attention deficit hyperactivity disorder. *Psychiatric Clinics of North America, 15*, 1–27.

Grinspoon, L., & Singer, S. B. (1973). Amphetamines in the treatment of hyperkinetic children. *Harvard Educational Review, 43*, 515–555.

Handen, B. L., Feldman, H., Gosling, A., Breaux, A. M., & McAuliffe, S. (1991). Adverse side effects of methylphenidate among mentally retarded children with ADHD. *Journal of the American Academy of Child and Adolescent Psychiatry, 30*, 241–245.

Handen, B. L., Janosky, J., McAuliffe, S., Breaux, A. M., & Feldman, H. (1994). Prediction of response to methylphenidate among children with ADHD and mental retardation. *Journal of the American Academy of Child and Adolescent Psychiatry, 33*, 1185–1193.

Hechtman, L. (1985). Adolescent outcome of hyperactive children treated with stimulants in childhood: A review. *Psychopharmacology Bulletin, 21*, 178–191.

Hechtman, L. (1989). Attention-deficit hyperactivity disorder in adolescence and adulthood: An updated follow-up. *Psychiatric Annals, 19*, 597–603.

Hedges, L. V., & Olkin, I. (1985). *Statistical methods for meta-analysis*. Orlando, FL: Academic Press, Inc.

Henker, B., & Whalen, C. K. (1989). Hyperactivity and attention deficits. *American Psychologist, 44*, 216–223.

Hentoff, N. (1972, May 25). Drug-pushing in the schools: The professionals. *The Village Voice*, pp. 20–22.

Hinshaw, S. P. (1991). Stimulant medication and the treatment of aggression in children with attentional deficits. *Journal of Clinical Child Psychology, 20*, 301–312.

Hinshaw, S. P., Buhrmester, D., & Heller, T. (1989). Anger control in response to verbal provocation: Effects of stimulant medication for boys with ADHD. *Journal of Abnormal Child Psychology, 17*, 393–407.

Hinshaw, S. P., Henker, B., Whalen, C. K., Erhardt, D., & Dunnington, R. E. (1989). Aggressive, prosocial, and nonsocial behavior in hyperactive boys: Dose effects of methylphenidate in naturalistic settings. *Journal of Consulting and Clinical Psychology, 57*, 636–643.

Horn, W. F., Ialongo, N. S., Pascoe, J. M., Greenberg, G., Packard, T., Lopez, N., Wagner, A., & Puttler, L. (1991). Additive effects of psychostimulants, parent training, and self-control therapy with ADHD children. *Journal of the American Academy of Child and Adolescent Psychiatry, 30*, 233–240.

Hoza, B., Pelham, W. E., Sams, S. E., & Carlson, C. (1992). An examination of the "dosage" effects of both behavior therapy and methylphenidate on the classroom performance of two ADHD children. *Behavior Modification, 16*, 164–192.

Hunt, M. (1997). *How science takes stock: The story of meta-analysis*. New York: Russell Sage Foundation.

Hunter, J. E., & Schmidt, F. L. (1990). *Methods of meta-analysis*. Newbury Park, CA: SAGE Publications, Inc.

Ialongo, N. S., Horn, W. F., Pascoe, J. M., Greenberg, G., Packard, T., Lopez, M., Wagner, A., & Puttler, L. (1993). The effects of a multimodal intervention with attention-deficit hyperactivity disordered children: A 9-month follow-up. *Journal of the American Academy of Child and Adolescent Psychiatry, 32*, 182–189.

Jackson, G. B. (1980). Methods for integrative reviews. *Review of Educational Research, 50*, 438–460.

Jacobvitz, D., Sroufe, A., Stewart, M., & Leffert, N. (1990). Treatment of attentional and hyperactivity problems in children with sympathomimetic drugs: A comprehensive review. *Journal of the American Academy of Child and Adolescent Psychiatry, 29*, 677–688.

Kavale, K. (1982). The efficacy of stimulant drug treatment for hyperactivity: A meta-analysis. *Journal of Learning Disabilities, 15*, 280–289.

Kavale, K. A. (1984). Potential advantages of the meta-analysis technique for special education. *Journal of Special Education, 18*, 61–72.

Klein, R. G. (1995). The role of methylphenidate in psychiatry. *Archives of General Psychiatry, 52*, 429–433.

Ladd, E. T. (1970, November 21). Pills for classroom peace? *Saturday Review*, pp. 66–68, 81–83.

Lahey, B. B., & Carlson, C. L. (1991). Validity of the diagnostic category of attention deficit disorder without hyperactivity: A review of the literature. *Journal of Learning Disabilities, 24*, 110–120.

Lambert, N. M., Windmiller, M., Sandoval, J., & Moore, B. (1976). Hyperactive children and the efficacy of psychoactive drugs as a treatment intervention. *American Journal of Orthopsychiatry, 46*, 335–352.

Loeber, R. (1990). Development and risk factors of juvenile antisocial behavior and delinquency. *Clinical Psychology Review, 10*, 1–41.

Matier, K., Halperin, J. M., Sharma, V., Newcorn, J. H., & Sathaye, N. (1992). Methylphenidate response in aggressive and nonaggressive ADHD children: Distinctions in laboratory measures of symptoms. *Journal of the American Academy of Child and Adolescent Psychiatry, 31*, 219–225.

Mostert, M. P. (1996). Reporting meta-analyses in learning disabilities. *Learning Disabilities Research and Practice, 11*, 2–14.

Murray, J. B. (1987). Psychophysiological effects of methylphenidate (Ritalin). *Psychological Reports, 61*, 315–336.

Nahlik, J. E. (1995). New thoughts on attention-deficit/hyperactivity disorder. *Hospital Practice, 30*, 49–50, 55.

Ottenbacher, K. J., & Cooper, H. M. (1983). Drug treatment of hyperactivity in children. *Developmental Medicine & Child Neurology, 25*, 358–366.

Pelham, W. E. (1993). Pharmacotherapy for children with attention deficit hyperactivity disorder. *School Psychology Review, 22*, 199–227.

Pelham, W. E., Bender, M. E., Caddell, J., Booth, S., & Moorer, S. H. (1985). Methylphenidate and children with attention deficit disorder. Dose effects on classroom academic and social behavior. *Archives of General Psychiatry, 42*, 948–952.

Pelham, W. E., Carlson, C., Sams, S. E., Vallano, G., Dixon, M. J., & Hoza, B. (1993). Separate and combined effects of methylphenidate and behavior modification on boys with attention deficit-hyperactivity disorder in the classroom. *Journal of Consulting and Clinical Psychology, 61*, 506–515.

Pelham, W. E., McBurnett, K., Harper, G. W., Milich, R., Murphy, D. A., Clinton, J., & Thiele, C. (1990). Methylphenidate and baseball playing in ADHD children: Who's on first? *Journal of Consulting and Clinical Psychology, 58*, 130–133.

Pihl, R. O. (1980). Hyperactivity in children: Is there a treatment of choice? *Psychology in the Schools, 17*, 500–508.

Rappoport, R., & Repo, S. (1971). The educator as pusher: Drug control in the classroom. *This Magazine Is About Schools, 5*, 87–112.

Rapport, M. D., Denney, C., DuPaul, G. J., & Gardner, M. J. (1994). Attention deficit disorder and methylphenidate: Normalization rates, clinical effectiveness, and response prediction in 76 children. *Journal of the American Academy of Child and Adolescent Psychiatry, 33*, 882–893.

Rapport, M. D., DuPaul, G. J., Stoner, G., & Jones, J. T. (1986). Comparing classroom and clinic measures of attention deficit disorder: Differential, idosyncratic, and dose-response effects of methylphenidate. *Journal of Consulting and Clinical Psychology, 54*, 334–341.

Rosenthal, R. (1984). *Meta-analytic procedures for social research*. Beverly Hills, CA: Sage.

Rostain, A. L. (1991). Attention deficit disorders in children and adolescents. *Pediatric Clinics of North America, 38*, 607–635.

Safer, D. J. (1995). Major treatment considerations for attention-deficit hyperactivity disorder. *Current Problems in Pediatrics, 25*, 137–143.

Safer, D. J., & Krager, J. M. (1988). A survey of medication treatment for hyperactive/inattentive students. *Journal of the American Medical Association, 260*, 2256–2258.

Schachar, R., & Tannock, R. (1993). Childhood hyperactivity and psychostimulants: A review of extended treatment studies. *Journal of Child and Adolescent Psychopharmacology, 3*, 81–97.

Schrag, P., & Divoky, D. (1975). *The myth of the hyperactive child.* New York: Pantheon.

Solanto, M. V. (1984). Neuropharmacological basis of stimulant drug action in attention deficit disorder with hyperactivity: A review and synthesis. *Psychological Bulletin, 95*, 387–409.

Sprague, R. L., & Sleator, E. K. (1973). Effects of psychopharmacologic agents on learning disorders. *Pediatric Clinics of North America, 20*, 719–735.

Sprague, R. L., & Sleator, E. K. (1977). Methylphenidate in hyperkinetic children: Differences in dose effects on learning and social behavior. *Science, 198*, 1274–1276.

Sroufe, L. A., & Stewart, M. A. (1973). Treating problem children with stimulant drugs. *New England Journal of Medicine, 289*, 407–413.

Stevenson, R. D., & Wolraich, M. L. (1989). Stimulant medication therapy in the treatment of children with attention deficit hyperactivity disorder. *Pediatric Clinics of North America, 36*, 1183–1197.

Stoner, G., Carey, S. P., Ikeda, M. J., & Shinn, M. R. (1994). The utility of curriculum-based measurement for evaluating the effects of methylphenidate on academic performance. *Journal of Applied Behavior Analysis, 27*, 101–113.

Swanson, J. M. (1993). The UCI ADD Center: Final report. *The effects of stimulant medication on children with ADD.* Washington, DC: U.S. Department of Education; University of California, Irvine, Attention Deficit Disorder Center.

Swanson, J. M., Cantwell, D., Lerner, M., McBurnett, K., & Hanna, G. (1991). Effects of stimulant medication on learning in children with ADHD. *Journal of Learning Disabilities, 24*, 219–230.

Sylvester, C. (1993). Psychopharmacology of disorders in children. *Psychiatric Clinics of North America, 16*, 779–791.

Tannock, R., Schachar, R. J., Carr, R. P., & Logan, G. D. (1989). Dose-response effects of methylphenidate on academic performance and overt behavior in hyperactive children. *Pediatrics, 84*, 648–657.

Thurber, S., & Walker, C. E. (1983). Medication and hyperactivity: A meta-analysis. *The Journal of General Psychology, 108*, 79–86.

Vinson, D. C. (1994). Therapy for attention-deficit hyperactivity disorder. *Archives of Family Medicine, 3*, 445–451.

Wachter, K. M., & Strat, M. L. (1990). *The future of meta-analysis.* New York: Russell Sage Foundation.

Wells, K. C. (1986). What do we know about the use and effects of behavior therapies in the treatment of ADD? *Journal of Children in Contemporary Society, 19*, 111–122.

Wender, P. H. (1971). *Minimal brain dysfunction in children.* New York: John Wiley & Sons.

Whalen, C. K., & Henker, B. (1976). Psychostimulants and children: A review and analysis. *Psychological Bulletin, 83*, 1113–1130.

Wilens, T. E., & Biederman, J. (1992). The stimulants. *Psychiatric Clinics of North America, 15*, 191–222.

Wolf, F. M. (1986). *Meta-analysis: Quantitative methods for research synthesis.* Beverly Hills, CA: Sage.

Wolraich, M. L., Lindgren, S., Stromquist, A., Milich, R., Davis, C., & Watson, D. (1990). Stimulant medication use by primary care physicians in the treatment of attention deficit hyperactivity disorder. *Pediatrics, 86*, 95–101.

DOES ONE-TO-ONE TUTORING WITH THE TEACH INTERVENTION MODEL IMPROVE AT-RISK CHILDREN'S BEHAVIOR PROBLEMS?

Panayota Mantzicopoulos and Delmont Morrison

ABSTRACT

This study investigated the behavioral effects of the TEACH tutoring program. Participants were 166 children, screened during kindergarten as at-risk for school failure. These at-risk children were randomly assigned into one of three intervention groups: perceptual training (TEACH), academic tutoring, and no-contact control. The tutoring interventions were administered to children in individual sessions during first grade. Post-intervention behavior measures were obtained at the end of first and second grade. No significant improvements in behavior problems resulted from one-to-one tutoring. However, at the end of second grade, girls who had received either TEACH or academic tutoring were rated lower on behavior problems than boys. Comparisons of at-risk and not-at-risk children at the end of first and second grade

Advances in Learning and Behavioral Disabilities, Volume 13, pages 167–181.

ISBN: 0-7623-0429-4

indicated that the at-risk children were rated significantly higher on problem behaviors. Ratings were most pronounced in the areas of attention problems and motor excess.

Early remediation of learning problems seems to be the best strategy for preventing later school failure. First, considerable research indicates that children's early school adjustment and achievement have long-term educational implications (Alexander & Entwisle, 1988; Lazar, Darlington, Murray, & Snipper, 1982; Schweinhart, Weikart, & Larner, 1986). Second, longitudinal evidence emphasizes the importance of intervening early and of understanding the factors related to early school achievement (Entwisle, Alexander, Cadigan, & Pallas, 1986).

While reading skills are critical to the development of children's academic competence, it is also well established that children with reading difficulties demonstrate more behavior problems than their peers who are learning at the expected level (Bruck, 1986; Mantzicopoulos & Morrison, 1994; Morrison, Mantzicopoulos, & Carte, 1989). Research has suggested that, these behavior problems (a) are present as early as kindergarten; (b) become progressively more pronounced as children move forward in the early school grades; and (c) have the potential for interfering with the acquisition of basic skills (Mantzicopoulos & Morrison, 1994).

One-to-one tutoring is the most effective form of instruction for first graders with reading problems (Slavin & Madden, 1989). However, effective one-to-one remediation programs (for a review of effective tutoring programs see Wasik & Slavin, 1993) are focused on the acquisition of reading skills without particular attention to co-occurring behavior problems.

One exception is the Prevention of Learning Disabilities (PLD) program developed at the Learning Disorders Unit of the Department of Psychiatry of New York University-Bellevue Medical Center (Silver, Hagin, & Beecher, 1978). Intended for children at-risk for reading failure, this program has primarily been implemented with children from low socioeconomic backgrounds (Arnold, Barnebey, McManus, Smeltzer, Conrad, Winer, & Desranges, 1977; Arnold, Smeltzer, & Barneby, 1981; Silver & Hagin, 1981; Silver, Hagin & Beecher, 1978). Research, based on samples of inner-city children has indicated that the program has a positive impact on both reading and behavioral skills (Arnold et al., 1977; Silver & Hagin, 1981). However, a study of middle-class at-risk children has concluded that the program does not significantly improve first-grade children's reading competence (i.e., Mantzicopoulos, Morrison, Stone, & Setrakian, 1992). Data from the same sample further established that at-risk readers also demonstrated significant behavior problems and that these problems were detected by teachers as early as kindergarten (Mantzicopoulos & Morrison, 1994; Morrison, Mantzicopoulos, & Carte, 1989). This investigation builds on our prior work with the PLD program and explores its long-term behavioral effects with a group of middle class children screened at kindergarten as at-risk for reading failure.

THE PREVENTION OF LEARNING DISABILITIES PROGRAM: DESCRIPTION AND OUTCOMES

Unlike other tutoring models that directly address the process of reading, the PLD program focuses on strengthening those neurophysiological processes that are believed basic to beginning reading (Hagin, Silver, & Beecher, 1978). The perceptual-deficit orientation of PLD is compatible with the perceptual training models that enjoyed some popularity among educators in the 1960s and 1970s (i.e., Hammill, 1972; Hammill, Goodman, & Wiederholt, 1974). However, this line of research yielded little supporting evidence for the benefits of visual and auditory training for reading. Silver and Hagin (1990), with their neurophysiological view of reading failure, appear to be the last proponents of the perceptual deficit hypothesis. Their program incorporates a screening battery (called SEARCH) and an educational intervention program (called TEACH).

SEARCH is based on the concept that the antecedents of reading failure may be found in delayed acquisition of spatial and temporal orientation (Silver & Hagin, 1981). It is individually administered and comprises 10 subscales that assess a child's visual and auditory performance, body image, and a range of perceptual modalities. Children screened by SEARCH as "vulnerable" for reading failure may be helped by TEACH, a program designed to prevent learning problems by "building the neuropsychological skills necessary for progress in reading, writing, and spelling" (Hagin et al., 1978, p. 54). Rather than providing direct reading instruction to at-risk readers, TEACH involves perceptual stimulation activities and can be used in small groups or individually. In a number of reports, Silver and his colleagues have presented clinical evidence for behavioral improvement in children who received the TEACH program (Hagin et al., 1978; Silver, Hagin, & Beecher, 1978). Moreover, school-level data have suggested that TEACH children, followed over a 12-year period, were less likely to be retained (Hagin, 1984; Silver & Hagin, 1990).

Thus far, the only published cross-validation study of the behavioral effects of the TEACH intervention has been conducted by Arnold and his colleagues (Arnold et al., 1977; 1981). That study provided behavior ratings of the children prior to the TEACH intervention and employed a no-contact control group and a phonetic intervention group. Before assignment to treatment conditions, at-risk children were rated as more hyperactive than the not-at-risk sample. However, by the end of second grade, children in the TEACH intervention evidenced significant decreases in hyperactive behaviors. Following a re-analysis of the same data, the authors further suggested that the TEACH intervention had direct effects on problem behaviors (Arnold, Smeltzer, & Barneby, 1981). Nevertheless, at least three major interrelated problems in the design of the Arnold and colleagues' (1977) study merit further attention. First, the sample of children in the two intervention groups was rather small ($N = 23$) and probably not representative of the at-risk hyperactive children that are generally found in kindergarten. Second, there were no data on the gender distribution in the sample. Although the experimental groups were matched for gender, there were no data on the actual numbers of boys and girls in each group. Moreover, the small number of children in each group would limit the possibility of examining the effects of gender. This is an important issue particularly in light of evidence that there are significant differences in the characteristics of boys and girls with attention deficit and hyperactivity (Berry, Shaywitz, & Shaywitz, 1985). Finally, no quantitative measure of socioeconomic status (SES) was obtained although it was mentioned that 60 percent of the at-risk children came from inner city schools.

To address the above mentioned issues, this study is based on prior work by Morrison and his colleagues (i.e., Morrison, Mantzicopoulos, & Carte, 1989; Morrison & Mantzicopoulos, 1990; Mantzicopoulos & Morrison, 1994; Mantzicopoulos et al., 1992). Our work with a large group of kindergarten children has indicated that (a) at-risk status in kindergarten is related to variables such as SES; and (b) hyperactivity as well as attention problems are also related to at-risk status.

Using the same sample of children, this study investigated the behavioral effects of the TEACH intervention which was implemented during first grade. To closely replicate Arnold and colleagues' (1977) design, we compared TEACH to academic tutoring and to a no contact control group. In addition, we examined the relationship between gender and behavior problems within each intervention program. Finally, to gauge the magnitude of the reported behavior problems, we compared at-risk children with their not-at-risk classmates.

METHOD

Participants

The participants for this study came from four school districts in Marin County, California. At the beginning of the study, all parents were contacted with a letter and approximately 78 percent (1,731) agreed to participate over a three-year period. Specifically, children were individually screened with SEARCH in kindergarten for three consecutive years (1984: $N = 444$; 1985: $N = 662$; and 1986: $N = 625$). Of the 1,731 children, 437 (approximately 25%) were designated at-risk (AR Group) on the basis of scores below the 33rd percentile (using local norms) on at least five of the nine valid SEARCH subtests (Hinshaw, Morrison, Carte & Cornsweet, 1986; Silver & Hagin, 1981). An equivalent number of not-at-risk control children (NARC) were randomly selected from each classroom, subject to the constraint that the groups had the same ratio of boys and girls and of Caucasian and non-Caucasian children as the at-risk sample within that classroom. Initial comparisons of the AR and NARC groups of children indicated that the at-risk group had significantly lower scores on SEARCH, cognitive ability, and preacademic achievement than the NARC group (Mantzicopoulos et al., 1992).

At the beginning of first grade, at-risk subjects who continued participation in the study were matched on SEARCH scores, sex, and cognitive ability, as assessed by the Kaufman Assessment Battery for Children (Kaufman & Kaufman, 1983). They were then randomly assigned to one of three intervention groups: (a) TEACH, (b) phonetic, or (c) control. Because of attrition, behavior data from 166 children were available at the one-year follow-up (end of second grade). Comparison of the characteristics of children remaining in the study and those who were lost to the study are provided later in this chapter. Of the 166 children, 55 (29 boys and 26 girls) were in the TEACH group, 53 (23 boys and 30 girls) in the phonetic group, and 58 (30 boys and 28 girls) in the no-contact control group. Because our analyses involved comparisons between AR and NARC children, a random sample of NARC children was drawn from our large sample of not-at-risk controls, matched to the at-risk control group on sex.

These procedures yielded a total sample of 224 children (166 at-risk and 58 not-at-risk) who were subjects for the study reported in this chapter. At the time of the SEARCH administration at kindergarten, this sample had a mean age of 69.3 months with a range of 63–80 months. There were 112 boys and 112 girls. The racial composition of the sample was as follows: 160 (72%) Caucasian, 18 (8%) Black, 12 (5%) Hispanic, 14 (6%) Asian, 12 (5%) Other, and 8 (4%) Unknown. Socioeconomic status (SES) data were available for 200 (89%) participants because not all parents returned the mailed questionnaire assessing SES information. Twenty-one (10%) children were in Class I, professional; 33 (17%) in Class II, upper middle; 74 (37%) in Class III, middle; 60 (30%) in Class IV, lower middle; and 12 (6%) in Class V, unskilled labor and unemployed.

Measures

Search

This screening instrument is designed for children between 63 and 80 months of age (Silver & Hagin, 1981). The individual administration takes approximately 20 minutes and the screen was given in February of the kindergarten year to each cohort. There are ten subtests that measure visual discrimination, immediate visual recall, visual-motor copying, rote sequencing, auditory discrimination, articulation, associating sounds with their visual symbols, directional orientation, finger schema, and pencil grip. As recommended by Silver and Hagin (1981), local norms for SEARCH were established and the procedures for administration and scoring were strictly followed. Although collected for the first cohort, the pencil grip subtest data were not used in the analyses, and this subtest was not given to the second and third cohorts. In the first cohort, 48 percent of the children demonstrated an appropriate pencil grip in contrast to the 75–79 percent found in the Silver and Hagin sample. Thus SEARCH was scored from 0 to 9 with scores of five or less indicating at-risk performance. Evidence for the construct and predictive validity of SEARCH is found in Hinshaw, Morrison, Carte, and Cornsweet (1986) and Morrison and Mantzicopoulos (1990).

Kaufman Assessment Battery for Children (K-ABC)

The K-ABC was administered in March of kindergarten. This test was selected for use in this research because it (1) is appropriate for children from ages 2 1/2 to 12; (2) provides a quantitative measure of the cognitive level of this sample of children; and (3) assesses simultaneous and sequential information processing skills that have been shown to be associated with the development of reading skills (Kaufman & Kaufman, 1983). The K-ABC yields a Mental Processing Composite scale (MPC), which is subdivided into Sequential and Simultaneous Processing scales. All scales provide a standard score with M = 100 and SD = 15 (Kaufman & Kaufman, 1983).

Revised Behavior Problem Checklist (RBPC)

This checklist was completed in April of each academic year by classroom teachers. Classroom teachers completed the RBPC on both the at-risk and not-at-risk children without knowledge of the child's status in the study. Because of the intervention procedures during first grade, the teacher may have been aware that some children were identified as at-risk. Since no interventions were provided in second grade, the behavior ratings were blind. The checklist provides six subscales: Conduct Disorder, Anxiety Withdrawal, Attention Problems, Motor Excess, Socialized Aggression, and Psychotic Behavior. However, for this sample of children, Psychotic Behavior is best described as immaturity because it is based on behaviors such as having an imaginary playmate. For children of this age range, such behaviors may be developmentally immature but probably not psychotic.

Behaviors are scored on a three-point scale where 0 reflects not a problem; 1, mild problem; and 2, severe problem (Quay & Peterson, 1983). Because of the age range of the children in this study, the Socialized Aggression scale was inappropriate and was not used.

Procedure

SEARCH and the K-ABC were individually administered to children at kindergarten. At the beginning of first grade, at-risk children, matched on SEARCH, sex, and K-ABC MPC, were randomly assigned to one of three groups: TEACH, phonetic tutoring, or no-contact control. The interventions were administered during first grade. Children in the control group simply participated in their regular first-grade curriculum without any supplementary tutoring. Children in the intervention groups received one-to-one tutoring twice a week, for a total of 50 half-hour sessions, with either TEACH or phonetic materials. The TEACH or phonetic sessions took place at the school during the school year. Each TEACH or phonetics session included a variety of activities that are described in detail in Mantzicopoulos, Morrison, Stone, & Setrakian (1992). The interventions were administered by licensed teachers, who all had Master's degrees, and were trained specifically in each approach by Elizabeth Stone, an experienced special education teacher, who assumed primary responsibility for the intervention implementation. Prior to the implementation of the intervention program, Ms. Stone was trained in the TEACH intervention by Rosa Hagin and kept in close contact with her throughout the intervention phase of the study. The tutors were then trained by Ms. Stone and were closely observed during the initial phases of the implementation to ensure compliance with the intervention protocol. Weekly supervision and consultation were provided throughout the implementation process.

During second grade, the children in this study participated in the regular school programs. The not-at-risk control children attended the regular school program for the duration of the study. In the month of April of each year, classroom teachers completed the RBPC for each child.

RESULTS

Overview of Analysis

A multivariate analysis of variance (MANOVA) was conducted to compare the three intervention groups and the not-at-risk group on behavior problems at baseline (end of kindergarten). Following this analysis two sets of MANCOVAs were conducted to investigate the effects of intervention and sex, while controlling for the effects of attention problems manifested during the kindergarten year. Because a fully crossed model was not of interest in this set of comparisons, we adopted a nested model. Thus the effects of sex were nested within each intervention group. To examine differences between at-risk and not-at-risk children after the intervention, we conducted MANOVAs at the end of first and second grade. We also evaluated differences between the groups expressed as effect sizes for each outcome variable. Effect sizes were computed by dividing the mean difference (or adjusted mean difference when appropriate) between the groups by the pooled standard deviation (Hedges & Olkin, 1985). Effect sizes were considered educationally significant when they were greater than +/– .20 standard deviation units (Cohen, 1988).

To investigate the extent to which attrition was systematic, a t-test analysis was computed to explore differences on the baseline measures between those children who left the study and children who served as subjects for this report.

Pre-intervention Comparisons

Pre-intervention comparisons at kindergarten were intended to examine the comparability of the TEACH, phonetic, control, and NARC groups and to explore

Table 1. Means and Standard Deviations for Children in the Teach, Phonetic, Control, and NARC Groups at the End of Kindergarten

	TEACH		*Phonetic*		*Control*		*NARC*	
	M	*Sd*	*M*	*Sd*	*M*	*Sd*	*M*	*Sd*
Conduct Disorder	3.13	4.97	3.53	7.66	2.31	5.60	2.37	6.99
Attention Problems	4.11	4.51	5.13	6.47	3.69	5.52	2.22	4.47
Anxiety-Withdrawal	1.94	2.46	2.74	3.68	2.14	3.67	1.32	3.04
Motor Excess	1.24	1.59	1.47	2.01	1.26	2.31	0.84	1.77
Immaturity	.31	1.03	.54	1.28	.28	1.07	0.40	1.40

gender differences. Although there were no gender effects, a nearly statistically significant group effect was identified ($F = 1.97$, $p = .08$). Post hoc comparisons indicated that the TEACH, phonetic, and control children were comparable on behavior problems at baseline. However there was a tendency for the at-risk children to be rated higher on behavior problems than the NARC children. Group means and standard deviations are presented in Table 1.

Post-intervention: First- and Second-Grade Comparisons

No significant intervention and no significant sex effects were identified at the end of first grade. However, a significant multivariate statistic was identified for the sex effect at the end of second grade. With the sex effect being nested within intervention group, it was suggested that males and females were affected differently within specific groups. Specifically, females were rated lower than males both within the TEACH and phonetic intervention groups. However, there were no consistent sex differences within the control group. These findings are clearly illustrated through an examination of effect sizes, computed by obtaining the difference between the adjusted means for males and females and then dividing this difference by the pooled standard deviation. As reported in Table 2, the effect sizes within the TEACH intervention group ranged from .25 for the Conduct Disorder subscale to .83 for the Motor Excess subscale. Similarly, within the phonetic intervention group, effect sizes ranged from .30 for the Anxiety-Withdrawal subscale to .75 for the Motor Excess subscale. However, the effect sizes for the control group did not exhibit a clear pattern of differences. Thus, participation in one-to-one tutoring was related to improved behavior problems for second-grade girls but not for boys.

Comparisons of At-Risk and NARC Children

Two MANOVAs were conducted to compare the at-risk control and NARC children on all behavior dimensions at the end of first and second grade. The effects

Table 2. Post-test Comparisons: Sex Differences within TEACH, Phonetic and Control Group at the End of Second Grade

		TEACH				*Phonetic*				*Control*			
		M	M_{Adj}	*Sd*	*ES*	*M*	M_{Adj}	*Sd*	*Es*	*M*	M_{Adj}	*Sd*	*ES*
Conduct Disorder	Male	5.03	5.17	6.84	0.25	5.57	5.55	6.39	0.31	3.31	3.42	4.52	0.33
	Female	3.42	3.55	5.76		3.50	3.20	8.49		1.82	2.15	2.73	
Attention Problems	Male	9.90	10.02	8.15	0.72	8.65	8.40	8.06	0.56	6.17	6.25	5.42	–0.18
	Female	4.38	4.53	6.92		4.83	4.47	6.15		7.07	7.46	7.92	
Anxiety-Withdrawal	Male	4.66	4.60	5.42	0.51	4.36	4.37	4.74	0.30	2.75	2.77	4.45	–0.24
	Female	2.27	2.32	3.34		3.17	3.05	4.23		3.57	3.70	3.35	
Motor Excess	Male	2.03	2.07	1.88	0.83	2.96	2.66	3.27	0.75	1.50	1.56	2.00	0.35
	Female	0.69	0.72	1.29		0.87	0.78	1.74		0.89	0.99	1.13	
Immaturity	Male	1.11	1.11	2.15	0.80	0.91	0.90	1.56	0.73	0.40	0.33	0.86	–0.23
	Female	0.23	0.23	0.59		0.13	0.13	0.35		0.61	0.62	1.57	

of sex and the group by sex interaction were also investigated in these analyses, but no significant results emerged for these factors. Significant multivariate group effects were identified both at the end of first ($F = 4.37$, $p = .001$) and second grade ($F = 3.69$, $p = .004$). Results are presented in Table 3.

At risk children's behavior ratings were significantly higher than the ratings of NARC children. The effect size analysis indicated that the groups consistently differed on all dimensions except one (Conduct Problems). The magnitude of the differences on Attention Problems was large ($ES = -.84$ and $-.69$ at first and second grade, respectively). On the remaining subcales the differences ranged from moderate to small.

Attrition Group Analyses

Of the original sample of at-risk children identified at kindergarten with SEARCH, there were complete data on the major study variables for 447 children. Of this group 280 (63%) left the study some time between the SEARCH screen and the final evaluations at the end of second grade. Comparisons between the at-risk children lost through attrition and those who completed the study are summarized in Table 4. In comparison to children who remained in the study, the attrition group was significantly different on every variable assessed in the present investigation. Specifically, attrition children had a lower SES rating and lower SEARCH, and cognitive ability (K-ABC MPC) scores. In addition, they were rated by their teachers significantly higher on problem behaviors than children who served as subjects for this report.

Table 3. Comparisons of NARC and At-Risk Control Children at the End of First and Second Grade

		NARC		*At-Risk Control*		
	Grade	*M*	*Sd*	*M*	*Sd*	*ES*
Conduct Disorder	1	2.41	5.94	2.77	5.64	0.06
	2	2.83	5.83	2.58	3.79	0.05
Attention Problems	1	1.48	2.27	5.90	7.09	0.84
	2	2.74	4.17	6.60	6.70	0.69
Anxiety-Withdrawal	1	1.40	2.22	2.40	3.64	0.33
	2	2.38	3.29	3.16	3.93	0.22
Motor Excess	1	0.67	1.57	1.39	2.02	0.40
	2	0.74	1.50	1.21	1.65	0.30
Immaturity	1	0.05	0.29	0.53	1.17	0.56
	2	0.17	0.53	0.50	1.25	0.34

Table 4. Comparisons between Children who Left the Study (Attrition Group) and Children who Remained in the Study (Study Group) at the End of Kindergarten

	Attrition Group		*Study Group*		
	M	*Sd*	*M*	*Sd*	*t*
Socioeconomic Status (SES)	3.37	1.04	3.14	0.99	2.10*
SEARCH Score	3.71	1.28	4.26	1.01	–5.01**
K-ABC MPC	98.31	12.57	101.03	10.37	–2.44*
Conduct Disorder	4.50	7.29	3.00	6.56	2.16*
Attention Problems	7.87	7.82	4.31	5.59	5.60**
Anxiety-Withdrawal	3.27	4.08	2.43	3.19	2.39**
Motor Excess	2.00	2.52	1.32	1.95	3.19**
Immaturity	0.72	1.57	0.36	1.10	2.81**

Notes: $^{*}p < .05$; $^{**}p < .01$

DISCUSSION

Using the same sample, an earlier study (Mantzicopoulos, Morrison, Stone, & Setrakian, 1992) attempted to systematically replicate the effects of TEACH on the low academic performance of the at-risk children. However, there was no evidence of improved performance on either group-administered or individually administered academic achievement batteries. Effects only favored a moderately at-risk group of children who received the phonetic intervention. Specifically, this moderatately at-risk group evidenced improvements in phonetic analysis, spelling, and word attack skills. The present research examined the effects of the TEACH and phonetic tutoring models on behavior but did not replicate the significant outcomes reported in prior research (e.g., Arnold et al., 1977).

Although the tutoring interventions had been provided for a year in first grade there were no significant differences between the AR control and the tutoring intervention groups on behavior problems. It is noteworthy that as early as kindergarten, all three at-risk groups were rated as demonstrating higher rates of behavior problems than a not-at-risk comparison group. A year after the intervention, at the end of second grade, the AR groups were not significantly different on teachers' behavior ratings but were rated significantly higher than the NARC group on problem behaviors. However, at the end of second grade, clear sex differences emerged for children in the two tutoring groups but not for children in the control group. Specifically, at second grade, teachers, who were blind to the status of the children in the study, rated the girls who had received tutoring as demonstrating fewer behavior problems than boys. These differences were not found in the control group. Thus it seems that one-to-one tutoring provided some benefits for girls but not for boys. Although sex differences have not been reported in previous work with the TEACH intervention, Arnold, Smeltzer, & Barneby (1981), in a reanalysis of their data, reported that boys benefitted from "any contact with tutors," (p. 198), while girls only benefitted from participation in TEACH. Once again, our findings are not consistent with those reported by Arnold (1981).

As noted earlier, at-risk children as a group were rated by their kindergarten teachers as demonstrating more behavior problems than not-at-risk children particularly in the area of inattention. In keeping with the results of an earlier study with a larger sample of this population (Morrison, Mantzicopoulos, & Carter, 1989), these findings suggest that at-risk status and inadequate preacademic skills are related to attention problems. Because attention problems occur as early as kindergarten, they may contribute to these children's early academic difficulties. Our first and second grade comparisons of AR and NARC children further substantiated that these behavior differences continue to exist through second grade. Moreover, as our previous analyses have shown (Mantzicopoulos & Morrison, 1994) these stable behavior differences are connected to differential academic outcomes. AR children perform significantly lower than NARC children on academic achievement tests over time.

Given the lack of significant differences between the tutoring intervention groups and the AR control group, we reasoned on a post hoc basis, that the intervention effects may vary either by risk level (as defined by SEARCH), and/or by SES level. We thus performed a series of analyses intended to identify effects for low and high SES children and for children with low SEARCH scores. However, no significant effects emerged from these analyses. Our findings, although not fully expected, are not unreasonable, particularly because the SEARCH/TEACH model does not provide a clear rationale about the specific mechanism through which TEACH contributes to improved classroom behaviors.

Attrition was an important concern in our study. The comparisons of those at-risk children who left the study with those who stayed indicated that the former came from lower SES families and had lower mental processing skills as well as lower preacademic skills. This trend continued with the behavioral ratings. For example, the ratings at kindergarten for attention problems were significantly higher for those children who left compared to those who stayed. A similar situation occurred in the ratings for motor excess. Additionally, attrition children had lower SEARCH scores. Although this difference was statistically significant, it is not clear that it would be clinically significant on a screening instrument like SEARCH (Morrison & Mantzicopoulos, 1990). Generally, those children who were more at risk left the study. This may in part account for the lack of effects of the interventions on behavior since those children who left may have needed the interventions and did not receive them. The attrition rate in the Arnold and colleagues' (1977) study was only 9 percent, considerably less than the rate in this study, and there were no data presented on the eight children who left the study. An argument could also be made that the more at-risk children would have a lower probability of responding positively to the interventions because of their more severe problems with attention and motor excess. In fact, our examination of the intervention effects for children of varying levels of risk status would support this inference.

The lack of replication of the effects of TEACH on attention problems and hyperactivity (Arnold et al. 1977) or behavior problems in general (Silver, Hagin, & Beecher, 1978) may be due to the fact that children representing the full range of SES were included in the interventions. For example, although quantitative estimates of SES were not available, 60 percent of the Arnold and colleagues' (1977) sample came from lower class schools. In the present study 40 percent of the intervention group came from the lower-middle and lower SES groups and 60 percent came from the middle and upper SES groups. When interventions for at-risk children have been effective, there are indications that they are most effective with children whose families are underprivileged and less economically affluent (Lazar, Darlington, Murray & Snipper, 1982; Woodhead, 1988). However, the reanalysis of our data taking into account SES differences in the groups yielded no significant intervention effects for SES.

Although it appears that the SES distribution for this sample was different from the one in the study by Arnold and his colleagues, the evidence on the subjects' academic performance differences is far from clear. The children in the study by Arnold and colleagues (1977) had reading scores in the low-average range. By the end of second grade their mean improved by 0.70 standard deviations and was at the national average. Arnold and colleagues (1977) do not report how these children performed locally (i.e., in comparison to their peers in their school district). In contrast, our earlier study indicated that the at-risk children performed above the national mean on group academic achievement tests (Mantzicopoulos, Morrison, Stone, & Setrakian, 1992). At the same time, their academic performance was significantly below that of the not-at-risk sample. However, when compared to other children in their districts, the at-risk children provided consistent indicators of academic vulnerability as they demonstrated significantly deficient performance on group tests of total reading. In addition, as the present investigation demonstrates, attention problems and hyperactivity were not reduced by the two interventions and the at-risk children were significantly more deviant in these two behaviors than children who were not identified as at-risk. The occurrence of these two behaviors in the at-risk children at kindergarten suggests that a behavioral intervention targeted to these problems (Sprague, 1983) combined with academic tutoring may be a more effective method of remediating at-risk children's deficits.

ACKNOWLEDGMENT

The order of authors' names is alphabetical. We wish to extend our appreciation to Elizabeth Stone and Win Setrakian for their administrative support and for their comments on earlier versions of this chapter.

REFERENCES

Alexander, K. L., & Entwisle, D. R. (1988). Achievement in the first two years of school: Patterns and processes. *Monographs of the Society for Research in Child Development, 53* (2, serial no. 218).

Amante, D. (1975). Visual-motor malfunction, ethnicity and social class position. *Journal of Special Education, 9*, 247–259.

Arnold, L. E., Barnebey, N., McManus, J., Smeltzer, D. L., Conrad, A., Winer, G., & Desgranges, L. (1977). Prevention by specific perceptual remediation for vulnerable first graders. *Archives of General Psychiatry, 34*, 1279–1294.

Arnold, L. E., Smeltzer, D. J., & Barneby, N. S. (1981). Specific perceptual remediation: Effects related to sex, IQ, and parents' occupational status; behavioral change patterns by scale factors; and mechanism of benefit hypothesis tested. *Psychological Reports, 49*, 198.

Barkley, R. A. (1985). The parent-child interaction patterns of hyperactive children: Precursors to aggressive behavior? In M. Wolraich and D. Routh (Eds.), *Advances in developmental and behavioral pediatrics*, (vol. 6, pp. 117–150), Greenwich, CT: JAI Press.

Berry, C. A., Shaywitz, S., & Shaywitz, B. (1985). Girls with attention deficit disorder: A silent minority? A report on behavioral and cognitive characteristics. *Pediatrics, 5*, 801–809.

Bruck, M. (1986). Social and emotional adjustments of learning disabled children: A review of the issues. In S. J. Ceci (Ed.), *Handbook of cognitive, social, and neuropsychological aspects of learning disabilities, 1*, 361–380, Hillsdale, NJ: Lawrence Erlbaum.

Cohen, J. (1988). *Statistical power analysis for the behavioral sciences* (Rev. ed). New York: Academic Press.

Entwisle, D., Alexander, K., Cadigan, D., & Pallas, A. (1986). The schooling process in first grade: Two samples a decade apart. *American Educational Research Journal, 23*, 587–613.

Hagin, R. A., Silver, A. A., & Beecher, R. (1978). Scanning, diagnosis and intervention in the prevention of learning disabilities: II. TEACH: Learning tasks for the prevention of learning disabilities. *Journal of Learning Disabilities, 2*(7), 54–58.

Hagin, R. A. (1984). Effects on first grade promotion practices of a program for the prevention of learning disabilities. *Psychology in the Schools, 21*, 471–476.

Hagin, R., Silver, A., & Kreeger, H. (1976). *TEACH: Tasks for the prevention of learning disability*. New York: Walker Educational Book Corporation.

Hammill, D. (1972). Training visual perceptual processes. *Journal of Learning Disabilities, 5*(10), 552–559.

Hammill, D., Goodman, L., & Wiederholt, J. L. (1974). Visual-motor processes: Can we train them? *Reading Teacher, 27*(5), 469–478.

Hedges, L.V., & Olkin, I. (1985). *Statistical methods for meta-analysis*. New York: Academic Press.

Hinshaw, S. P., Morrison, D., Carte, E. T., & Cornsweet, C. (1986). Factor composition of the SEARCH scanning instrument in kindergarten. *Journal of Psychoeducational Assessment, 4*, 95–101.

Hollingshead, A. B. (1957). *Two factor index of social position*. Unpublished manuscript. New Haven, CT: Yale University.

Kaufman, A., & Kaufman, N. (1983). *Kaufman assessment battery for children: Administration and scoring manual*. Circle Pines, MN: American Guidance Service.

Lazar, I., Darlington, R., Murray, H., & Snipper, A. S. (1982). Lasting effects of early education: A report from the Consortium for Longitudinal Studies. *Monograph of the Society for Research in Child Development, 47*, 195 (Serial No. 2–3).

Mantzicopoulos, P., & Morrison, D. (1994). A comparison of boys and girls with attention problems: Kindergarten through second grade. *American Journal of Orthopsychiatry, 64*(4), 522–533.

Mantzicopoulos, P., Morrison, D., Stone, E., & Setrakian, W. (1992). Use of the SEARCH/TEACH tutoring approach with middle class students at risk for reading failure. *The Elementary School Journal, 92*(5), 573–586.

Mantzicopoulos, P., & Morrison, D. (1990). *Children at risk for reading failure: Two-year academic effects of a perceptually based and a phonetic intervention.* Paper presented at the AERA annual meeting, April, Boston, MA.

Morrison, D., & Mantzicopoulos, P. (1990). Predicting reading problems at kindergarten for children in second grade: SEARCH as a screen. *Remedial and Special Education, 11*(4), 29–36.

Morrison, D., Mantzicopoulos, P., & Carte, E. T. (1989). Preacademic screening for learning and behavior problems. *Journal of the American Academy of Child Psychiatry, 1*, 101–106.

Morrison, D., Mantzicopoulos, P., & Stone, E. (1988). Screening for reading problems: The utility of SEARCH. *Annals of Dyslexia, 38*, 181–192.

Quay, H. C., & Peterson, D. (1983). *Revised behavior checklist: Interim manual.* Coral Gables, FL: University of Miami.

Schweinhart, L. J., Weikart, D. P., & Larner, M. B. (1986). Consequences of three preschool curriculum models through age 15. *Early Childhood Research Quarterly, 1*(l), 15–45.

Silver, A., & Hagin, R. (1981). *SEARCH manual.* New York: Walker Educational Book Corporation.

Silver, A. A., & Hagin, R. A. (1990). *Disorders of learning in childhood.* NY: John Wiley & Sons.

Silver, A., Hagin, R., & Beecher, R. (1978). Scanning, diagnosis, and intervention in the prevention of reading disabilities. *Journal of Learning Disabilities, 7*, 437–449.

Slavin, R. E., & Madden, N. A. (1989). What works for students at risk: A research synthesis. *Educational Leadership, 4*(1), 4–13.

Sprague, R. L. (1983). Behavior modification and education techniques. In M. Rutter (Ed.), *Developmental neuropsychiatry.* New York: The Guilford Press.

Wasik, B. A., & Slavin, R. E. (1993). Preventing early reading failure with one-to-one tutoring: A review of five programs. *Reading Research Quarterly, 28*(2), 179–200.

Werry, J. S., & Quay, H. (1971). The prevalence of behavior symptoms in younger elementary school children. *American Journal of Orthopsychiatry, 41*, 136–140.

Woodhead, M. (1988). When psychology informs public policy: The case of early childhood intervention. *American Psychologist, 6*, 443–454.

SELECTIVE MUTISM:
DEVELOPMENTS IN DEFINITION, ETIOLOGY, ASSESSMENT AND TREATMENT

Frederick J. Brigham and Jane E. Cole

ABSTRACT

In this chapter, we summarize the developments in definition, assessment and treatment of selective mutism (SM). First, the two major diagnostic guidelines of SM are compared. Several unresolved issues relating to the definition of SM are also described. Second, we describe the current understanding of the etiology of SM with particular attention to theories relating it to the continuum of anxiety disorders. Third, we describe the rationale for improved practices in assessment of SM. Adaptations of common assessments as well as SM-specific assessment protocols are included in this section. Also, we discuss procedures for determining whether or not intervention is needed for any child who displays SM or similar conditions. Finally, we summarize the recent intervention literature from the psychodynamic, speech and language, medical, and behavioral approaches. It is argued that because SM is probably a multiply determined condition, treatment packages employing two or more approaches are most likely to yield successful intervention results.

I think that he must have been some kind of a challenge to my sense of reality, because I couldn't stop watching him. Maybe I thought, sooner or later, I was going to pick up on something that somebody else had missed (Randle, 1995, p. 22).

Advances in Learning and Behavioral Disabilities, Volume 13, pages 183–216.

ISBN: 0-7623-0429-4

The narrator in the quote above is a fictional adolescent female who, upon moving to a new school, meets an individual who is capable of speech and apparently quite bright but does not speak to anyone outside his home. Given that humans are such social creatures, it is difficult to imagine children who are "seen and not heard" to the point that it interferes with their education and social development. Yet such children do exist and people who have encountered them usually respond with an interest which is disproportionate to the prevalence of the condition (Bayley, 1991). Such children are referred to by a number of terms including elective mutism, speech inhibition, speech avoidance, speech phobia, functional mutism, and the currently more popular term, selective mutism (Kratochwill, 1981).

Selective mutism (SM) is a rare disorder identified in children who, although they are able to produce speech, speak only to certain individuals or in certain environments. The condition was first described in 1877 by Kussmaul, a German physician, who termed it "aphasia voluntaria." The term elective mutism did not appear in the literature until 1934 (Silver, 1989) and actual systematic research regarding the condition was rare before the 1950s (Porjes, 1992). Currently, the term selective mutism is favored because it recognizes that children with the condition can and do speak but within a very limited audience or environment. SM can seriously and negatively affect the lives of children who exhibit it as well as those of their family members and teachers (Cline & Baldwin, 1994).

Because SM is rare, it is unlikely that many individuals have much experience on which they can rely when working with children with SM (Cline & Baldwin, 1994). Additionally, the resistance to treatment demonstrated by many children with SM can lead to feelings of ineptitude or anger on the part of the child's teacher (Bow, 1997). SM may be even more detrimental to educational progress than it was in the past because currently popular constructivist approaches to education (e.g., Marlowe & Page, 1998) require more active verbal interaction with teachers and peers than traditional, teacher-led classrooms. Taken together, these observations suggest that educators working with children who have SM are likely to recognize it as a factor which seriously interferes with the child's education but unlikely to possess relevant knowledge and skills for dealing with it. Therefore, the purpose of this chapter is to provide a summary of the definitions, methods of identification, and treatments associated with elective mutism for teachers, parents, and other individuals who are involved with identification and treatment of children with SM.

Kratochwill's (1981) text was the only systematic review of the literature in the field up to its date of publication. Kratochwill clearly summarized the psychodynamic and behavioral treatment literature regarding SM and described the major ideas regarding definition and assessment of SM. Three years later, Labbe and Williamson (1984) published an extensive review of behavioral treatments for SM. Therefore, this chapter will concentrate on developments in the field since 1984. Because most children with SM are identified first by educators when the children enter school (Baldwin & Cline, 1991), we will emphasize treatments which are likely to be carried out in school or involve educators in some way.

DEFINITIONS OF SELECTIVE MUTISM

A variety of definitions appear in the literature regarding SM. The essential feature of all definitions is that the individual is capable of speech but does not speak or speaks in only a limited number of situations or to a limited number of people. Variation in the duration of the condition necessary for diagnosis and the severity of mutism are the most common differences among definitions. Two clinical guides, the *Diagnostic and Statistical Manual of Mental Disorders* (DSM-IV) (American Psychiatric Association, 1994) and *The ICD-10 Classification of Mental and Behavioral Disorders* (ICD-10) (World Health Organization, 1992), provide definitions and descriptions of SM.

DSM-IV Criteria

The DSM-IV definition contains the following five major points:

1. Consistent failure to speak in specific social situations (in which there is expectation for speaking, e.g., at school) despite speaking in other situations
2. The disturbance interferes with educational or occupational achievement with social communication
3. The duration of the disturbance is at least one month (not limited to the first month of school)
4. The failure to speak is not limited to a lack of knowledge of, or comfort with, the spoken language required in a social situation
5. The disturbance is not better accounted for by a Communication Disorder (e.g., stuttering) and does not occur exclusively during the course of a pervasive developmental disorder, schizophrenia, or other psychotic disorder (American Psychiatric Association, 1994, p. 115).

According to DSM-IV, SM is estimated to affect less than 1 percent of individuals seen in mental health settings. In addition to these diagnostic criteria, SM may be associated with a variety of other features and disorders such as negativism, social isolation, controlling or oppositional behavior, and anxiety disorders. Additionally, some children with SM are teased or scapegoated by their peers who have normal verbal skills. The condition has a typical onset before the age of five, but may not be diagnosed until the child enters school. SM is somewhat more common in girls than it is in boys.

Some children do not speak because of a communication disorder such as a phonological disorder or stuttering. In these cases, the communication disorder should be considered more descriptive of the child's communication status rather than SM because it is likely to be a pervasive characteristic across settings. Children who have recently immigrated to another country and who are unfamiliar with the language may frequently refuse to or be reluctant to speak with others in their new environment; however, the DSM-IV guidelines indicate that this should not be considered an indication of SM because these children do not possess the necessary knowledge of their language or may be uncomfortable with the language.

The ICD-10 Definition

The ICD-10 definition (World Health Organization) uses the term elective mutism. This definitions states:

> The condition is characterized by a marked, emotionally determined selectivity in speaking, such that the child demonstrates his or her language competence in some situations but fails to speak in other (definable) situations. Most frequently, the disorder is first manifest in early childhood; it occurs with approximately the same frequency in the two sexes, and it is usual for the mutism to be associated with marked personality features involving social anxiety, withdrawal, sensitivity, or resistance. Typically, the child speaks at home or with close friends and is mute at school or with strangers, but other patterns (including the converse) can appear (World Health Organization, 1992, p. 278).

The ICD-10 definition presupposes an adequate ability to comprehend language and use language for expressive purposes along with evidence that the child speaks in a normal or nearly normal manner in some situations. The conditions can coexist with other conditions such as language or communication disorders provided the child exhibits fluency in some situations but not in others. Emotional problems such as social anxiety, social withdrawal, and oppositional behavior can coexist with selective mutism but are not essential features of the condition. The term includes selective mutism and excludes pervasive developmental disorders, specific developmental disorders of speech and language, and transient mutism as part of separation anxiety in young children.

Features of the Definitions

The central feature of both the DSM-IV and the ICD-10 definitions is the persistent refusal to speak in some but not all situations despite adequate expressive and receptive language abilities, which persists for a substantial amount of time and cannot be accounted for by other physical or emotional problems. Both definitions indicate that SM can often be accompanied by other problems, particularly anxiety disorders and oppositional behavior; however, comorbidity is unnecessary for identification of SM in either condition. Both definitions suggest that SM has an early age of onset but is often not identified until the child enters school. The DSM-IV definition explicitly precludes identification of SM in children who lack language facility because of recent immigration to a country which uses a language different from their own. The ICD-10 guidelines require that the child possesses adequate ability to speak and comprehend the language for social communication, thereby excluding children whose language is different from the dominant language of their environment by inference.

Unresolved Definitional Issues

One of the major unresolved issues in defining SM is the meaning of the term persistent. The DSM-IV definition indicates that the condition must persist for one month (outside of the first month of school). The ICD-10 definition gives no time parameters. Because children can have a variety of transient adjustment reactions which affect their willingness to speak, the time over which the condition is displayed can dramatically affect the number of children in which it is observed (Kolvin & Fundudis, 1981). Researchers have defined their populations of selectively mute children using a variety of measures of persistence which range from one month (DSM-IV) to two years (Kolvin & Fundudis, 1981). When overly loose criteria are employed, too many children are identified with the condition. This clouds the validity of the treatment and diverts resources and attention away from more severe cases by including children who, because their mutism is transient, are likely to improve without treatment or less intensive treatments than are required for selectively mute children (Cline & Baldwin, 1994).

The extent to which the child's condition is detrimental to educational and social development seems to be important in both definitions, yet neither definition provides much guidance as to how detrimental the condition should be before it is identified in a given individual. Variations in teacher tolerance, peer group patterns of interaction and parental expectations could all be expected to influence judgments regarding the severity of impact of SM on a child's development. Some selectively mute children are socially isolated and incompetent in their interactions with other individuals while other selectively mute children are able to attain social goals and avoid peer rejection through sophisticated use of nonverbal communicative behaviors such as gestures, shrugs, and head nods (Cline & Baldwin, 1994). It is unclear under what circumstances distinctions should be made between these groups of selectively mute children.

ETIOLOGY OF SELECTIVE MUTISM

Selective mutism is sometimes ascribed to a single factor such as pathology in the relationship between the child and his or her mother; however, it is more likely that it is rooted in multiple risk factors which affect different children in varying degrees (Baldwin & Cline, 1991). Risk factors associated with selective mutism include but are not necessarily limited to: hereditary tendencies, family interaction patterns, and recent immigration.

The colloquial nature of the term "mutism" also adds to the confusion surrounding SM. For example, a search of the Psychlit data base for selective mutism yielded a case study of a young woman who is clearly dissimilar to children with SM. Amy's case (Ratner, 1995) presents a young woman with Down syndrome who uses a private language to communicate and only began to show withdrawal from general interaction when she was 20 years old. It is clear that SM can coexist with mental retardation (Klin & Volkmar, 1993). Although considered to be "mute" by her therapist, Amy does not fit the criteria for SM. Her late onset and use of private language are very different from the pattern of development of SM. However, naive readers of the literature are likely to assume that this case is representative of the children with SM when it is not.

The specific cause or causes of SM remain unknown. Among the problems in identifying causes of SM include the number of other conditions which appear similar to SM and the "folklore" surrounding SM. There are many reasons why people may avoid talking which are different from selective mutism. Anyone who has committed a blunder in a close relationship is well aware of one kind of transient selective mutism and almost everyone has experienced such an event. Another example of mutism occurs in shy children who do not warm easily to strangers but interact reasonably well with familiar individuals. However, despite similar topography with SM, such episodic breaks in communication are far different from the long-term, deeply entrenched behavior exhibited by children who have SM. Failure to distinguish between SM and other communication problems adds to the uncertainty which surrounds diagnosis of this condition.

Traumatic Events and SM

One of the more commonly held beliefs about the origin of SM is that it is related to some intense traumatic event in the child's history (Halpern, Hammond, & Choen, 1971; Hayden, 1980). The usual assumption is that the event happened in the home. However, Hadley (1994) noted that if the traumatic event occurred in the home, it would be more likely for the child to speak outside of the home and remain mute in the home. This is almost always the opposite pattern of behavior displayed by children with selective mutism. Nevertheless, the folklore surrounding SM is often resilient to the research about SM. For example, in response to a diagnostic study by Black and Uhde (1995) which suggested that social anxiety was a more likely root of SM than trauma, Szabo (1996) indicated that traumatic events should remain a probable cause of SM. Szabo's support for this was that several years earlier he had worked with a child who was reported to have stopped talking following the murder of her mother. When the child was finally told what had happened to her mother and allowed to visit the grave, she reportedly began speaking freely again. Although traumatic and painful events are important in understanding a given child, trauma and bereavement do not appear to be common factors in the etiology of selective mutism (Black, 1996; Black & Uhde, 1995).

Jacobsen (1995) reported the case of a 15 year-old male who was referred for treatment of SM. He had been both physically and sexually abused during infancy and had witnessed the murder of a sibling at age four. Just before he entered high school, his best friend was murdered and he ceased speaking with other people. Through four years of individual psychotherapy, it was determined that the individual had dissociative identity disorder (DID) which had resulted in the development of alternate identities as a mechanism to adapt to traumatic circumstances. One of the identities was reported to have "told the therapist that he thought it best to 'shut the boy up completely' to save him from death, too" (p. 865). Jacobsen concluded that the mutism in this case was a manifestation of DID rather than SM because the onset was later than suggested in the definitions, no progress was made when the individual was treated directly for SM, and the young man's statements indicated that his SM was directly related to DID. For example, he stated that he wanted to speak but believed that he should not. Jacobsen concluded that this case like other trauma-based cases involving mutism was better explained by another condition than by SM.

In another examination of children with SM, Kopp and Gillberg (1997) screened children aged seven to 15 years in 101 classes in Switzerland for SM according to DSM-IV (American Psychiatric Association, 1994) criteria. They found that there were no major traumatic events reported in connection with onset of SM in the children they identified with the condition.

Heredity and SM

Twin studies would be the most beneficial for identifying genetic links to SM. However, given the small numbers of children observed with SM, it is unlikely that sufficient numbers of twins could be identified for such a study. Steinhausen and Adamek (1977) examined the family history data for 38 children identified with SM according to the ICD-10 definition and 31 children who, although not identified with SM, were diagnosed with an emotional disorder and had either an articulation or expressive language disorder. Although this procedure cannot control for the effects of family environment and differential sensitization toward reporting shyness or mutism in the families of SM, the authors contended that observations of significantly greater numbers of family members with speech avoidant behaviors in the SM group than in the control group could indicate the presence of a genetic role in the etiology of SM. Steinhausen and Adamek (1997) found that "taciturnity" ("a person with very little if any spontaneous speech, restricted length of spoken sentences and long periods with no verbal communication at all," p. 108) discriminated best between samples. Taciturnity was 2.5 times more likely to show up in first degree relatives compared to third degree relatives. Despite the definition of the control group as specifically children with articulation or expressive language disorders, there was no difference in the rate of manifestation of speech and language disorders between the two groups. Steinhausen and Adamek (1997) concluded that, although it was impossible to rule out family environment contributions in their study, the results suggested a polygenetic mode of transmission of a generalized speech avoidant factor which differentially interacts with the environment to produce SM in some children but not in others.

Black and Uhde (1995) also noted a strong relationship between a first degree family history of social phobia, avoidant disorders and SM. Most of the parents interviewed in this study reported that while they experienced a decrease in speech reluctance across adolescence, they continued to experience high levels of social anxiety and avoidance even into adulthood.

Simons, Goode, and Fombonne (1997) reported the case of a 55-month-old female who was given a diagnosis of selective mutism. Language development problems had been identified as early as 24 months and continued across settings (preschool and home). IQ and language scores were all reported to be in the low average range. A chromosome analysis revealed deletion of the short arm of Chromosome 18. According to the authors deletions of the long arm of Chromosome 18 are associated with severe developmental delays. Deletion of the short arm of Chromosome 18 is associated with variable expressions of less severe conditions which can include mental retardation and autism. While only one case linking this disorder to SM has been reported, it is significant to note that the symptoms in this case appeared at a very early age and could not be explained by other factors in the child's background. In such children, it is possible that specific chromosomal abnormalities underlie SM.

Anxiety and SM

The idea that SM is an extreme form of anxiety disorder or social phobia has gained credibility, particularly in the 1990s. In an early case study, Shreeve (1991) concluded that the SM of one four-year-old was rooted in stranger anxiety which was a projection of a hostile mother-child relationship onto outsiders. Given the descriptive psychodynamic case study method employed by Shreeve, it is difficult to determine the generality of his suggestions. However, Shreeve's suggestion that the SM is initially derived from a "freeze reflex" emitted to perceived danger is in line with thinking that various forms of anxiety may underlie SM.

Black and Uhde (1992) examined the relationship between the syndromes of SM and social phobia (SP) in the case of a 12-year-old girl who was considered to exhibit both syndromes of behavior. The child had already received one year of outpatient psychotherapy starting at age five and failed to show improvement. Therefore, a single blind medication trial without any other family therapy or psychotherapy was conducted. A three-week placebo condition yielded no change in her behavior and was followed by treatment with desipramine starting at 25 mg daily and increasing over three weeks to 200 mg daily. Although some positive changes were noted in her behavior, they were minimal. The desipramine was discontinued for one month and then treatment with fluoxetine was begun at 20 mg every other day for seven days and then 20 mg daily. After four weeks of fluoxetine treatment, the child was reported to be speaking freely with adults in a variety of settings, interacting freely with classmates and teachers at school and attending school parties and dances without distress. Interestingly, she continued to refuse to speak with her therapists. Because the child's symptoms responded to treatment with fluoxetine, a medication shown to be effective in the treatment of SP, it is suggested that elective mutism or reluctance to speak in unfamiliar social situations may be a manifestation of SP rather than a separate diagnostic syndrome in both children and adults. Black and Uhde suggested that SM may be a more common reaction of children with SP than adults with SP because adults are more often able to control their environments and avoid situations where they are likely to be called upon to speak.

Black and Uhde (1995) assessed the characteristics of 30 children aged 5.3 to 12.8 years with selective mutism with parent and teacher rating scales as well as structured diagnostic interviews. Ninety-seven percent of the children were diagnosed with social phobia, avoidant disorder of childhood or adolescence, or both. Thirty percent of the sample also were identified with simple phobias. Parent and teacher rating scales showed high levels of social anxiety and low levels of other psychiatric symptoms. Social anxiety severity correlated with SM severity. The authors concluded that SM may, therefore, be a symptom of social anxiety rather than a distinct diagnostic syndrome. The link between anxiety disorders, phobias, and SM appears to be the best supported of the suggested causes for SM which have appeared in the literature to date (Black, Leonard, & Rapport, 1997).

Vulnerability to SM

Steinhausen and Juzi (1996) suggested a vulnerability model to explain the variations in characteristics across a population of 100 children with SM. In general, it was found that the condition appeared more frequently in girls, was associated with children who were recent immigrants as well as with children who had a history of problems in motor development, toilet training, and speech and language disorders. Steinhausen and Juzi concluded that when children who are predisposed toward SM are confronted with stresses, such as acquiring a new language, they manifest their difficulties by developing SM. Although this theory has appeal, it remains unsupported by empirical data.

ASSESSMENT OF SELECTIVE MUTISM

Many children referred because of SM have failed to receive systematic evaluations because clinicians believed that the children were untestable due to lack of verbal responding or because the clinicians did not believe that systematic assessment was necessary (Dow, Sonies, Scheib, & Moss, 1995). Although structured methods for assessing psychological, medical and behavioral aspects of an individual have been developed in the last half of the twentieth century, they are not popular nor are they commonly used by clinical practitioners (Klien, 1988).

Possibly because SM, in contrast to most other psychiatric diagnoses, has existed for many years with little change or debate, the diagnostic criteria and assessment strategies associated with it have had only minor change over the last century (Hooper & Linz, 1992). This, in part, could explain why few, if any, standardized procedures for assessment appear in the published case studies of SM (Hooper & Linz, 1992).

These observations suggest that identification of SM is a highly variable proposition with little protection from error and little hope of replication across evaluators or individual children. Additionally, it is now known that many disorders can coexist with SM or can possess the same behavioral topography of SM; therefore, evaluators must be aware that mutism is a nonspecific symptom which can be associated with other conditions which may require different treatment than SM (e.g., social phobias, speech and language disorder, oppositional-defiant disorder) (Weckstein, Krohn, & Wright, 1995). Clearly, it is in the best interest of children suspected of having SM to improve the procedures employed to identify and classify them for treatment.

Several authors have suggested general guidelines for assessing children suspected of having SM. In many assessments of behavioral and psychological problems of school-aged children, a great deal of information can be gathered through first-hand interviews with the target child. However, it is likely that most children with SM will refuse to cooperate with an unknown evaluator particularly on tasks which require verbal responses. Therefore, structured parent interviews, rating scales, and nonverbal standardized cognitive assessments are frequently employed when considering SM (Hooper & Linz, 1992). The following sections contain descriptions of the components which have been suggested for assessment of children with SM. It is unlikely that a standard battery for assessing this condition can be recommended with any certainty. For some children, many aspects of assessment can be carried out at the screening level. For others, far more in-depth assessment than is described here may be necessary.

Medical Examination and History

It is essential to review the child's medical history because physical problems such as neurological insult, frequent ear infections, or frequent or prolonged illness can underlie mutism (Dow et al., 1995). It may also be useful to obtain a summary of the family's medical history, particularly the extent to which SM, shyness, or anxiety disorders have occurred in close relatives (Dummit, Rachel, Tancer, & Asche, 1997). Much of this information can be collected through parent interviews and record reviews. Particular attention should be given to the possibility that oral sensory, motor ability or neurological difficulties are contributing to the child's reluctance to speak. Physical aspects such as muscular asymmetry, tongue or lip weakness, abnormal gag reflexes, and difficulties in sucking and swallowing can indicate difficulties in producing the movements necessary for speech (Dow et al., 1995).

Parent Interviews

Several authors suggested that the parent interview is a critical part of assessment for SM. Among the topics to be included in the parent interview are (a) a social history of the child and the family; (b) the history of the SM, including onset, duration and any suspected precipitants as well as (c) a description of the environments where the SM is displayed and those in which it is not a problem. Information obtained from interviews must be combined with other results in order to provide relevant insight to the person, behaviors, or conditions under consideration (Sattler, 1992).

Advantages and Concerns Regarding Interviews

For some children, a parent interview may be the only means of obtaining personal information. The interview can offer several advantages over other assessment procedures. It can be directed at specific target behaviors. It can provide affective information to observers who note the respondent's verbal (e.g., tone of voice, hesitancy) and nonverbal behaviors (e.g., facial expressions, posture) (Sattler, 1992).

Sattler also cautioned that reliability and validity can be difficult to establish for interviews. Some respondents may provide inaccurate information or react to subtle cues from the interviewer to alter their responses in some way, and cultural bias can often play a part in the information revealed as well as the interpretation of the interview results. Additionally, Herjanic and Reich (1982, 1997) cautioned that using only reports from parents and teachers provides no control of the extent to which these individuals may have psychiatric or behavioral disturbances themselves.

Whenever possible multiple sources of information including reports from the child should be obtained. Disagreements between sources indicates need for additional assessment and probing to determine the nature or severity of the problem being considered.

Structured Interviews

In order to structure the interview and increase the consistency, researchers and clinicians sometimes use pre-established psychiatric interview protocols. The structured interview is a standardized procedure. It allows all respondents to be asked the same questions (Sattler, 1992). Standardization allows comparisons among respondents and interviewers and helps to ensure that important topics are not overlooked due to oversight of the interviewer. Additionally, standardized interview formats lead to more definitive diagnoses than do informal interviews (Sattler, 1992). Examples of structured interview formats which have been developed for use with children are the Diagnostic Interview Schedule for Children (Costello, Edelbrock, Kalas, Kessler, & Klaric, 1982; Costello, Eldelbrock, & Costello, 1985) and the Diagnostic Interview for Children and Adolescents (Herjanic & Reich, 1982). Several researchers have developed interview protocols specific to SM. For example Dummit, Klien, Tancer, Asche, Martin, and Fairbanks (1997) employed the Diagnostic Interview Schedule for Children, Parent version (National Institute of Mental Health, 1991) to obtain information regarding their children. Hooper and Linz (1992) developed a checklist of characteristics of SM which could also be employed during parent interviews.

Audiology, Speech, and Language

Audiology

Because even mild audiological problems can have a negative effect on speech and language development (Fundudis, Kolvin, & Garside, 1979), an audiological examination should be a part of the identification procedure for any child suspected of having SM. Tests of peripheral sensitivity (using speech sounds and pure tone audiometry) are usually adequate to detect problems in hearing. In addition, middle ear functioning should be assessed with tympanometry and acoustic reflex testing (Dow et al., 1995).

Speech and Language

Adequate speech and language evaluations for children with SM will require a variety of approaches including standardized tests of receptive abilities, information obtained from parent interviews, and analysis of audiotapes of the child speaking (usually at home) (Dow et al., 1995). The *Peabody Picture Vocabulary Test* (Dunn & Dunn, 1997) can be administered nonverbally to children as young as two years old. Other standardized instruments which can be used to assess receptive language include the *Token Test for Children* (DiSimoni, 1978) and the *Test of Language Development* (Hammill & Newcomer, 1982). A variety of other instruments designed to measure receptive language in individuals who are nonverbal are also available. It appears appropriate to include at least one of these measures early in the identification procedure to ensure that target children possess sufficient language abilities to respond to the treatments which will subsequently be employed.

Actual speech production in children with SM is typically assessed through prerecorded audiotapes made in the environment where the child speaks freely or with the people to whom the child speaks. A speech and language clinician can use the audiotape to determine phonological ability, mean length of utterances, grammatical construction, pragmatics such as turn-taking in conversations, and aspects of voice such as volume, quality, and inflection (Dow, et al., 1995; Hooper & Linz, 1992; Schill, Kratochwill, & Gardner, 1996).

Intellectual Assessment

Because ability interacts with language facility and production (Beirne-Smith, Patton, & Ittenbach, 1994; Zigler & Hodapp, 1986), it may be useful to obtain some form of intellectual assessment. Clearly tests requiring verbal responses will either be unadministrable to children with SM or obtain underestimates of intellectual ability. However, several nonverbal measures of ability are available for this task. Among these are the Comprehensive Test of Nonverbal Intelligence (Hammill, Pearson, & Weiderhold, 1996), and the Leiter Intentional Performance Scale-Revised (Roid & Miller, 1997). These measures should be considered as only rough guides and not as good predictors of school achievement which is the more common purpose for intelligence testing. This is partly because schools are highly verbal places and much of the acquisition and demonstration of knowledge and skills is in the verbal domain (Ausubel, 1963). The differences between the response formats of nonverbal assessments and the performance requirements of most classrooms limit the predictive ability of these instruments. Nevertheless, nonverbal tests of ability can help to rule out factors such as mental retardation as a cause or contributing factor for the SM. In cases where ability assessments indicate problems such as low IQ, it may be that the primary intervention should be related to mental retardation with SM considered as a secondary feature which may or may not, depending on the individual case, require specific treatment.

Academic Achievement

Even for fairly young children, identification and remediation of achievement deficits is a primary concern in school programs. Therefore, at least a screening for achievement concerns is a necessary part of evaluation of children with SM. Because children with SM are unlikely to participate in assessments which require oral responses, any procedures for assessment of SM should capitalize on formats which allow for silent responding. The Peabody Individual Achievement Test-Revised (PIAT-R) (Markwardt, 1989) is presented in a multiple choice format which allows children to point at responses.

Curriculum-based measurement procedures (Fuchs, Fuchs, Hamlett, Walz, & Germann, 1993) for mathematics, reading, and spelling can allow evaluators to compare children's performance to that of agemates in the same classes, schools, and communities (Hasbrouck & Tindal, 1992). Some children with SM will read a book out loud but refuse to speak to strangers. Other children will read but only to parents. For such children reading fluency measures can be obtained through tape recordings and compared to local standards as suggested for arithmetic and spelling. Children who display deficits in academic achievement should be considered for remedial programs along with treatment for the SM. Some evidence suggests that children with achievement deficits perceive themselves to be quite alienated from the school and their peers (Fulk, Brigham, & Lohman, in press). Without a good foundation in academic skills, it is unlikely that children with SM will find school a comfortable environment even after their SM is treated.

Direct Observation

Observations of the child in a variety of settings should be conducted in addition to clinical assessments. Black and Uhde (1992, 1995) caution that the severity of the child's mutism in clinical settings is not likely to be a valid indicator of symptom severity across other settings. Further, change or lack of change in the clinical setting may not correspond to changes or lack of changes in other environments. Children with SM have been known to resolve their symptoms outside of the clinic yet maintain their SM with their clinician (Black & Uhde, 1992).

Specific Assessment Protocols

Two assessment protocols that have been developed specifically for assessment of SM were found in the literature. Both are related more to the behavioral than the medical or psychodynamic models, but appear to have good utility when used with many models of intervention. Hooper and Linz (1992) presented a model for assessment referred to as the "multisetting, multisource, multi-instrument model." Although sensible and clearly more systematic than other methods of assessment for SM, the multisetting, multisource, multi-instrument model is presented without supporting data. Schill, Kratochwill, and Gardner (1996) presented a procedure for conducting a functional analysis of the variables which are maintaining the SM. The validity of their protocol was demonstrated with one eight-year-old child. Both procedures are described briefly in the following sections.

Multisetting, Multisource, Multi-Instrument Model

In order to increase reliability of the diagnosis, the multisetting, multisource, multi-instrument model collects two or more measures of the same characteristic within settings and also collects measures across multiple settings. By combining these measures, some sources of error can be eliminated or cancel each other out.

It is relatively easy to identify relevant settings for assessment of children with SM. "Generally, the chosen settings should include those of importance or relevance to the child, and those with characteristics that could differentially affect the child's behaviors (e.g., marital/family environment). Setting variance may be the single most crucial data point in the diagnosis of this disorder" (Hooper & Linz, 1992, p. 446).

Most often, the home, school, and clinical settings are assessed in this model. Within two parent homes, the mother and the father are the most likely sources of information, although it is possible to collect data from siblings and other family members who may be present frequently in the home. In the school, two teachers or a teacher and a paraprofessional who interact frequently with the child are good sources of information. Observations in the clinical setting can be carried out by two clinicians with similar or, in some cases, complementary training (e.g., a psychologist and a social worker or two psychologists).

The multi-instrument component of this plan is substantially more difficult to achieve. Because few instruments relevant to assessment of SM are developed with parallel forms, Hooper and Linz suggested that evaluators must approximate the "spirit of this third component by using multiple assessment methods with each information source" (p. 447).

Among the assessment procedures suggested by Hooper and Linz (1992) are structured observations of the child in the home, school, and other social settings. Tape recordings of the child's speech obtained in environments or with persons not affected by the SM are used to evaluate quality and quantity of speech and language.

Assessment of SM in this model includes rating scales such as the *Child Behavior Problem Checklist* (Quay & Peterson, 1987), and the *Child Behavior Checklist* (CBCL) (Achenbach & Edelbrook, 1983). Hooper and Linz also suggested that measures of personality (e.g., Personality Inventory for Children, Wirt, Lachar, Klinedist, & Seat, (1977), anxiety (e.g., Revised Children's Manifest Anxiety Scale, Reynolds & Richmond, 1985), and depression (e.g., Children's Depression Inventory, Kovacs & Beck, 1977) be included in identification of SM. Because all of these instruments are developed for use with general populations and may be differentially affected by the presence of SM, the scheme of multiple ratings seems highly appropriate.

In addition to personality and behavior evaluations, Hooper and Linz suggested that nonverbal measures of language (e.g., Peabody Picture Vocabulary Test—Revised, Dunn & Dunn, 1997), achievement (e.g., Peabody Individualized Achievement Test—Revised, Markwardt, 1989) and cognitive ability (e.g., The Comprehensive Test of Nonverbal Intelligence, Hammill, Pearson, & Weiderholt, 1996) be included in the assessment package for SM. Measures of family functioning and parental adjustment may also be useful in identification of SM and related features. Among the instruments that Hooper and Linz suggested were the Parenting Stress Index (Abidin, 1983), the McMaster Family Assessment (Miller, Epstien, Bishop, & Leitner, 1985) and the Minnesota Multiphasic Personality Inventory (Hathaway & McKinley, 1989).

Hooper and Linz also developed a checklist of 45 symptoms derived from the case study literature on SM. Each symptom on the scale is rated according to a three point Likert-type scale to indicate whether the behavior is (0) Not Similar, (1) Somewhat Similar, or (2) Very Similar to the child. The entire scale appears in Hooper and Linz (1992) along with permission to reproduce and use the scale. The authors stated that no normative data is presently available for this scale. Therefore, the scale can serve as a prompt to consider the many aspects of SM in a thorough evaluation, but cannot in itself provide sufficient information for a clear diagnosis.

Functional Assessment using Parents as Facilitators

Schill, Kratochwill, and Gardner (1996) presented a method of functional analysis of the variables suspected of maintaining SM. First, the CBC (Achenbach & Edelbrook, 1983) was administered to obtain a description of the child's behavioral characteristics and to identify any other childhood behavioral disorders. Next, a Functional Diagnostic Protocol (FDP) (Cole & Gardner, 1993) was developed for

SM and administered to the parents as an informal interview. The FDP included assessment of environmental and personal variables involved in the instigation of the condition as well as acquisition and persistence of aberrant behaviors (Schill, Kratochwill, & Gardner, 1996). The information gained from the FDP was used to generate hypotheses about the variables maintaining the SM. These hypotheses were then tested in an analog assessment.

Before the analog assessment was conducted with the child, parents were consulted about tasks which would be of interest to the child and potential reinforcers for the child. Additionally, the Treatment Evaluation Inventory-Short Form (Kelly, Heffner, Gresham, & Elliot, 1989) was administered to obtain the parent's perceptions of the acceptability and effectiveness of the treatments considered for the child. Finally, a questionnaire requesting the child's opinions about the analog assessment procedure was administered with the parent's assistance. These procedures allowed the researchers to identify a body of interesting tasks and potential reinforcers which could be combined with treatments and which were acceptable to both the child and the parents.

The dependent variable observed across the evaluations was the number of words spoken per minute during five- to ten-minute sessions. Audible whispers were counted as words.

The evaluation was conducted in three phases: baseline (no demand), initial assessment, and replication assessment. After the baseline phase established levels of speech across settings, the child was assessed under both high and low demand conditions for each of six functional hypotheses derived for the child. The functional hypotheses included were that: "Certain requests, directives, and task demands are aversive and SM is negatively reinforced by removal of these aversive demands" and "the child's self-perceptions that she is unable to perform certain tasks to perfection (e.g., oral reading) are related to the SM through negative reinforcement" (Schill, Kratochwill, & Gardner, 1996, p. 11). For example, the easy-demand reading condition involved having the child read a book either to the parents or together with the parents. In the high-demand reading condition, an unfamiliar adult was added to the reading task. The low and high demand situations were employed because the authors suspected that, for some children, a given strategy may be effective in producing speech under low-demand circumstances but ineffective under high-demand conditions.

By testing each hypothesis, the researchers were able to identify several consistent aspects of the child's mutism. In this case, the child clearly demonstrated reluctance to read orally (one of the functional hypotheses) and greatly decreased speech under high-demand conditions across environments. Treatment recommendations were generated based on the data gathered through the parent interview, the FDP, and the analog assessments. According to Schill, Kratochwill, and Gardner, identification of SM based on DSM-IV criteria often leads to a treatment deadend. Therefore, these authors suggested that analog assessment protocol procedure is an improvement over other diagnostic measures because it directly links treatment to diagnosis.

Summary

From this discussion, it appears that the best practice for identification of SM in children is to consider the cluster of symptoms as a whole while remaining sensitive to other conditions (e.g., language difference, communication disorder) which could account for the behavior. Finally, one of the outcomes of the assessment procedure should be a clear decision about whether or not to intervene with the child's SM. In making decisions regarding whether or not to intervene, educators and other service providers along with the child's parents should weigh the benefits and risks of intervention versus doing nothing. In the next section several criteria which can help make this determination are presented.

Deciding Whether or Not to Intervene

When dealing with a child who displays SM, it is important to make a conscious decision whether or not intervention is necessary (Powell & Dalley, 1995). Lumb and Wolff (1988) noted that most of the studies they reviewed reported no discussion of the need to intervene with the child's SM. Such a decision is important because intervention with SM is difficult to carry out and poorly implemented interventions often lead to exacerbation of the condition. Also, some children remit their symptoms without treatment. In cases where the child would improve without treatment, the expense and inconvenience of intervention is questionable.

Barrios, Hartman, and Shigetomi (1981) suggested that part of the determination to intervene should be based on examination of the views of the child and the adults regarding the behavioral issues, the relationship of the problem behavior to other problem behaviors or potential for behavioral problems, and the anticipated costs and benefits associated with available treatments. To assist in this decision, they provided a set of questions to guide professionals in making the decision to intervene with children who display anxieties and fears. These questions are easily applicable to children with SM. Table 1 presents the questions that Barrios, Hartman, and Shigetomi (1981) suggested with a brief explanation of the rationale for each question. Even if the answers to these questions support the decision to directly intervene, several determinations which are directly related to identification of SM remain.

Porjes (1992) presented a four-stage approach for treatment of children with SM. In the first two stages, one collects data to (a) determine if SM exists in the child, and (b) to determine if the mutism is transient or persistent. According to DSM-IV, the behavior must persist for a substantial period of time in order to be considered SM. Although some authors (e.g., Paez, 1988; Silver, 1989) have contended that it is possible to discriminate between transient and persistent forms of SM the definitions discussed earlier in this chapter appear to suggest that transient forms

Table 1. Questions to Determine the Need for Intervention with Selective Mutism

Question	*Rationale*
Who is complaining?	• Children may be unmotivated or unwilling to participate in treatment. In such cases treatment may be inordinately difficult. • In some cases, the child's behavior may actually be appropriate and the referring adult rather than the child may be the more appropriate target for treatment.
How is the behavior really a problem?	• Intervention is justified only when the behavior interferes with normal development, or learning experiences and results in curtailment of behavioral choices and results in discomfort in the target individual.
How are fears related to other areas of the child's behavior?	• Sometimes the behavior identified in the referral is not the problem that needs modifications. The presence of other associated difficulties may signal that a problem other than the one indicated in the referral (e.g., mental retardation, speech and language deficits) should be treated or that both problems should be treated together.
What are the costs of treatment, assuming that there are effective interventions for the problems?	• Particularly for behaviors which are resistant to treatment, it is wise to consider the time, money, effort, and disruption of regular activities before beginning an intervention. Haphazard, poorly applied, and nonsystematic interventions appear to be associated with subsequent increased resistance to treatment.
What would be different for the child in his or her natural environment without the problem?	• Intervention is justified if the expected changes in behavior can be considered a positive event for all involved. • The long and short-term consequences of allowing the problem behavior to remain unchanged must be weighed. If a child is likely to spontaneously remit, little risk is associated with non-treatment. However, if the behavior is likely to continue and result in limits in social, academic, or vocational opportunities, intervention is more warranted.

Note: Adapted from Barrios, Hartman, & Shigetomi, 1981

of speech withholding are not properly classified as SM. Porjes (1992) suggested that "transient mutism" was a more appropriate term to describe the behavior of children under the age of five whose mutism (a) has lasted less than six months, (b) is intermittent, and (c) is restricted to only one environment. Children with transient mutism may require evaluations in other areas (e.g., medical, speech and language, or family, parent, or teacher interviews, Rutter, 1977; Weckstein, Krohn, & Wright, 1995) to rule out other possible problems. Additionally, the child should be monitored for improvement of the condition, with possible intervention at a later date. For children older than five whose mutism (a) has lasted more than six months, (b) is consistent, and (c) occurs in more than one environment, an identification of "persistent mutism" is warranted and intervention is needed (Porjes, 1992).

In sum, if a child's refusal to speak in some areas or to some people is severely detrimental to his or her development, socialization, family life, or education; has persisted for a lengthy period of time; and occurs age five or later, planned systematic intervention is clearly justifiable. Intervention with younger children is less clearly warranted. However, in some cases, the severity of a young child's condition may require it. In the next section, several intervention strategies are reviewed.

CURRENT APPROACHES TO INTERVENTION WITH SELECTIVE MUTISM

The majority of interventions for SM fall into the categories of psychodynamic and behavioral (Kratochwill, 1981; Wright, Holmes, Cuccaro, & Leonhardt, 1994). Other forms of interventions for SM include medical intervention with drugs and treatment of SM as a speech and language disorder.

Few intervention studies with SM contain a substantial number of subjects. Krohn, Weckstein, and Wright (1992) found that only five studies reported data for more than ten cases. It is, therefore, somewhat difficult to draw solid conclusions regarding the kinds of treatments which are most likely to yield improvement. Another problem in the treatment literature is the likelihood of differential reporting of successful versus unsuccessful treatments. Because unsuccessful treatments are less likely to be reported, the small case studies may not be particularly accurate indicators of responses to various treatments (Krohn, Weckstein, & Wright, 1992). Additionally, small case studies may use lax diagnostic criteria, particularly in regard to duration which may result in the inclusion of a substantial number of children with transient forms of SM or children whose SM may spontaneously improve (Krohn, Weckstein, & Wright, 1992). Despite these problems, professionals and parents dealing with a child with SM must make decisions about the variety of treatments available. Therefore, the next sections present summaries of the tactics used in these approaches to treatments.

Psychodynamic Interventions

Psychodynamic treatments are the most time-consuming interventions for SM (Black, Leonard, & Rapoport, 1997). Few psychodynamic studies include data regarding the severity of the SM or the amounts of speech noted in different environments after treatment (Brigham & Cole, 1997). It is, therefore, difficult to determine the overall effectiveness of the psychodynamic approaches to interventions with SM. Previous reviews (e.g., Black, Leonard, & Rapoport, 1997; Kratochwill, 1981; Silver, 1989) have concluded that it is the least effective of the intervention approaches available for SM.

Play Therapy

Because SM is most often identified in early childhood, play therapy is sometimes recommended for treating children with SM. Play therapy seeks to allow children to work through anxiety and self-restriction (Cook, 1997) and is, therefore, considered a psychodynamic treatment.

Barlow, Strother, and Landreth (1986) conducted individual and sibling-group play therapy sessions and provided counseling to the rest of the family of a child with SM. They reported that the primary function of the sibling play therapy sessions was to allow the target child to develop intrapersonal communication skills and social skills. Lesser-Katz (1988) conducted play therapy with the target child alone and with the target child and selected classmates. She reported that once the child felt comfortable with his therapist and was sure that he would be accepted, he began to improve his communication skills. Carr and Afnan (1989) conducted play therapy along with individual child therapy and family therapy with a six-year-old who refused to speak to anyone outside of the family. Atlas (1993) used play therapy with dolls and games to engage a child with SM in treatment. He concluded that symbolic play had enabled the four-year-old child to resolve intrapsychic conflicts which included a "burgeoning of her feminine identity" (p. 1081). Reasons to suspect that a four-year-old child would have clear awareness of femininity were not presented.

Roe (1993) conducted group therapy with children who had SM. Among the techniques used in her group were copying the actions of another person as if one was standing in front of a mirror, rolling a ball between members of a group sitting on the floor after saying the recipient's name, storytelling with puppets, and, finally, storytelling and reading to the group without puppets. Participation in the group was continued "until sustained improvement in the child's social interactions was observed" (p. 136). Cook (1997) reported a general format for play therapy with children who have SM. She suggested that through careful choice of materials, play themes, and actions, the child will be able to derive important understandings about himself or herself without the need to wait for or provoke verbal expression. Bow (1997) concluded that play therapy can be an effective intervention because it (a) offers children a natural way to communicate, (b) employs play as a symbolic language, and (c) creates a comfortable environment which can be less threatening than other forms of therapy.

Because play therapy is a highly specialized form of intervention which relies primarily on the judgment of specially trained therapists, it is unlikely that it can be implemented in school settings as a primary intervention for SM. Several aspects of play therapy (e.g., differential response to verbal communication) may be present in other forms of intervention, particularly behavioral interventions. Play therapy does present the opportunity to structure pleasant interactions between the child, adults, and other children. It is likely that elements of play therapy can be combined with behavioral or medical treatments to provide increased opportunities for the child to engage in and receive reinforcement for verbal behavior.

Family Therapy

Family therapy is often recommended for children with SM because of the assumption that the SM is rooted in a struggle for autonomy between the child and his or her parents in which the child exerts control over the environment and punishes his or her parents by refusing to talk (Trad, 1989), although no evidence in support of this theory could be located in the empirical literature. Family therapy is often combined with other approaches but is distinguished by work primarily intended to alter the interactions and relations among family members (Harris, 1996).

Several studies described treatments intended to reduce psychological problems in both the parent(s) and the child. Atoynatan (1986) concluded that improvements in a target child's speech were the result of his mother's resolution of difficulties communicating with men coupled with threats to place the child in a residential treatment program unless he began to speak. In another report, the target child, a member of a lesbian stepfamily, began to speak after she was released from a "vow of secrecy" regarding her family (Baptiste, 1995). Baptiste suggested that the child (age nine) was placed in a "we-versus-they" situation when her mother divorced her alcoholic and abusive husband and entered a family relationship with another woman. The late onset of this case and the specific circumstances surrounding it, however, render the diagnosis of SM somewhat questionable. In fact, in a commentary on the report Rae (1995) suggested that the case was better considered to be about homosexuality than SM.

Other family interventions involve examination and alteration of patterns of interaction which may be supporting the SM. For example, Carr and Afnan (1989) worked to develop a trusting relationship between the parents and the therapist so that they would allow directive treatment of their child. Tatem and DelCampo (1995) worked with the parents to give the child more "floor time" to speak, reduce the enmeshment between the child and her mother, encourage the child to take the lead in interactive play between herself and her parents, and not ask her "to be so correct so much of the time and during play not to 'teach' her anything" (Tatem & DelCampo, 1995, p. 190).

Some form of family involvement is wise to include in any form of intervention because family dynamics may be involved in maintaining the mutism (Meyers, 1984) and because parents can support or hinder any form of intervention. Family therapy requires special training and a great deal of time, so it is unlikely that educators will adopt this treatment as a primary intervention. However, because SM is usually most problematic outside of the family, it may be important to enlist the help of the family in supporting whatever intervention is proposed. Many of the ideas described in family therapy can be useful when working with parents of children with SM. In some cases, it may be wise to enlist the help of a social worker or mental health consultant to serve as a liaison between the home and the school, particularly during the initial stages of referral and treatment (Hoffman, 1996).

Summary of Psychodynamic Intervention Tactics

Psychodynamic therapies work to resolve conflicts which prevent children from expressing themselves. Toward that end, supportive environments which emphasize therapeutic interactions between a trained clinician and the child or the child and his or her family are created and adapted to intervene with the SM. These treatments typically lack assessment or outcome data (Brigham & Cole, 1997), require a great deal of time and appear to be far less effective than more behavioral interventions (Black, Leonard, & Rapoport, 1997).

Speech and Language Interventions

Speech and language (SL) problems have been noted in some children with SM (Beitchman & Inglis, 1991; Tancer, 1992). Although SL concerns do not appear to be a primary cause of SM (Black, Leonard, & Rapport, 1997; Dummit, Klein, Tancer, Asche, Martin, & Fairbanks, 1997; Steinhausen & Juzi, 1996), they may contribute to the likelihood that a given child will display SM (Beitchman & Inglis, 1991; Steinhausen & Juzi, 1996; Steinhausen & Adamek, 1997). Additionally, it is possible that the SM is a learned pattern of communication which will respond to interventions aimed at improving the quantity and quality of speech in other children who have communication disorders.

Few studies using SL interventions to treat SM were located in the literature. Despite the importance of SL to child development, relatively few intervention studies of language disorders which manifested themselves in the preschool years appear in the literature (Scruggs, Mastropieri, Forness, & Kavale, 1988).

Schmerling and Kerins (1987) combined SL intervention with dance/movement therapy and chanting to improve the ability of a seven-year-old boy to "communicate his wants and needs verbally and nonverbally" (p. 33). Because the treatment is only vaguely described in terms of general goals, it is impossible to determine the effectiveness of the various components in the package. Several techniques which appear to be behavioral in nature (e.g., stimulus generalization) are described in the report although they do not appear to be regarded as behavioral intervention by the authors.

Functional Language Training

Pecukonis and Pecukonis (1991) provided a remarkably detailed report of a functional language intervention with a seven-year-old boy. Their treatment was evaluated with a multiple baseline design across behaviors. The functional language package included four language behaviors: (1) non-verbal attending, (2) non-verbal imitation, (3) verbal imitation, and (4) functional language training. Functional language training emphasizes conversational skills and generalization of these skills across people, settings, and situations (Pecukonis & Pecukonis, 1991). By providing direct and explicit reinforcement of successive approximations of each of these skills, the child was able to move from a general state of non-interaction through the various stages of imitation (e.g., "This is a baseball, say baseball.") to generalized responding to open ended questions (such as "What do you like about baseball?"). The authors reported a that 90 percent positive response criterion was attained for each of the training areas. However, the rate of functional language decreased to 80 percent during the maintenance and generalization phase of the study. Despite the small regression in functional language, generalization of spontaneous speech was noted in observations conducted in non-treatment settings.

Summary of Speech and Language Intervention Tactics

Few speech and language studies appear in the SM literature. When students receive SL training, it appears that they are being explicitly taught to use communication skills and also taught how, when, and where to use them. These SL components appear to be based on behavioral learning principles although they focus primarily on the acquisition and improvement of communication skills. However, the task of increasing language in children with SM may be far more difficult than it appears. Scruggs, Mastropieri, Forness, and Kavale (1988) noted that outcomes associated with increased language use were, on the whole, lower than outcomes addressing language acquisition. Nevertheless, for some children the SL approach appears to hold a great deal of promise. It may be advantageous to approach some resistant children and families from the perspective of training needed skills embodied in this literature rather than the psychological pathology model embodied in psychodynamic therapies.

Medical Interventions

Medical treatment of SM with drugs is a relatively recent addition to the literature. We found no reports of intervention for SM using drugs before 1990. Two classes of drugs, tricyclic antidepressants (TCAs) and selective serotonin reuptake inhibitors (SSRI), another form of antidepressant, have been employed with children who have SM. The mechanism of action for antidepressants is believed to be the blocking of reuptake of neurotransmitters in the brain (Biederman, Spencer, & Wilens, 1997). Biederman, Spencer, and Wilens point out that although drug treatment should begin with the lowest possible dose, it is likely that some children and adolescents will require full adult doses of antidepressants because they metabolize the drugs more efficiently than do adults.

Before beginning any drug treatment, it is important to explain the risks and benefits of the treatment as well as the alternative treatments which may be available. One adverse effect of antidepressant drugs in some but not all children receiving this intervention is behavioral disinhibition, which can lead to problems which are worse than those that prompted the referral in the first place. When considering medical intervention, it is critical to have a complete assessment of the child available. Because symptoms can be associated with different syndromes which respond differently to drugs, treatment of symptoms alone can be dangerous (Koplewicz & Williams, 1987). Therefore, use of these medications in the absence of specific indications of need is ill-advised and may worsen the clinical picture for a given child (Biederman, Spencer, & Wilens, 1997).

Three drugs have been reported in the literature, desipramine and phenelzine, both TCAs, and fluoxetine, an SSRI. Golwyn and Weinstock (1990) treated a seven-year-old girl with a two-year history of SM with phenelzine. They reported positive effects of the drug on the child's speaking over the course of a 16-week treatment. Weight gain and mild constipation were reported as negative effects of the treatment. No recurrence of mutism was observed at a five-month follow-up. Black and Uhde (1992) began treatment of a 12-year-old female with SM with desipramine, another TCA. After increasing the dose from 10 to 200 mg daily and continuing the treatment for 10 weeks, they observed no tangible improvement in the child's behavior. Therefore, a treatment with fluoxetine, an SSRI was begun with 20 mg every other day, increasing to 20 mg daily. The authors reported that after four weeks of treatment with fluoxetine, the child began to speak freely in school and other environments. Medication was discontinued at the beginning of the summer vacation. Also, her improved behavior was noted in observations taken at one month and seven months after the treatment ended.

Fluoxetine has been the drug of choice in most treatments of SM. It has been shown to yield improved communicative behavior over placebo treatments in a controlled, double blind study (Black & Uhde, 1994). However, teacher behavior ratings of the target children showed no significant differences between treatment groups over the 12-week course of the drug therapy. In contrast, Motavalli (1995) reported that a 12-year-old female treated with fluoxetine began speaking freely after two weeks of 20 mg daily fluoxetine treatment. However, this report is in the form of a letter to the editor and must be viewed with some caution. Dummit, Klien, Tancer, Asche, and Martin (1996) examined the consistency of positive responding to fluoxetine in a group of 21 children who had all been identified as having SM and anxiety disorders. In order to minimize the number of children who were likely to spontaneously improve, each child received four weeks of behavioral therapy before the drug treatment began. Seventy-six percent of the children treated in this study responded positively to the fluoxetine. However, two children experienced behavioral disinhibition severe enough to require discontinuation of the medication. Additionally, it was found that older children whose SM had persisted longer were less likely to respond positively to the fluoxetine treatment.

A partial explanation to the variable responding to the medication may be in the behavioral and communicative skills of the target children. Many children with SM have learned maladaptive coping behaviors as a result of their condition (Wright & Cuccaro, 1994). Wright, Cuccaro, Leonhardt, Kendall, and Anderson (1995), found that it was necessary to combine fluoxetine with family therapy, play therapy, and specific behavior management skills to elicit the desired changes in the target child. Wright and colleagues (1995) concluded in the absence of adaptive coping strategies, the child would continue to demonstrate maladaptive and oppositional behavior even with the drug. In this case, the medication was seen as allowing the child to "be available to learn and execute skills acquired in other modalities (i.e., play or behavior therapy)" (Wright et al., 1995, p. 861).

Summary of Medical Interventions

"In cases where anxiety appears salient and psychosocial therapies do not produce appreciable gains, the use of medication should be considered" (Wright et al., 1995, p. 861). Currently fluoxetine appears to be the most promising drug for treatment of SM. Because some children may develop behavioral disinhibition, it is important to monitor the child after the treatment has begun. For older children whose SM has persisted a long time, the medication may be ineffective. It appears that other interventions (e.g., behavioral and play therapies) are important to consider along with drug treatment for any child in order to ensure that they possess the necessary skills to profit from the drugs.

Behavioral Interventions

Probably, the interventions most frequently employed with children displaying SM are from the behavioral school (Harris, 1996). Kratochwill (1981) reported that behavioral approaches were at least as effective as and often more effective than psychodynamic approaches. In two separate reviews, Cunningham, Cataldo, Mallion, and Keyes (1983) and Labbe and Williamson (1984) concluded that behavioral approaches whether or not they were combined with family interventions were more effective than purely psychodynamic approaches. In a comprehensive review of behavioral interventions for SM, Labbe and Williamson (1984) categorized treatments as: (a) contingency management, (b) stimulus fading with reinforcement, and (c) response initiation procedures. Only papers published after that review will be considered in this section. In addition to these forms of treatments, a newer technology based intervention, self-modeling, has also been employed with children who have SM. Recent studies in each of these areas are described in the next sections.

Contingency Management Procedures

Contingency management procedures are best used with children who speak to most people in most situations but with very low frequency (Labbe & Williamson, 1984). Because the child is emitting the target behavior with some regularity, reinforcement procedures can be expected to be of value. General contingency management procedures continue to be reported in the literature. They are generally associated with children who have already established some level of speaking (Lachenmeyer & Gibbs, 1985). In some cases reinforcement is also paired with extinction of nonverbal communication or general nonresponding. In more extreme cases punishment for failure to speak has also been paired with reinforcement of speech (Louden, 1987).

One source of contingency management support can be found in the student's peer group. Peers can provide models for acceptable verbal behavior. Additionally, they can be trained to deliver reinforcement for speaking and to extinguish nonverbal communication. These techniques have been validated in two separate interventions (Matson, Box, & Francis, 1992; Porjes, 1992).

Contingency management can also incorporate active participation of the target child in establishing treatment goals and procedures. For example, Watson and Kramer (1992) gave the child in their study the choice to move to the next step in a 21-step treatment program. In addition to the gradual shaping program, multiple positive reinforcers were combined with mild punishment for silence and extinction of nonverbal forms of communication. In all, the treatment yielded small improvement after 11 weeks but considerable improvement after 27 weeks with the target student speaking to all other students in the school at various times. The improved behavior was maintained at a six-month follow-up observation.

In cases where the target child is extremely reluctant to speak in one important environment such as school, contingency management procedures have been combined with stimulus fading procedures (Masten, Stacks, Caldwell-Colbert, & Jackson, 1996; Richburg & Cobia, 1994). Typically members of the student's class are introduced to the settings in which the child speaks freely to promote speech in the school.

Stimulus Fading with Reinforcement

If a child will speak to at least one person in one environment, stimulus fading procedures are considered the treatment of choice for establishing communication behavior in new environments and with new people (Labbe & Williamson, 1984). After speech is established in the target settings, it can be maintained with contingency management.

Holmbeck and Lavigne (1992) first established verbal interactions in a clinical setting and then introduced classmates of the target child to the treatment sessions. Once the children were interacting with each other, the child's teacher was also introduced to the clinical sessions. Verbal interactions in the school were then supported by contingency management programs. Richburg and Cobia (1994) first established verbal communication between a target child with SM and a resource teacher in a small group setting. After the child was speaking freely in the small group setting, the teacher and her group of students moved their sessions to a general education classroom. In this case, however, the general education classroom was not conducive to the instructional goals of the students in the small group, so they eventually returned to the resource room setting.

Self-modeling Procedures

Self-modeling procedures are a recent development in the behavioral literature. In self-modeling, the target child views a videotape of himself or herself which has been edited to show the child exhibiting only the target behaviors (Dorwick & Dove, 1980). Three studies (Holmbeck & Lavigne, 1992; Kehle, 1990; Pigott & Gonzales, 1987) employing self-modeling with children who had SM were identified in the literature. Two studies (Kehle, 1990; Pigott & Gonzales, 1987) employed edited video tapes so that the child appeared to be talking in settings or to people to whom he or she usually did not. For example, Kehle, Owen, and Cressy (1990) had the child's mother come to the classroom and ask a set of nine prearranged questions when the classroom was empty. Later, the teacher was taped asking the same questions and her tape was spliced with the child's to make it appear that the child was speaking to the teacher. It appears that it is essential to remove all instances of the nontarget behavior(s) and to provide long segments which show the target child speaking. Videotapes of the child performing the target behavior can also be used as reinforcement for continued improvement (Holmbeck & Lavigne, 1992).

Response Initiation Procedures

If the child is unresponsive to contingency management, stimulus fading, or self-modeling procedures, more extreme steps may be necessary to establish initial communication. Labbe and Williamson (1984) suggested that shaping, response cost, reinforcement sampling and escape procedures could all be used to initiate speech. Three recent studies were identified which used these procedures to establish initial communication.

Shaping is probably the least intrusive procedure used to establish initial communication with children who have SM. Unfortunately, it appears to require far more time and patience than other initial communication procedures. Bayley and Hirst (1991) shaped speech by first having the child write yes or no to respond to questions. In the next phase of treatment, the child was required to whisper responses to questions. Next, she was prompted to read a book to her teacher and subsequently to her class in a full voice. In this case, after the child read her book to the teacher, she was reported to continue to speak freely and in normal volume to her classmates and teacher. It appears likely that in this case, with each approximation of typical verbal communication, the child came under increasing control of natural reinforcers for speaking which subsequently maintained her improved verbal behavior.

Two studies (Krohn, Weckstein, & Wright, 1992; Lysne, 1995) employed escape behaviors to establish initial communication with children who had SM. In an escape procedure, the individual conducting the intervention first builds some level of trust and rapport with the child even if the child does not speak. Part of the rapport-building includes clear communication that the child will be expected to speak before leaving the room at some set point in the future. On the established day, the child is told that he must say a certain number of words before he or she can leave. The task of the interventionist is then to ensure that the child speaks before leaving the room. Cautions that although this technique is effective, it is not to be considered lightly appear in both reports. The procedure is often quite unpleasant for the child and failed escape procedures are associated with increased resistance to subsequent treatments. Both reports also clearly state that establishing initial communication with a child needs to be followed up with additional treatments (e.g., contingency management, stimulus fading). A third report (Mosak, 1995) of successful use of escape procedures to establish speech was found in the literature. The clients in this report, however, were adults with schizophrenia. Nevertheless, the escape procedure established communication where other methods had previously failed.

Summary of Behavioral Interventions

In general, the behavioral literature is the most straight forward approach to treatment available to children with SM. It requires little special equipment. Practitioners and lay persons can be trained to implement it, particularly if professional supervision is a part of the treatment package. Seven general recommendations emerge from the behavioral literature:

1. Reinforce speech or communicative behavior in environments where it is currently exhibited
2. Increase verbal interactions with target person in current "speech environment," then transfer target person to non-speech environment
3. Use stimulus fading to transfer speech from target individual to natural stimuli
4. Use successive approximation of speech act (e.g., move from yes/no questions to more open-ended questions)
5. Extinguish non-verbal behavior which serves same function as speech (e.g., head gestures for yes and no)
6. Consider technology to provide self-modeling experiences to support increased verbalizations
7. If the child fails to respond to less intensive initial communication prompts, escape procedures should be carefully considered.

CONCLUSION

Selective mutism remains a somewhat mysterious condition which affects a very small number of children. It continues to evoke interest which is disproportionate to its rate of occurrence. Early reports of SM contain sketchy assessment and identification information at best. Although this remains a characteristic of the literature, a number of researchers have adapted traditional assessment devices to SM or developed SM-specific assessment protocols. The improved assessment procedures are likely to refine the SM construct by allowing discrimination between SM and conditions with similar behavioral manifestations. A particularly promising development in assessment for children with SM is found in the application of functional assessment to determine the likely environmental supports for the SM. Functional assessments of the environmental supports of SM are likely to more effectively link intervention to identification procedures.

Another development in the consideration and treatment of children with SM is in the etiological link between SM and anxiety disorders, hereditary factors, and models of multiply determined vulnerability. SM appears to be moving away from more traditional psychodynamic theories which place the cause of the condition on the shoulders of the parents or at the foot of some traumatic event to a more open position which considers the family as a part of the treatment team. This is not to say that children with SM never come from dysfunctional homes. Certainly some do and the strain of raising a child with SM is likely to affect the family in a variety of ways which have yet to be identified. However, it currently appears that like autism, SM has a far more complicated etiology than dysfunctional interactions with the family.

The most common forms of intervention for SM continue to be from the psychodynamic and behavioral schools. Behavioral treatments continue to outperform the psychodynamic treatments in terms of overall effectiveness and efficiency. Two additional forms of intervention appear to hold promise for certain children with SM, interventions to establish functional speech and language skills and interventions employing anti-anxiety drugs such as fluoxetine. Given the probability that SM is a multiply determined condition, it is likely that treatment packages employing two or more of these approaches will, in the long run, prove to be most efficacious for most children with SM.

Despite progress in a number of areas, much remains to be learned about SM. A robust mythology exists to fill the voids in our knowledge base. Many of these myths are counterproductive and misdirect attention from more effective pursuits. Therefore, practitioners hold the dual responsibility of intervening effectively with children who have SM and correcting misconceptions of other professionals, parents, and sometimes, even the children themselves regarding the nature and causes of SM. One thing that is unlikely to change is the challenge such children present to their families, educators, and other concerned individuals.

REFERENCES

Abidin, R. (1983). *Parenting stress index.* Charlottesville, VA: Pediatric Psychology Press.

Achenbach, T. T., & Edelbrook, C. (1983). *Manual for the child behavior checklist and revised child behavior profile.* Burlington, VT: University of Vermont, Department of Psychiatry.

American Psychiatric Association. (1994). *Diagnostic and statistical manual of mental disorders-IV*. Washington, DC: Author.

Atlas, J. A. (1993). Symbol use in a case of elective mutism. *Perceptual & Motor Skills, 76*, 1079–1082.

Atoynatan, T.H. (1986). Elective mutism: Involvement of the mother in the treatment of the child. *Child Psychiatry and Human Development, 1*(17), 15–27.

Ausubel, D. P. (1963). *The psychology of meaningful learning*. New York: Grune and Stratton.

Baldwin, S., & Cline, T. (1991). Helping children who are selectively mute. *Educational and Child Psychology, 8*(3), 72–83.

Baptiste, D. A. (1995). Therapy with a lesbian stepfamily with an electively mute child: A case report. *Journal of Family Psychotherapy, 6*(1), 1–14.

Barlow, K., Strother, J., & Landreth, G. (1986). Sibling group play therapy: An effective alternative with an elective mute child. *School Counselor, 34*(1), 44–50.

Barrios, B. A., Hartman, D. P., & Shigetomi, C. (1981). Fears and anxieties in children. In E. J. Mash & L. G. Terdal (Eds.), *Behavioral assessment of childhood disorders* (pp. 259–304). New York: Guilford Press.

Bayley, S., & Hirst, S. (1991). A child who did not speak at school: The constructive use of a support worker for behaviour. *Maladjustment and Therapeutic Education 9*, 104–110.

Beirne-Smith, M., Patton, J. R., & Ittenbach, R. (1994). *Mental retardation*. New York: Merrill.

Beitchman, J. H., & Inglis, A. (1991). The continuum of linguistic dysfunction from pervasive developmental disorders to dyslexia. *Psychiatric Clinics of North America, 14*(1), 95–111.

Biederman, J., Spencer, T., & Wilens, T. (1997). Psychopharmacology. In J.M. Wiener (Ed.), *Textbook of child and adolescent psychiatry* (2nd ed., pp. 779–812). Washington, DC: American Psychiatric Press.

Black, B. (1996). Reply to Szabo (1996): Selective mutism and social anxiety. *Journal of the American Academy of Child & Adolescent Psychiatry, 35*, 555.

Black, B., Leonard, H., & Rapoport, J. L. (1997). Specific phobia, panic disorder, social phobia, and selective mutism. In J.M. Wiener (Ed.), *Textbook of child and adolescent psychiatry* (2nd ed., pp. 491–506). Washington, DC: American Psychiatric Press.

Black, B., & Uhde, T. W. (1992). Elective mutism as a variant of social phobia. *Journal of the American Academy of Child and Adolescent Psychiatry, 31*, 1090–1094.

Black, B., & Uhde, T. W. (1994). Treatment of elective mutism with fluoxetine: A double-blind, placebo-controlled study. *Journal of the American Academy of Child and Adolescent Psychiatry, 33*, 1000–1006.

Black, B., & Uhde, T. W. (1995). Psychiatric characteristics of children with selective mutism: A pilot study. *Journal of the American Academy of Child and Adolescent Psychiatry, 34*, 847–856.

Bow, J. N. (1997). Play therapy with the resistant child. In H.G. Kaduson, D. Cangelosi, & C. E. Schaefer (Eds.), *The playing cure: Individualized therapy for specific childhood problems* (pp. 317–336). Northvale, NJ: Jason Aronson Press.

Brigham, F. J., & Cole, J. E. (1997, April). *Children with selective mutism: Definition, identification, and intervention*. Paper presented at the annual meeting of the Council for Exceptional Children, Salt Lake City, UT.

Carr, A., & Afnan, S. (1989). Concurrent individual and family therapy in a case of elective mutism. *Journal of Family Therapy, 11*, 29–44.

Cline, T., & Baldwin, S. (1994). *Selective mutism in children*. San Diego: Singular.

Cole, C. L., & Gardner, W. I. (1993). Psychotherapy with developmentally delayed children. In T. R. Kratochwill & R. J. Morris (Eds.), *Handbook of psychotherapy with children and adolescents* (pp. 426–471). New York: Pergamon.

Cook, J.-A. L. (1997). Play therapy for selective mutism. In H. G. Kaduson, D. M. Cangelosi, & C. E. Schaefer (Eds.), *The playing cure: Individualized play therapy for specific childhood problems* (pp. 83–115). Northvale, NJ: Jason Aronson, Inc.

Costello, A. J., Edelbrock, C. S., Kalas, R., Kessler, M. K., & Klaric, S. A. (1982). *N.I.M.H. Diagnostic interview schedule for children.* Bethesda, MD: National Institute of Mental Health.

Costello, E. J., Edelbrock, C. S., & Costello, A. J. (1985). Validity of the NIMH Diagnostic Interview Schedule for Children: A comparison between psychiatric and pediatric referrals. *Journal of Abnormal Child Psychology, 13,* 579–595.

Cunningham, C. E., Cataldo, M. F., Mallion, C., & Keyes, J. B. (1983). A review and controlled single case evaluation of behavioral approaches to the management of elective mutism. *Child & Family Behavior Therapy, 5*(4), 25–49.

DiSimoni, F. (1978). *The token test for children.* Boston, MA: Teaching Resources Corporation.

Dorwick, P. W., & Dove, C. (1980). The use of self-modeling to improve the swimming performance of spina bifida children. *Journal of Applied Behavior Analysis, 13,* 51–56.

Dow, S. P., Sonies, B. C., Scheib, D., & Moss, S. E. (1995). Practical guidelines for the assessment and treatment of selective mutism. *Journal of the American Academy of Child and Adolescent Psychiatry, 34*(7), 836–846.

Dummit, E. S., Klein, R. G., Tancer, N. K., Asche, B., & Martin, J. (1996). Fluoxetine treatment of children with selective mutism: An open trial. *Journal of the American Academy of Child and Adolescent Psychiatry, 35,* 615–621.

Dummit, E. S., Klein, R. G., Tancer, N. K., & Asche, B. (1997). Systematic assessment of 50 children with selective mutism. *Journal of the American Academy of Child and Adolescent Psychiatry, 36,* 653–660.

Dunn, L. M., & Dunn, M. (1997). *Peabody picture vocabulary test-III.* Circle Pines, MN: American Guidance Service.

Fuchs, L. S., Fuchs, D., Hamlett, C. L., Walz, L., & Germann, G. (1993). Formative evaluation of academic progress: How much growth can we expect? *School Psychology Review, 22*(1), 27–48.

Fulk, B. J. M., Brigham, F. J., & Lohman, D. A. (in press). Motivation and self-regulation: A comparison of students with learning and behavior problems. *Remedial and Special Education.*

Fundudis, T., Kolvin, I., & Garside, R. (1979). *Speech retarded and deaf children: Their psychological development.* London: Academic Press.

Golwyn, D. H., & Weinstock, R. C. (1990). Phenelzine treatment of elective mutism: A case report. *Journal of Clinical Psychiatry, 51*(9), 384–385.

Hadley, N. H. (1994). *Elective mutism: A Handbook for educators, counselors, and health care professionals.* Norwell, MA: Kluwer Academic Publishers.

Halpern, W. I., Hammond, J., & Choen, R. (1971). A therapeutic approach to speech phobia: Elective mutism reexamined. *Journal of the American Academy of Child Psychiatry, 10,* 94–107.

Hammill, D. D., & Newcomer, P. L. (1982). *The test of language development.* Austin, TX: PRO-ED.

Hammill, D., Pearson, N., & Weiderholt, L. (1996). *Comprehensive test of nonverbal intelligence.* Austin, TX: PRO-ED.

Harris, H.F. (1996). Elective mutism: A tutorial. *Language, Speech, and Hearing Services in Schools, 27,* 10–15.

Hasbrouck, J. E., & Tindal, G. (1992). Curriculum-based oral reading fluency norms for students in grades 2 through 5. *Teaching Exceptional Children, 24*(3), 41–44.

Hathaway, S. R., & McKinley, J. C. (1989). *Minnesota Multiphasic Personality Inventory-2.* Minneapolis, MN: National Computer Services.

Hayden, T. L. (1980). Classification of elective mutism. *Journal of the American Academy of Child Psychiatry, 19,* 118–133.

Herjanic, B., & Reich, W. (1982). Development of a structured psychiatric interview for children: Agreement between child and parent on individual symptoms. *Journal of Abnormal Child Psychology, 10,* 307–324.

Herjanic, B., & Reich, W. (1997). Development of a structured psychiatric interview for children: Agreement between child and parent on individual symptoms. *Journal of Abnormal Child Psychology, 25*(1), 21–31.

Hoffman, J. A. (1996). Not with a bang but a whisper: Mental health consultation with a selectively mute child. *Early Childhood Education Journal, 23*, 207–210.

Holmbeck, G. N., & Lavigne, J. V. (1992). Combining self-modeling and stimulus fading in the treatment of an electively mute child. *Psychotherapy, 29*, 661–667.

Hooper, S. R., & Linz, T. D. (1992). Elective mutism. In S.R. Hooper, G. W. Hynd, & R. E. Mattison (Eds.), *Child psychopathology: Diagnostic criteria and clinical assessment* (pp. 409–459). Hillsdale, NJ: Lawrence Erlbaum Associates.

Jacobsen, T. (1995). Case study: Is selective mutism a manifestation of dissociative identity disorder? *Journal of the American Academy of Child and Adolescent Psychiatry, 34*, 863–866.

Kehle, T. J. (1990). Self-modeling for children's emotional and social concerns. In P. W. Dowrick (Ed.), *Practical guide to using video in the behavioral sciences* (pp. 244–255). New York: John Wiley & Sons.

Kehle, T. J., Owen, S. V., & Cressy, E. T. (1990). The use of self-modeling as an intervention in school psychology: A case study of an elective mute. *School Psychology Review, 19*(1), 115–121.

Kelly, M. L., Heffner, R. W., Gresham, F. M., & Elliott, S. N. (1989). Development of a modified Treatment Evaluation Inventory. *Journal of Psychopathology and Behavioral Assessment, 11*, 235–247.

Klien, R. G. (1988). Childhood anxiety disorders. In C. J. Kestenbaum & D. T. Williams (Eds.), *Handbook of clinical assessment of children and adolescents* (Vol. 2, pp. 722–742). New York: New York University Press.

Klin, A., & Volkmar, F. R. (1993). Case study: Selective mutism and mental retardation. *Journal of the American Academy of Child and Adolescent Psychiatry, 32*, 860–864.

Kolvin, I., & Fundudis, T. (1981). Elective mute children: Psychological development and background factors. *Journal of Child Psychology and Psychiatry, 22*, 219–232.

Koplewicz, H. S., & Williams, D. T. (1987). Psychopharmological treatment. In C. J. Kestenbaum & D. T. Williams (Eds.), *Handbook of clinical assessment of children and adolescents* (Vol. 2, pp. 1084–1110). New York: New York University Press.

Kopp, S., & Gillberg, C. (1997). Selective mutism: A population-based study: A research note. *Journal of Child Psychology & Psychiatry & Allied Disciplines, 38*, 257–262.

Kovacs, M., & Beck, A. (1977). An empirical-clinical approach toward a definition of childhood depression. In J. Schulterbrandt & A. Raskin (Eds.), *Depression in childhood: Diagnosis. treatment, and conceptual methods* (pp. 1–26). New York: Raven Press.

Kratochwill, T. (1981). *Selective mutism: Implications for research and treatment*. Hillsdale, NJ: Lawrence Erlbaum.

Krohn, D. D., Weckstein, S. M., & Wright, H. L. (1992). A study of the effectiveness of a specific treatment for elective mutism. *Journal of the American Academy of Child & Adolescent Psychiatry, 31*, 711–718.

Labbe, E. E., & Williamson, D. A. (1984). Behavioral treatments of elective mutism: A review of the literature. *Clinical Psychology Review, 4*, 273–292.

Lachenmeyer, J. R., & Gibbs, M. S. (1985). The social-psychological functions of reward in the treatment of a case of elective mutism. *Journal of Social and Clinical Psychology, 3*, 466–473.

Lesser-Katz, M. (1988). The treatment of elective mutism as stranger reaction. *Psychotherapy, 25*, 305–313.

Louden, D. M. (1987). Elective mutism: A case study of a disorder of childhood. *Journal of the National Medical Association, 79*, 1043–1048.

Lumb, D., & Wolff, D. (1988). "Mary doesn't talk." *British Journal of Special Education, 15*, 103–106.

Lysne, A. (1995). Elective mutism: Special treatment of a special case. *Scandinavian Journal of Educational Research, 39*(2), 93–97.

Markwardt, F. (1989). *Peabody individual achievement test—revised*. Circle Pines, MN: American Guidance Service.

Marlowe, B. A., & Page, M. L. (1998). *Creating and sustaining the constructivist classroom.* Thousand Oaks, CA: Corwin Press.

Masten, W. G., Stacks, J. R., Caldwell-Colbert, A. T., & Jackson, J. S. (1996). Behavioral treatment of a selective mute Mexican-American boy. *Psychology in the Schools, 33*(1), 56–60.

Matson, J. L., Box, M. L., & Francis, K. L. (1992). Treatment of elective mute behavior in two developmentally delayed children using modeling and contingency management. *Journal of Behavior Therapy & Experimental Psychiatry, 23*, 221–229.

Meyers, S.-V. (1984). Elective mutism in children: A family systems approach. *American Journal of Family Therapy, 12*(4), 39–45.

Miller, I., Epstien, N., Bishop, D., & Keitner, G. (1985). The McMaster Family Assessment Device: Reliability and validity. *Journal of Marital and Family Therapy, 11*, 345–356.

Mosak, H. H. (1995). Drugless psychotherapy with schizophrenics. *Individual Psychology: Journal of Adlerian Theory, Research & Practice, 51*(1), 61–66.

Motavalli, N. (1995). Fluoxetine for (s)elective mutism. *Journal of the American Academy of Child & Adolescent Psychiatry, 34*, 701–702.

National Institute of Mental Health. (1991). *NIMH diagnostic interview schedule for children.* Rockville, MD: National Institute of Mental Health.

Paez, P. (1988). Oppositional disorder and elective mutism. In C. J. Kestenbaum & D. T. Williams (Eds.), *Handbook of clinical assessment of children and adolescents* (pp. 800–811). New York: New York University Press.

Pecukonis, E. V., & Pecukonis, M. T. (1991). An adapted language training strategy in the treatment of an electively mute male child. *Journal of Behavior Therapy and Experimental Psychiatry, 22* (1), 9–21.

Pigott, H. E., & Gonzales, F. P. (1987). Efficacy of videotape self-modeling in treating an electively mute child. *Journal of Clinical Child Psychology, 16*, 106–110.

Porjes, M. D. (1992). Intervention with the selectively mute child. *Psychology in the Schools, 29*, 367–376.

Powell, S., & Dalley, M. (1995). When to intervene in selective mutism: The multimodal treatment of a case of persistent selective mutism. *Psychology in the Schools, 32*, 114–123.

Quay, H. C., & Peterson, D. R. (1987). *Manual for the revised behavior problem checklist.* Coral Gables, FL: Authors.

Rae, G. (1995). "Therapy with a lesbian stepfamily with an electively mute child": A comment. *Journal of Family Psychotherapy, 6*(1), 15–20.

Randle, K. D. (1995). *The only alien on the planet.* New York: Scholastic.

Ratner, J. F. (1995). Amy: A young woman chooses to be mute. In M. A. Blotzer & R. Ruth (Eds.), *Sometimes you just want to feel like a human being: Case studies of empowering psychotherapy with people with disabilities* (pp. 135–149). Baltimore, MD: Paul H. Brookes.

Reynolds, C. R., & Richmond, B. O. (1985). *Revised children's manifest anxiety scale.* Los Angeles: Western Psychological Services.

Richburg, M.-L., & Cobia, D.-C. (1994). Using behavioral techniques to treat elective mutism: A case study. *Elementary School Guidance and Counseling, 28*, 214–220.

Roe, V. (1993). An interactive therapy group. *Child Language Teaching & Therapy, 9*(2), 133–140.

Roid, G., & Miller, N. (1997). *Leiter international performance scale—Revised.* Chicago: Stoelting.

Rutter, M. (1977). Delayed speech. In M. Rutter & L. Hersov (Eds.), *Child psychiatry: Modern approaches.* Oxford, UK: Blackwell Scientific.

Sattler, J. M. (1992). *Assessment of children.* (3rd ed.). San Diego, CA: Jerome M. Sattler Publisher.

Schill, M. T., Kratochwill, T. R., & Gardner, W. I. (1996). An assessment protocol for selective mutism: Analogue assessment using parents as facilitators. *Journal of School Psychology, 34*(1), 1–21.

Schmerling, J. D., & Kerins, M. R. (1987). Stimulating communication in a child with elective mutism: Collaborative interventions. *American Journal of Dance Therapy, 10*, 27–40.

Scruggs, T. E., Mastropieri, M. A., Fomess, S. R., & Kavale, K. A. (1988). Early language intervention: A quantitative synthesis of single subject research. *Journal of Special Education, 22*, 259–282.

Shreeve, D. F. (1991). Elective mutism: Origins in stranger anxiety and selective attention. *Bulletin of the Menninger Clinic, 55*, 491–504.

Silver, L. B. (1989). Elective mutism. In H. I. Kaplan & B. J. Sadock (Eds.), *Comprehensive textbook of psychiatry* (5th ed., Vol. 2, pp. 1887–1889). Baltimore: Williams and Wilkins.

Simons, D., Goode, S., & Fombonne, E. (1997). Elective mutism and chromosome 18 abnormality. *European Child & Adolescent Psychiatry, 6*, 112–114.

Steinhausen, H. C., & Adamek, R. (1997). The family history of selective mutism: A research report. *European Journal of Adolescent Psychiatry, 6*, 107–111.

Steinhausen, H. C., & Juzi, C. (1996). Elective mutism: An analysis of 100 cases. *Journal of the American Academy of Child and Adolescent Psychiatry, 35*, 606–614.

Szabo, C. P. (1996). Selective mutism and social anxiety. *Journal of the American Academy of Child and Adolescent Psychiatry, 35*, 555.

Tancer, N. K. (1992). Elective mutism: A review of the literature. *Advances in clinical child psychology, 14*, 265–278.

Tatem, D. W., & DelCampo, R. L. (1995). Selective mutism in children: A structural family therapy approach to treatment. *Contemporary Family Therapy: An International Journal, 17*, 177–194.

Trad, P. V. (1989). *The preschool child: Assessment and treatment*. New York: Wiley.

Watson, T. S., & Kramer, J. J. (1992). Multimethod behavioral treatment of long-term selective mutism. *Psychology in the Schools, 29*, 359–366.

Weckstein, S. M., Krohn, D. D., & Wright, H. L. (1995). Elective mutism. In A. R. Eisen, C. A. Kearney, & C. E. Schaefer (Eds.), *Clinical handbook of anxiety disorders in children and adolescents* (pp. 169–194). Northvale, NJ: Jason Aronson Inc.

Wirt, R., Lachar, D., Klinedist, J., & Seat, P. (1977). *Multidimensional description of child personality: A manual for the Personality Inventory for Children*. Los Angeles: Western Psychological Services.

World Health Organization (1992). *The ICD-10 classification of mental and behavioural disorders: Clinical descriptions and diagnostic guidelines*. Geneva, Switzerland: Author.

Wright, H. H., & Cuccaro, M. L. (1994). Selective mutism continued. *Journal of the American Academy of Child and Adolescent Psychiatry, 33*, 593–594.

Wright, H. H., Cuccaro, M. L., Leonhardt, T. V., Kendall, D. F., & Anderson, J. H. (1995). Case study: Fluoxetine in the multimodal treatment of a preschool child with selective mutism. *Journal of the American Academy of Child and Adolescent Psychiatry, 34*, 857–862.

Wright, H. H., Holmes, G. R., Cuccaro, M. L., & Leonhardt, T. V. (1994). A guided bibliography of the selective mutism (elective mutism) literature. *Psychological Reports, 74*, 995–1007.

Zigler, E., & Hodapp, R. M. (1986). *Understanding mental retardation*. New York: Cambridge University Press.

FROM EARLY INFANTILE AUTISM TO AN AUTISTIC SPECTRUM: AN ANALYSIS OF THEORETICAL PERSPECTIVES

Ina van Berckelaer-Onnes and Daniela Lucangeli

ABSTRACT

Since Kanner's famous article about autism (1943), many researchers and clinicians have attempted to solve the enigma of this complex disorder. In this chapter, an overview of the different viewpoints are given, with the emphasis on recent cognitive theories. Will the theory of mind, the central coherence theory, executive functioning, or the coming personal relatedness theory offer bridges between behavior, mind, and brain? We are closer to the nature of the autistic disorder, but further research is still needed.

The autistic disorder is today considered to be a neurobiological disorder characterized by certain behavioral features. The severity and the nature of behavior in autistic disorders have attracted the interest of many researchers and clinicians. Although relatively rare (around 4 cases in every 10,000 births), its symptoms have a major impact on the child, the family, the school, the community, and society.

Advances in Learning and Behavioral Disabilities, Volume 13, pages 217–244.

ISBN: 0-7623-0429-4

The autistic disorder has been and today still is a challenge in all fields of interest and research connected with child development. A survey of studies on autism reveals that our present understanding of autism derives from different areas of research. Some studies are concerned with the biological and physiological causes, some with its psychological aspects, others with its social implications, and again others with childrearing questions.

AN HISTORICAL PERSPECTIVE

In 1801, for the first time, a child who was probably autistic became the subject of re-education in every sense. Jean Itard, doctor at the Institute for the Deaf and Mute of Paris, took up the challenge to educate a "wild boy," Victor, found abandoned in the Ayeron forest. Itard believed he had before him a pure human being, uncontaminated by culture, to whom the pedagogical principles of Jean-Jacques Rousseau could be applied. Reading the notes left by Itard with the knowledge of today, the boy described may have been an autistic child abandoned by his parents (Brauner & Brauner, 1978).

In the last century psychiatrists did not recognize a specific pathology for children affected by autism. Psychotic children, especially if they were autistic, were grouped together with the mentally retarded and without appropriate treatment they soon behaved like them.

It was only at the beginning of this century that childhood psychosis was mentioned. It was described as precocious dementia (Heller, 1909), which was explicit acknowledgement of a mental status different from that of the mentally retarded; but the term precocious was used to emphasize the early age of onset of an adult disease, while the concept of dementia implied a once normally developed psychological organization.

In 1933 Potter used the concept schizophrenia in children, indicating a disorder specific to children. However, the simple semiotic transfer from adults to children failed, because the model based on adult pathology was applied without modification to children. It was not until 1943 that Kanner, an American child psychiatrist of Austrian origin, reported eleven cases of children with a very particular symptomatology:

> Since 1938, there have come to our attention a number of children whose condition differs so markedly and uniquely from anything reported so far, that each case merits—and, I hope, will eventually receive—a detailed consideration of its fascinating peculiarities (Kanner, 1943, p. 217).

Kanner proposed the term "early infantile autism" for this symptomatology (Kanner, 1943). The common denominator for all of these patients was the inability from birth to establish normal relationships. In the same period, and quite independently, the Austrian Asperger (1944) described a group of children using the concept "autistic psychopathy." Kanner and Asperger were both born in Austria and trained in Vienna, but they never met each other. They both used the term autism, which was coined by Bleuler (1911) describing the condition of schizophrenic patients. Derived from the Greek "autos," meaning "self," the word autism was used to describe an erosion of relationships with people and the outside world that was so severe that it seemed to lead to the exclusion of everything except the person's own self. The word clearly reflects one of the most evident symptoms described in the earliest clinical reports. It was Kanner who changed the approach to the study of childhood autism by abandoning the common practice of referring to standards used for adults. He formulated the first behavioral descriptions that are still fundamental for the diagnosis of autism today.

In his publication of 1943, and in later observations, Kanner refers to a very specific symptomatology characterized by distinct behavioral traits. Kanner's cases exhibited the following symptoms in the early years of life:

1. *An extreme autistic aloneness*: the subjects seem to be mentally alone:

> From the beginning the tendency towards an extreme autistic solitude is present, that whenever possible, inhibits access to anything that reaches the child from the exterior. He has a good relation with objects; he can play with them for hours . . . the relation of the child with people is totally different. . . A deep solitude dominates his whole behaviour. . . . An autistic child's relationship with people is very peculiar. He passes them by without trying to establish any communication; when he establishes relationships they prove to be fragmented. He does not demonstrate any reaction to the loss of his parents and seems to ignore them, he does not participate in collective play with other children (Kanner, 1943, p. 220).

Kanner noticed certain characteristics of the autistic child: self-absorption, inaccessibility, solitude and an inability to form human relationships. From the case of Frederick (case 2 described by Kanner), "I could leave him alone and he'd entertain himself very happily . . . . I have never known him to cry in demanding attention" (p. 221). Charles' mother, from case 9, stated, "I can't reach my baby. . . . He would pay no attention to me and show no recognition of me if I entered the room. . . . The most impressive thing is his detachment and his inaccessibility" (p. 223).

2. *An anxiously obsessive desire for the preservation of sameness*, shown by simple repetitive movements, utterances, thoughts, by elaborate routines and by an extreme narrowing of interests. The desire for changelessness is shown by an obsessive and anguished reaction to every change in the surrounding environment. The compulsive desire for changelessness cannot be overcome by anyone except the child himself. "The noises, movements and other actions of the child are monotonously repeated just like his verbal expressions. There is an enormous limitation in his spontaneous actions" (p. 230).

> When John's parents began to move to a new house, the child went crazy when he saw the movers roll the carpet in his room, and remained very deranged until the carpet was placed in the same

way as before; only then he appeared satisfied, the anxiety disappeared rapidly and he began to turn about the carpet caressing every piece of it (p. 232).

An autistic child grasps details but is not able to understand the totality of the structure. His thoughts are based on appearances instead of functions: he establishes only formal relationships. From the case of Frederick (case 2 described by Kanner):

> To a certain extent, his mother said, he likes to stick to the same things. On one of the bookshelves at home there were three pieces in a certain arrangement. Whenever this was changed, he always rearranged it in the old pattern. By the age of six, he could count up into the hundreds and read numbers, but he was not interested in numbers as they applied to objects (p. 221).

From the case of Virginia (case 6 described by Kanner): "The child will amuse herself for hours putting picture puzzles together, sticking to them until they are done" (p. 234). From the case of Charles (case 9 described by Kanner): "When he was one and half years old, he began to spend hours spinning toys and lids of bottles and jars" (p. 237).

3. *The presence of islands of ability such as excellent rote memory*, recollection of complex patterns and sequences, and astounding vocabulary, apart from the use of pronouns. The author observes:

> The astonishing vocabulary of children that speak, the excellent memory for situations many years before, the exceptional memory for poems and names, and the precise remembrance of complex modality and sequences, denote good intelligence in the sense in which this word is commonly used (p. 220).

From the case of Donald (case 1 described by Kanner): "He was encouraged by the family in learning and reciting short poems, and even the Twenty-third Psalm and twenty-five questions and answers of the Presbyterian Catechism" (p. 224). From the case of Charles (case 9 described by Kanner): "He could discriminate between eighteen symphonies. He recognized the composer as soon as the first movement started" (p. 237). From the case of Elaine (case 11 described by Kanner): "She reads very well, but she reads fast, jumbling words, not pronouncing clearly, and not making proper emphases. Her range of information is really quite wide, and her memory almost infallible" (p. 241).

4. *The great delay in or lack of speech acquisition*. Speech, when acquired (autistic children are often mute), rarely performs a communicative function, consisting instead of a repetitive echo of words overheard:

> There were no essential differences between those who spoke and those who did not. . . . When phrases are formed, they are for a long time repeated parrot-like combinations of words; sometimes the children make an echo immediately, but often they conserve them and they pronounce them one after the other. If one wishes he can speak about echolalia (p. 224).

Comparing Kanner's and Asperger's descriptions of autistic children, it is clear that many of the standards still used today to describe the characteristic traits originate from their early work. In their case descriptions both Kanner and Asperger

- stressed the difficulties of social adaptation;
- pointed out the isolated interests, often in bizarre or idiosyncratic objects;
- paid particular attention to stereotypic movements or expressions such as the marked resistance to change;
- were impressed by occasional performances which displayed narrow intellectual ability;
- described the lack of flexible imaginative play.

Kanner and Asperger differed in their view of

- language skills (in Kanner's subjects language was not used communicatively, but Asperger detailed evidence of fluent speech);
- motor abilities (clumsy only in gross motor skills, in Kanner's opinion; clumsy in both gross and fine motor skills, according to Asperger);
- learning abilities (Kanner thought the children learned by rote; Asperger described them as abstract thinkers).

The hypotheses about the causes of autism and the standards used for its clinical diagnosis derive from these early observations.

TOWARDS A DIAGNOSIS

Different systems have been used for the diagnosis of autism. These include the original Kanner (1943) criteria, the nine points of Creak (1961), Rutter's (1978) definition, and the Rutter and Schopler update of that of the National Society for Autistic Children (NSAC, 1978). Although widely used for clinical research, these five systems have not been combined into a formal rating scale (see Schopler & Mesibov, 1988).

Historically Kanner's definition (1943) constitutes the first system for the diagnosis of childhood autism. In the years following Kanner's publications, many authors described children who showed similar characteristics, thus creating controversy about the basic symptoms and leading to the proposal of additional diagnostic elements.

In 1961, the British Working Party directed by Creak defined nine specific standards in order to expand the description of autism into a fuller definition that would also incorporate child schizophrenia. The standards of the British Working Party were, however, widely criticized. In the first place, they were based on behavioral observations rather than on the construction of a reference theory. Second, they were difficult to use because they were not quantitative. Third, the lack of reference to development made them particularly difficult to apply to young children.

In 1978, reviewing the diagnosis of autism by conducting a survey of over 100 studies of autistic children, Rutter extrapolated four criteria present in almost all cases (Rutter 1978, p. 156):

1. an onset before the age of 30 months;
2. impaired social development that has a number of special characteristics and is out of keeping with the child's intellectual level;
3. a delayed deviant language development that also has certain defined features and is out of keeping with the child's intellectual level;
4. insistence on sameness, as shown by stereotyped play patterns, abnormal preoccupations or resistance to change.

In the same year, the National Society for Autistic Children (NSAC) published an article about the diagnosis of autism in which a delay in development and an abnormal response to sensory stimuli were included among the diagnostic symptoms. Of all of these definitions, Rutter's (1978) proved to be the most useful for diagnostic purposes, probably because, like the original description by Kanner (1943), the points of reference were more closely related to clinical experience.

It is beyond the scope of this review to summarize the development of the clinical debate about the diagnostic criteria for autism. It is, however, important to note that the most recent classification systems were formulated by the American Psychiatric Association (APA), and by the World Health Organization (WHO), but that there is still disagreement about the criteria used. The APA has included the autistic disorder in the Diagnostic and Statistical Manual of Mental Disorders since 1980 (APA DSM-III 1980). In 1992 the World Health Organization provided a categorical definition (ICD-10) which differed from that in DSM-III and DSM-IIIR. In ICD-10, the diagnosis of autism is established on the basis of four features:

1. onset before the age of three, defined by delayed or deviant communication, social interaction, and/or play;
2. qualitative impairment of social interaction;
3. qualitative impairment of communication;
4. restricted repetitive and stereotyped patterns of behavior, interests, and activities.

The ICD X includes also different categories for individuals with other forms of pervasive developmental disorders (e.g. Rett syndrome, Asperger syndrome, Childhood Disintegrative Disorder), attachment disorders, schizophrenia, specific developmental language disorders with secondary socio-emotional problems, and mental retardation with associated emotional/behavioral disorders.

However, the most widely used diagnostic standard today is DSM-IV (1994). This places autism within the clinical disorders of axis I and bases diagnosis on the following standards:

- qualitative impairment of social interactions;
- qualitative impairment of communication;
- limited patterns of behavior, repeated and stereotyped interests and activities.

Moreover, with onset prior to three years, delay or abnormality will be seen in at least one of the following areas: social interactions, speech as a means of social communication, symbolic and imaginative play.

It is interesting to observe that in the 1980 edition of the DSM (DSM-III), the autistic syndrome was classified in axis I (Clinical Disorders), whereas in the 1987 edition (DSM-IIIR) it was put in axis II (Personality and Developmental Disorders); in the latest edition (DSM-IV) (1994), it is again classified in axis I. These changes reflect the ongoing debate about the nature of autism and emphasize the abnormal aspects of development as distinct from mental abnormalities that appear in adulthood (Rutter & Schopler, 1987). Since fewer than 20 percent of autistic children have an IQ within the normal range, the autistic syndrome must also be distinguished from mental handicap, which is another clinical problem that the different classification systems have only partially solved.

In view of the difficulties of diagnosis, Wing (1980, 1993, 1996) recommended an assessment based on the DSM criteria which could be used to identify the specific characteristics of autism. She refers to a spectrum of autistic disorders that must be accompanied by the triad of impairments of social interaction, communication, and imagination. These symptoms are also associated with rigid and repetitive behavior. Wing suggests checking for the presence of other associated disturbances: developmental, physical or psychiatric (a frequent example is an associative depression disorder).

It appears from literature as well as clinical observation that neither the DSM-IV nor the ICD-10 is sufficient in itself for complete formulation of a diagnosis of autism. The assessment must include other values. However, the classification of a clinical disorder is based only on behavioral features and not the whole person, although every case is different and requires individual attention (Van Yperen, Van Berckelaer-Onnes, & Rispens, 1992). This is particularly true in the case of autism.

ETIOLOGICAL ISSUES

What are the causes of the autistic disorder? Theorists and investigators have put forward theories about the origin and development of the autistic disorder that can be divided into three basic approaches: psychogenetic hypothesis; biological factors (genetic and organic); and cognitive approach.

Psychogenetic Hypothesis

There are some theoretical premises or clinical descriptions in which the surroundings, that is to say, the parents and social interactions, play an important role in the onset of the autistic disorder. These hypothetical origins of the disorder are not always exclusive; other constitutional, organic, hereditary or acquired factors may combine with them.

The first evidence that social surroundings can affect development of the pathology comes from Kanner (Kanner, 1943; Eisenberg & Kanner, 1956). He was the first to provide a psychological profile of the parents of 11 children whom he observed in his early studies. The author describes these parents as highly intellectual and socially cultured individuals who formed cold and obsessive affective relationships. The term "refrigerator parents" was coined to describe the cold personality of these parents. Kanner did not believe that cold parents were the only cause of autism in their children. He believed that the disorder might be traced to bio-social causes (inborn affective disturbance), for example the combination of an organic predisposition with an unfavorable environment.

Most of the literature that interprets the actual behavior of the autistic syndrome in terms of affective causality is mainly of the psychoanalytical orientation. The psychogenetic approach to the aetiology of autism has been subscribed by many authors, particularly between 1943 and 1960. Research in this field continues today.

Spitz (1946), the first to attempt a psychoanalytical interpretation of autism, postulated that a lack of affection together with the absence of adequate stimulation can induce an anaclitical depression (an expression introduced by the author to indicate the disturbances that afflict a child who is deprived of his mother after having spent at least six months of his life with her) in the child in addition to severe affective and intellectual retardation.

Mahler (1952, 1965) formulated her hypothesis on childhood autism in evolutional terms: the most apparent symptom is that the mother, as a representative of the outside world, doesn't seem to be perceived as such by the child. She doesn't seem to exist as the living light of the orientation of the real world. The child's own self, and his own body do not seem to be distinct from the inanimate objects of the surroundings. According to Mahler, autism appears to be the basic stance of those children for whom the mother does not exist functionally. The lack of emotional bonds makes them unable to face the complexity of external stimuli.

Bettelheim (1967) accuses Mahler of failing to understand that autism is an autonomous reaction of the child conditioned by the mother to those life experiences, not a reaction to the totality of his lifetime experiences, of which the mother is in fact only a single part: "I think that the initial cause of the autistic withdrawal is the correct interpretations from the child of the negative attitude with which he approaches the most significant figures of his environment" (p. 47). The author interprets childhood autism as a withdrawal of the child from contact with his mother, detaching himself from her and becoming "encapsulated," the one purpose being to "protect his life by not doing anything that requires a relationship with reality" (p. 56).

Goshen (1963) expanded the study of autism to include the family nucleus and emphasizes the negative effects that a mother who is unable to stimulate and send coherent signals to her child during the critical periods of infancy (particularly between the sixth and eighteenth months) can have. The child may not manage to grasp the meaning of speech and, in some cases, can subside into a condition of mental feebleness.

Although such psychoanalytical models cannot and should not be evaluated by means of the key interpretations that belong to other areas of psychological research, it is true that starting from about the 1970s the principles which they took for granted were challenged on the basis of experimental evidence provided by studies on the affective characteristics of parents of autistic children (Freeman & Ritvo, 1984; Rutter, Bartak, & Newman, 1971). The most important evidence appeared to show that the parents of autistic children are not different from those of normal children: autism afflicts every type of family irrespective of socio-economic status and/or severe internal conflicts (Schopler & Reichler, 1979; Wing, 1980).

Biological and Genetic Factors

Particular emphasis has been placed on the importance of biological factors in the etiology of autism, since it has become increasingly evident that autistic children have neurological, biochemical, and genetic abnormalities. In line with these findings, epidemiological research has both theoretical and practical goals. It tells us about the nature and prevalence of disorders and provides the potential to test hypotheses about causality (see Bryson, 1996). The first review placed the prevalence of autism at 4–5 per 10,000 births (see Wing, 1993). More recent estimates are generally at least twice this, indicating a frequency of about 1 per 1,000.

This discrepancy in rate most likely reflects changes in diagnostic criteria and wider recognition of the expression of autism in more capable individuals (Bryson, 1996, p. 165). The ratio of male to female is 3-4:1. Most autistic subjects show evidence of cognitive impairment: 20–25 percent score within the normal or near-normal range on standard tests of intelligence (Bryson, Clark, & Smith, 1988). One-third of those affected have no speech, and as many as 50 percent have significant behavioral, additional psychiatric, and/or medical problems. Many are aggressive towards themselves or others and suffer depression and/or anxiety, epilepsy, and/or sensory impairment (Bryson, 1996).

Genetic Factors

Today it is commonly accepted that a genetic factor is involved in autism (Rutter, Bailey, Bolton, & Le Couteur, 1993), and the possibility of a genetic cause of autism is one of the more credible hypotheses under investigation. In his first report,

Kanner (1943) described autism as an inborn disorder, and he suggested that genetic factors could be responsible only in terms of a predisposition to development of the syndrome. Yet for many years little attention was paid to possible genetic factors (because it is very rare to have two autistic children in the same family and because early chromosome studies failed to reveal any abnormalities). Three fields of study have changed the direction of research radically: first, the evidence obtained from family and twin studies; second, associations with specific genetic disorders (Fragile X syndrome and tuberous sclerosis); and third, associations with single gene medical disorders (see Bailey, Phillips, & Rutter, 1996). The family and twin studies suggest that genetic influences play a substantial role in the pathogenesis of the autistic syndrome. In his pioneering study, Rimland (1964) evaluated 14 cases of twins, 11 of which were monozygotes, both being autistic. Numerous investigators subsequently produced evidence of a probable genetic cause of autism. There are three twin studies of idiopathic autism. They found a 36 percent (Folstein & Rutter, 1977), 91 percent (Steffenburg, Gillberg, Helgren, Anderson, Gillberg, Jakobsson, & Bohman, 1989) and 69 percent (Bailey, Le Couteur, Gottesman, Bolton, Simonoff, Yuzda, & Rutter, 1995) pair-wise concordance rate for monozygotic twins and a 0 percent rate for dizygotic twins of the same sex, respectively (see Bailey, Phillips, & Rutter, 1996). These results might indicate a strong genetic component for the autistic syndrome, "but several issues need to be tackled before concluding that the genetic effect is as strong as it seems" (Bailey, Phillips, & Rutter, 1996, p. 95). There is a problem with what is genetically transmitted. Family studies have shown that family members of autistic children have language or social cognitive deficits more often than expected. Although there are some inconsistencies between the studies, the twin and family studies together strongly suggest that the autism phenotype extends well beyond the traditional diagnosis. It includes characteristics which are quite similar to autism in quality but not in degree and are also found in individuals of normal intelligence (Bailey, Phillips, & Rutter, 1996, p. 96). As far as the association of specific genetic disorders with autism is concerned, recent hypotheses focus especially on the Fragile X syndrome and tuberous sclerosis. The Fragile X syndrome is a specific abnormality of the genetic structure, which occurs with about the same frequency as autism; it is associated with mental retardation. The first reports on the Fragile X syndrome and autism suggested that the anomaly occurred in at least 16 percent of patients with autism (Gillberg & Wahlstrom, 1985). Current estimates put the true incidence at about 2.5 percent, almost certainly below 5 percent (Bailey, Bolton, Butler, Le Couteur, Murphy, Scott, Webb, & Rutter, 1993; Piven, Gayle, Landa, Wzorek, & Folstein, 1991). The fact that the incidence of the Fragile X syndrome in autism is so much lower than originally stated can be explained by a publishing bias, small sample size in the early studies, use of very low rates for Fragile X expression (1–3%), and inclusion of individuals identified by clinical impression rather than systematic standardized assessment. Probably it is not justifiable to conclude that there is a specific association between the Fragile X syndrome and autism. The association is too weak to constitute a strong indicator of a genetic mechanism involved in autism.

Tuberous sclerosis is a single gene, autosomal, dominant, neurocutaneous disorder, occurring in about 1 per 7,000 individuals (Bailey, Phillips, & Rutter, 1996). Hunt and Dennis (1987) using a checklist approach, reported that 50 percent of children with tuberous sclerosis showed autistic behavior. Current estimates put the true rate between 3 percent (Smalley, Tanguay, Smith, & Gutierrez, 1992) and 9 percent for the proportion of autistic subjects with tuberous sclerosis. Again, following Bayley's suggestions (1996), "the question must be raised as to what the association means. It is likely to be causal in some way (because of its relative strength) but it is noteworthy that the main association occurs with tuberous sclerosis that is accompanied by both mental retardation and epilepsy" (p. 94).

As far as the association of autism with single gene medical disorders is concerned, literature includes reports on autistic features in individuals with phenylketonuria (Folstein & Rutter 1988), neurofibromatosis and other genetically determined conditions (see the review by Gillberg & Coleman, 1992). There have been different hypotheses but there are no systematic studies that allow any estimate of the validity or strength of the association. The studies of Gillberg and Coleman (1992) hypothesize that a chromosomal alteration may be the cause of an abnormal cerebral development (causing abnormal neurons at the level of the dopaminergic system and epilepsy). In this way studies of genetic factors begin to approach those of organic factors.

Organic Factors

Neither Eisenberg nor Kanner (Eisenberg & Kanner, 1956) attributed any importance to organic factors for the etiology of childhood autism. In the 100 cases which they investigated they refer only occasionally to neurological abnormalities which, to their knowledge, were not related to the behavior problem. After years of dedicated work in search of organic abnormalities in early infantile autism, today there are many findings which appear to demonstrate the existence of neurological and neuropsychological abnormalities. However, neither the location nor the effects of these abnormalities have yet been identified.

In 1971 Rimland suggested that autistic children cannot respond to external stimuli because of a lesion in the reticular system. And in 1978 Damasio and Maurer proposed an explanatory theory from a neurological standpoint. They hypothesized damage to the dopaminergic system, which acts especially at the level of the basal ganglia but also partly on the frontal and temporal lobes. Although the dopaminergic system affects a limited part of the brain, its influence may be rather extensive. Damasio and Maurer's theory focuses on the symptoms associated with autism: a peculiar way of walking, slamming or twisting of the hands, repeated actions, lack of spontaneity, fixation of objects, and social deficits. Some of the earliest evidence supporting an organic cause of the autistic syndrome came from the report of epileptic seizures in nearly one third of adolescent autistic patients (for a review, see Gillberg & Steffenburg, 1987). A recent study by Elia, Musumeci, and Ferri (1995) of autistic subjects concludes that the risk of epilepsy depends on aetiological factors. According to these authors the association of autism with epilepsy demonstrates the severity of the underlying pathological processes. Other evidence of organic causes of autism was provided by neuropsychological research. Today extensive literature on the neuropsychology of autism exists. Dawson (1996) suggests that this literature is complex and sometimes inconsistent:

> The complexity comes in part from the fact that an understanding of neuropsychology of autism depends upon knowledge of the development and assessment of normal brain functioning, a nascent and challenging topic itself. In particular, developmentally sensitive neuropsychological tests across a wide range of functional domains are lacking. The inconsistency found across studies arises for at least two reasons. First, tremendous heterogeneity exists in the behavioral expression of autism, and studies differ substantially in the subject populations they examine. . . . Second, whether or not impairments are found in a given study is dependent upon the comparison group used . . . and the variables on which the groups are matched" (p. 179).

Despite these difficulties, some basic conclusions can be derived. Most studies reveal large individual differences in certain neuropsychological domains. Most autistic people have frontal lobe impairments (Ozonoff, Pennington, & Rogers, 1991; Rumsey & Hamburger, 1988). Language difficulties may range from mutism to pragmatic (see Dawson, 1996) and memory difficulties may range from visual recognition memory, mediated by the medial temporal lobe (Barth, Fein, & Waterhouse, 1995), to working memory and verbal encoding, which are indicative of higher cortical dysfunctions (Minshew & Goldstein, 1993; Ozonoff, Pennington, & Rogers, 1991).

Another finding is that autistic children have more difficulties if the tasks involve social information and theory of mind. This pattern of findings raises the question of whether or not autism involves dysfunction of a cerebral system meant for social cognition. Animal and human studies led some investigators to the hypothesis that parts of the temporal lobe (amygdala, hippocampus, entorhinal cortex) and the orbital frontal lobe are likely to constitute such a brain system (Allman & Brothers, 1994; Damasio, 1994; LeDoux, 1994). The amygdala and related cerebral structures appear to mediate attentional, motivational and representational processes required for social orientation, imitation, joint attention, and empathy (Bachevalier, 1994). Courchesne, Chisum, and Towsend (1994) propose a model in which cerebellar dysfunction is presumed to affect the development of limbic regions with many effects on cognitive performance (see Bauman 1996 for a review of neuroanatomical observations of the brain in pervasive developmental disorders). It is clear from the main findings of all of this research that individuals with autism suffer from a neurological and neuropsychological impairment in a wide range of domains as autism involves dysfunctions in multiple regions rather than only one cerebral region. "It is almost certain that different neuro-

FACTS	High genetic risk High incidence of associated medical disorders High incidence of mental retardation, neurological abnormalities, etcetera.	*Biological*
QUESTION	WHAT UNDERLIES THE BEHAVIORAL SYMPTOMS ?	*Cognitive*
FACTS	Manifestation of triad of impairments varies with age and ability: core symptoms in areas of socialization, communication and imagination	*Behavioral*
FACTS	Interpersonal problems: problems in family and peer group relationship, no friendships, no marriage, emotional repercussions, social avoidance	*Social*

Figure 1. Levels of Description Relevant to Autism

psychological profiles will exist for individual functioning at each end of the autistic spectrum. The challenge of the future is to characterize those profiles in order to pinpoint more effective and individualized intervention strategies for persons with autism" (Dawson, 1996, pp. 183–184).

In view of the different biological abnormalities reported, what can be considered critical for the emergence of autism? At present, it is not possible to describe the definitive biological symptomatology of the autistic disorder, since none of the abnormalities reported occur in all children. In addition there is not a clear relationship between the biological abnormalities and the phenotype. It is here that psychological research plays a major role because it specifies the nature of the psychological deficits. However it is very important to integrate the research data from both fields. Figure 1 described in Frith, Morton, & Leslie (1991, p. 434) summarizes the different descriptive levels used for autism.

Cognitive Approach

> There is good evidence of a basic cognitive deficit in autism. This deficit involves impaired language, sequencing, abstraction and coding functions generally. . . . The extent and severity of the social deficit are powerful predictors of outcomes. Treatment can do much to reduce the social and behavioural problems shown by autistic children, but it does little to alter cognitive development (Rutter, 1979, p. 261).

Since the pioneering work of Hermelin and O'Connor (1970), in which it was suggested that autism stems from the inability to encode stimuli meaningfully, it has been accepted that autistic children suffer from a basic cognitive deficit (DeMyer, Hingtgen, & Jackson, 1981). While the cognitive deficit is very evident, it is still difficult to understand more specifically the characteristics of this deficit.

The experimental findings are insufficient to provide an authoritative answer to the etiological question. The current scientific debate is dominated by research into the biological origins of autism. As already explained, the findings point to a variety of genetic and organic causes which lead to abnormal development of the nervous system. Current neuropsychological opinion holds that a direct link between behavioral manifestations and the cerebral structure cannot be made. Consequently, autism can be diagnosed only in behavioral terms. The most widely used definition for autism at present is that provided by DSM-IV (American Psychiatric Association, 1994), which identifies three principal areas of behavioral deficit: qualitative impairment of social interactions, communication and behavior (i.e., limited interests, repetitive and stereotyped activity).

In order to achieve a better understanding of autism today, it may be useful to move from a behavioral definition to a definition which includes the cognitive mechanism as an integral part. The term cognition usually refers to those functions that permit an organism to adapt to the surroundings or to change the surroundings in relation to its own needs. Often processes such as perception, attention, learning, memory, and thoughts are grouped together under the term cognitive functions. As shown by Surian and Frith (1993), when shifting the analysis from a behavioral to a cognitive perspective, the meaning of the word cognitive must not be confused with its traditional definition, the opposite of affective, since the ability to understand and express emotions and to develop social and affective relationships involves a cognitive level of representation and processing of information. The main lines of current research into the cognitive factors that prevent an autistic child from understanding events and their interaction which a normal child comprehends are:

- The central coherence hypothesis (e.g. Frith, 1989a, 1989b, 1991);
- The executive functioning deficit (e.g. Ozonoff, 1995);
- The theory of mind (e.g. Baron-Cohen, Leslie, & Frith, 1985, 1986; Baron-Cohen, 1991a, 1991b, 1991c, 1994);
- The personal relatedness perspective (e.g. Hobson, 1989a, 1990, 1993a, 1993b).

Each of these will be briefly discussed.

The Central Coherence Hypothesis

One hypothesis for the nature of intellectual dysfunctioning in autistic subjects was formulated by Frith (1989b). According to Frith, normal people have a built-in form to coherence over as wide a range of stimuli as possible and to generalize over as wide a range of contexts as possible (Frith, 1989b, p. 100). Autistic persons, in contrast, lack this capacity to form coherence. In the normal process of central coherence, priority is given to understanding meaning. This mentalizing ability can be seen as a cohesive interpretative device par excellence. It brings complex information from different sources together in a meaningful pattern and helps one to make sense out of the world.

A pervasive dysfunction at the central level would inevitably have wide repercussions in all of the main psychological domains: in cognition, in emotion, in behavior, and in social relations (Frith, 1989b, 1991). As far as cognitive characteristics are concerned, autistic individuals have particular difficulty with perception, attention, and generalization. These difficulties affect their comprehension of and interaction with events. The problem they have with generalization, for example, which is characteristic of their slow learning process, stems not so much from an inability to categorize or to see similarities despite differences but rather from an inability to see the need for generalizations across differences (Frith, 1991; Happè, 1994b).

Their problems with perception involve the ability to focus attention on what is salient. People pay attention to things they perceive as important, meaningful or relevant; these adjectives describe experiences of structure. In this sense, a stimulus is important or meaningful because it belongs to a set, and for this reason the individual pays attention. If so, attention is under the control of central thought processes. For those with a weak central control but an intact attention mechanism, patterns of attentive behavior will be odd rather than impaired, as in the case of autism (Frith, 1991). Because of defects in the central thought processes, autistic children experience sensations as fragmentary perceptions and they plan and execute action in the fragmentary form. This fragmentation does not allow them the possibility of seeing the parts in relation to the whole.

In the autistic insistence on sameness, Frith also recognized a type of local coherence that seems to be extremely limited in scope and quite self-contained, a preoccupation of a highly repetitive nature. If the information content is not a coherent whole, but remains a complex set of disconnected pieces of information, it will be difficult for anyone to make any sense out of it. Autistic children lack the ability to integrate vast amounts of information from events, objects, people and behavior. They interpret the world in a literal fashion. Intentions, which create alternative meanings, pose difficulties for them. This inability to take others into account may be the cause of the difficulties autistic individuals have in relating to other people normally. They do not experience the normal ability to integrate mind and behavior in order to achieve coherence.

Their social impairment derives also from their inability to absorb information from different levels into their mental process coherently. In his explanation of communication failures typical of autism, Frith distinguished two kinds of communication. The first—fully intentional communication, in which mental states and information are related and information is evaluated—is of higher priority in normal individuals. The second concerns the transmission of basic messages, which calls for accurate encoding-decoding of speech only at the input and output stages. In autism, real intentional communication is impaired. Consequently, many of the tools (i.e. tone of voice, whole range of non-verbal body language) which enable communication to develop to a highly sophisticated level have not been mastered (see Sperber & Wilson, 1986). The poor performance of autistic individuals in gesticulative communication may be traced to the same cognitive deficit. Autistic subjects seem to be able to understand and use gestures with an instrumental purpose (i.e. those designed to make someone else do something immediately), but they are unable to comprehend the intention underlying expressive gestures which convey states of mind and feelings. Intentional communication is particularly ingenious and distinctive to humans: we can be efficient transmitters, but so can machines; we can relate socially and affectively to other people, but all higher animals can relate, too. What makes humans different is that they can share a wide inner world of relationships and meanings in which risks are constantly taken. Prevented by their handicap from taking such risks, autistic individuals cannot fully participate in this inner world. It may fascinate or terrify them, but it will not really admit them as players (Frith, 1989b).

In conclusion, the capacity for mentation may be the best way to describe the function of cohesion: it brings complex information from widely different sources together in meaningful configurations. The same ability that enables us to know the world may enable us to make sense out of events.

Evidence from neuropsychological studies seems to confirm the presence of this central coherence deficit in autism. In fact, Ozonoff, Pennington, and Rogers (1991) have observed that autistic people have difficulties with tests requiring the use of central executive functions. On the basis of these results, Frith and Happè (1994b) suggest that executive functioning deficits are factors of primary importance in autism if one considers that such functions are necessary in order to process information from the external world into a coherent whole. We will discuss this in the next paragraph.

Executive Functioning

The executive functions are cognitive constructs used to describe the neurological processes thought to be mediated by the frontal lobes. Behavior characteristic of executive functions includes planning, inhibition of the strongest but not correct reply, the preservation of situation, organized search, and flexibility of thought and action (Ozonoff, 1995). What all the components of executive function seem to share is the ability to free the mind from the immediate situation and from the external context in order to guide behavior through mental models or internal representations (for example, planning objectives or script).

Some behavioral traits characteristic of autism, such as perseverance and inflexibility, resemble deficits shown to be caused by abnormalities of the executive functions due to a lesion in the frontal lobes (Luria, 1966). Autistic children are disturbed by changes in their surroundings and persist in routine actions, they have limited interests and stereotypic behavior (Kanner, 1943). Even when they are in possession of sufficient information to solve a problem, they are unable to apply this knowledge; they focus on the details and are unable to see the whole situation (Ozonoff, 1995). On the basis of neurological research, Ozonoff, referring in particular to studies of the frontal lobes (Damasio & Maures, 1978), showed how this area, and particularly the prefrontal cortical region, is involved in the regulation of social and emotional behavior. Recent studies have shown that damage to the frontal lobes may produce a deficit in the ability to understand another's point of view and to show appropriate emotional reactions (Grattan & Eslinger, 1992). In their social behavior, their communicative abilities and their problem-solving ability, therefore, autistic subjects show similarities to those with lesions of the frontal lobe.

Moreover, a deficit in the executive functions may explain the difficulty in imitating which is characteristic of autistic children (Rogers & Pennington, 1991). In order to imitate the body movements of another person one needs to be able to represent those movements at the mental level and to be able to modify the various actions that make up a movement. This type of research seems to augur well for the development of a more convincing perception of autism. By combining a psychological hypothesis with neurological studies, it provides the key to a new interpretation of the different levels of the autistic disorder. However, similar impairments in the executive functioning are found in a variety of other conditions (see Ozonoff, 1997). More research has to be done to explore the hypothesis of an executive dysfunction in autism.

The Theory of Mind

A cognitive theory on autism, known as the "theory of mind," has been particularly influential during the past decade. To develop a theory of mind is to accept the view that a distinction may be drawn between mental states and physical events. Understanding mental states (such as desires, beliefs, imagination, and the same nature of mind) amounts to progressing from a non-representational to a representational understanding which is acquired during development.

So theory of mind is taken to mean capability by means of which the individual attributes mental states to himself and to others. "A system of inferences of this kind is properly viewed as a theory, first, because such states are not directly observable and, second, because the system can be used to make predictions, specifically about the behavior of other organisms" (Premack & Woodruff, 1978, p. 515).

Indicators of this natural development of a mind theory can be observed by studying the characteristics of speech. In spontaneous speech, for example, from age two to three, children begin to talk about their internal psychological (e.g., wants, thoughts, dreams, etc.) and physiological (e.g., hunger) states and about their emotions (e.g., fear, happiness, etc.). Bretherton and Beeghly (1982) saw children using words like "I want" or "mad" in appropriate causal fashion; Huttenlocher and Smiley's studies (1987) on the comprehension and use of action verbs concluded that, before age three, children construe the actions of others as the result of internal states. But to have a belief means to assume that something is a true representation of the world and to understand belief means to conceive of it as a representational mental state that influences people's actions in different ways.

The acquisition of this construct radically transforms the naive psychology of the young child, who progresses from simple, internal, individual-specific dispositions to the first coherent understanding of mental representational states. This acquisition is matched by the development of the distinction between ideas or beliefs and facts. According to Dennett (1978), one can attribute a theory of mind to an individual as long as one is able to demonstrate an understanding of false beliefs (by proving the ability to distinguish one's own belief from somebody else's). Wimmer and Perner (1983) published their famous study on the understanding of false beliefs in normal three- and four-year-old children and introduced the innovative Maxi test. In this test, an object (a bar of chocolate) is moved from its original position while the protagonist, Maxi, is not looking. The child's task is to say where he thinks Maxi will look for the chocolate. The results showed that only children over three years of age were able to pass this test. Baron-Cohen, Leslie, and Frith (1985) performed the same test with autistic children; their results led to the theory that many features of the deficit at the core of autism can be explained in terms of a metarepresentational deficit. A series of very impressive and controlled studies has documented deficits in autistic children by means of a wide range of converging measures of theory of mind: false belief tasks, appearance/reality tasks, and story sequence tasks (Baron-Cohen, Leslie, & Frith, 1985, 1986; Dawson & McKissick, 1984; Harris & Muncer, 1988; Baron-Cohen, 1988, 1989a, 1989b, 1989c, 1991a, 1991b; Leslie & Frith, 1987; Ozonoff, Pennington, & Rogers, 1991; Leekam & Perner, 1991; Russel, Mauthner, Sharpe, & Tidswell, 1991; Charman & Baron-Cohen, 1992; Happè, 1994a, 1994b). The rate of failure among autistic subjects (around 80%) is impressively high in contrast to the rate of success (again around 80%) for both mentally retarded and non-retarded subjects. Thus, the theory of mind hypothesis about autism holds that in autistic children, the ability to conceive that other people know, want, feel or believe things is not developed in a normal way, resulting in social and communicative abnormalities. The results have been duplicated by many authors and by means of different methods. Shaw (1989) used the child's mother as investigator, thus ruling out stranger-anxiety as a cause of the child's failure; Perner, Frith, Leslie, and Leekam (1989) proposed the Smarties box test; Reed and Peterson (1990) used a story similar to that of Wimmer and Perner presented by a puppet; and Swettenham (1992) used a computer-graphic presentation of the original Maxi task, ruling out the possibility that failure was due to social factors in the laboratory.

The theory of mind hypothesis presupposes that the autistic child is able to form a primary representation of another person's physical self (just as he would form a representation of a table or a chair). It presupposes that the autistic child cannot understand another's mental state because he cannot form a secondary representation, metarepresentation, or mental representation of another's mental state.

The mind of a normal infant is already equipped from birth with fundamental knowledge about important features of the world (including objects and people) and how to respond to them. Of course the infant has to learn the specific features of his world, but he can do this because he is able to form representations of people, things and events; representations bring the world into his mind. The inability to represent other people's internal experiences, particularly to predict their behavior, is a great social disadvantage. The social environment is unpredictable and incomprehensible to autistic subjects. Leslie (1987, 1988) suggests that, in order to prevent the interference of pretence with knowledge of the real world, a child must possess two different kinds of representation: one of things as they really are in the world, the other a metarepresentation which is used to fictionalize things. Leslie observes that autistic children do not spontaneously engage in imaginary play and points out that pretence is an extraordinarily complex behavior which emerges early in normal development. During the second year of life, a child begins learning, for example, what a telephone is, that bananas are good to eat, and the names for these things; but he also will understand when the mother picks up a banana and holds it to her ear, saying: "Look, mom's on the telephone!" To summarize, the theory of mind perception of autism is focused on the critical triad of impairments of socialization, communication, and imagination (Wing & Gould, 1979). It has not only helped to make sense of this triad but has also provided us with a highly sensitive diagnostic tool. It must be emphasized, however, that theory of mind cannot explain all the features of autism and that there is more to autism than the classic triad of impairments.

The Personal Relatedness Perspective

There is much evidence of an innate ability in all higher animals to understand the expression of emotions and it could be supposed that this ability in humans is closely related to an innate mechanism that enables the establishment of relationships between people. Echoing an original idea of Kanner, Hobson suggests that, in autism, the mechanism of personal relatedness is defective. In his view, autism is primarily an affective and interpersonal impairment (1989a, 1989b, 1990, 1993a, 1993b, 1993c) which cannot be defined without reference to the child's relationship with his caregivers. Performing experiments to test the ability of autistic children to understand emotions, Hobson (1986) was surprised, given their age, ability and education, to find that many of them failed. The results proved that they had some specific difficulties in recognizing emotions which seemed to be independent of general intellectual ability.

The central thrust of Hobson's argument is that knowledge and understanding of persons are acquired through the individual's experience with affectively patterned, intersubjectively coordinated relationships with other people. A young child comes to know about people's psychological states through sharing them with someone else. This may mean that children derive the concept of mind from their experience with people. Very young children begin with innately constituted propensities and capacities to relate to and experience other people in a particular way and follow a socio-developmental path along which they acquire concepts about people's feelings, intentions, thoughts, and beliefs.

The whole process pivots around the child's experience of personal relatedness (realized in such a way as to effect interpersonal engagement and communication with people) and, more specifically, around the qualities of this experience. From the personal relatedness perspective, autism constitutes a profound disruption of those forms of patterned interpersonal interchange that affect sharing, conflict, or other modes of coordinated experience between the child and others (see Roth & Leslie, 1991). Autistic children lack an essential part of what is biologically given to effect intersubjective coordination with other people. They are deprived of what it takes to acquire knowledge of people and to understand minds.

Personal relatedness is characterized by the potential to express forms of behavior and experience that promote primary intersubjectivity (Trevarthen, 1979); the perception of personal meanings involves the ability to react to such meanings in the appropriate way. Because perception is relational (Hobson, 1989a, 1989b), there is not a radical developmental distinction between the perception of bodies or behavior and grasping the concept of mind. Aspects of mind are perceived in various aspects of expressive behavior. From this perspective, to know oneself is to know oneself among others. With regard to the development of self, it is important to bear in mind that:

- the patterning of an infant's observable exchanges with other people appears to be qualitatively different from his observable exchanges with objects;
- self-reflective awareness is achieved in progressive stages, through the development of a more elaborated sense of self.

When a child establishes intersubjective connectedness through which he perceives a person's bodily orientation to be expressive of psychological orientations, he also relates to things and events as shared. This is what Tomasello, Kruger, and Ratner (1993) consider to be the beginning of cultural learning: "the cognitive representation that results from cultural learning includes something of the perspective of the interactional partner . . . (an) internalization or appropriation of perspectives" (Tomasello, Kruger, & Ratner, 1993, p. 124).

Normal human beings can learn to imitate ways of feeling, acting and thinking through others. Autistic children, on the other hand, seem unable to engage in mutual eye gaze and to pay attention to and orient towards others; intercoordinated affective and motor exchanges with other people (Lord & Magill, 1989; Mundy, Sigman, Ungerer, & Sherman, 1986, 1987; Sigman, Mundy, Sherman, & Ungerer, 1986; Lord & Hopkins, 1986; Lord & Garfin, 1986; Lord, 1984). They also seem to have specific problems with "I-You" relatedness and with the development of an interpersonal self (Hobson, 1990, 1993a; Neisser, 1988).

From a developmental point of view, the interpersonal negotiation of attitudes and intentions provides the child with a configuration of experience that is necessary for, and essential to, self-reflective awareness, creative symbolization, and referential aspects of language. When the child comes to recognize, and then exercise, his own potential to attribute person-dependent rather than object-specific meanings, he acquires the ability to symbolize. This ability is an important social development.

The child perceives how other people can have an emotional attitude towards an object and registers something of the contrast between that attitude and his own feelings towards the same object. Thus, a single object or event may have several meanings-for-persons. An infant's ability may also have developmental significance in terms of her later ability to modify her own psychological attitude and attributions in creative symbolic play. Autistic children rarely manifest protodeclarative gestures of giving or showing things to others (Curcio, 1978; Loveland, Landry, Hughes, Hall, & McEvoy, 1988). They appear to have difficulty in understanding such gestures and they rarely engage in other forms of social referencing, the tendency to imitate is also weak, and the general subjective orientation towards other people is abnormal.

Autistic children are limited in their experiences of sharing and, therefore, of communicating with others; consequently they are slow in appreciating what it means to communicate intentionally. They are especially handicapped in grasping the meaning of a reference to something for someone else by means of interpersonally agreed linguistic symbols (see the problematic use of the pragmatics of language; the difficulties in grasping deietic terms such as "I" and "you," "this" and "that," "now" and "then," which are anchored in the position and the stance of the speaker, and the difficulty in understanding metaphors, the clearest example of replacement of the habitual meaning of words with a new meaning determined by the speaker's attitude). In other words, autistic behavior, language, and social incompetence seem to be related to a general cognitive deficit: autistic children are limited in their capacity for self-reflective awareness. They are not, or only partially, aware of themselves in others' minds (Bosch, 1970; Neuman & Hill, 1978; Dawson & McKissick, 1984; Spiker & Ricks, 1984; Hobson, 1987, 1990, 1993a, 1993b).

Hobson (1993c) suggests that autistic people are slow to develop higher cognitive functions. Their difficulty is closely linked to their lack of engagement not only with other people but also with themselves as selves. This is more evident when we consider cognitive competence in the use of beliefs. When believing, a person adopts the attitude that a given description (or representation) of a state of affairs is true. In order to understand what belief is, one has to understand that:

a. the interpretation of reality may derive from different descriptions;
b. people have attitudes towards objects and events as represented;
c. every kind of attitude holds reality as true.

Even those autistic individuals who achieve something of this understanding exhibit little concern with or scrutiny of their own and others' attitudes.

This lack of attentiveness to people's ways of representing is part and parcel of their failure to engage and identify with others and to recognize the intentionality of communication. In Hobson's opinion, the research of Fernyhough (1992) clearly demonstrates the social impairment of autistic individuals. He has contrasted their computer-like, monological thought with the dialogical mode of flexible thinking that stems from the ability of normal subjects to bring alternative perspectives into relation with one another. In this sense, autistic thought could be interpreted as a monological system with a degree of cognitive potential which cannot be realized.

Summarizing, four cognitive approaches attempt to explain the autistic disorder. The central coherence theory and the executive functioning theory can be seen in a broad perspective in the way that they propose a cognitive abnormality that influences a broad range of psychosocial functions while the other two show a narrow perspective (Bailey, Phillips, & Rutter, 1996). There are many questions about their mutual relationship. Is the central coherence theory encompassing the theory of mind theory? What is the relation between executive functioning and theory of mind? Is the theory of mind theory connected with Hobson's personal relatedness? Are we really discussing cognitive theories or is the term psychological theories better, like Russell (1997) prefers, as he wants "this explanatory level to encompass not only information-processing and epistemic states but also phenomenology" (p. 256). It is important to seek an explanation for the impairments in autism, but we have to keep in mind "that the brain is an open system whose development not only determines experience but is determined by it" (Russell, 1997, p. 256).

Future Prospects of the Etiological Explanations

An important question for future research is the following: Are any of the explanations indicative for special interventions? To treat persons with an autistic disorder means to treat *individuals* with autism. A treatment program must always appreciate this consideration. Thus, for instance, an autistic mentally retarded child needs a different program than a bright autistic child. Gillberg noted that the multiple aetiologies may call for a wide variety of different treatments in the future, depending on the exact aetiology in each individual case (Gillberg et al., 1992, p. 212). However, at present, most of the autistic individuals do not have an exact etiology. The present treatment programs for persons with autism are focused mostly on the behavioral features. Although the individual differences are enormous, there are some general objectives, which should be part of every treatment program. First, a full diagnostic assessment is necessary. This means not only a classification (including the possibility of comorbidity), but also an individual assessment and a family survey. What is the intellectual possibility of this child, what are his interests, does he have special skills or possibly special fears? How is his behavior, and can his family cope with it? Second, a home-based treatment program must be offered. Parents need to be supported in their difficult task of rearing their children. They have to learn how they can cope with the behavior of their child and how they can stimulate their development. Third, special education is needed.

Howlin (1997) indicates that appropriate treatment and education are essential in helping to minimize or avoid secondary behavioral problems and to ensure that children develop their existing skills to the full (p. 69). The prognosis of autism is not good, in the sense that there is no evidence of any cures for autism. However, intervention can have an essential impact on the development and behavior of children with autism (Howlin, 1997; Van Berckelaer-Onnes, Buysse, & Dijkxhoorn, 1997). Autism is a complex disorder that has been the subject of different disciplines, such as child psychiatry, neurology, psychology, childcare, special education, and others. An integration of the findings of different disciplines is needed to gain more insight into and a better understanding of the processes that underlie the clinical features in order to increase the quality of life of individuals with an autistic disorder.

REFERENCES

Allman, J., & Brothers, L. (1994). Faces, fear, and the amygdala. *Nature, 372*, 613.

American Psychiatric Association (1980). *Diagnostic and statistical manual of mental disorders*, 3rd ed. (DSM-III). Washington, DC: Author.

American Psychiatric Association (1987). *Diagnostic and statistical manual of mental disorders* (DSM-IIIR) (3rd ed., rev.). Washington, DC: Author.

American Psychiatric Association (1994). *Diagnostic and statistical manual of mental disorders* (DSM-IV) (4th ed.). Washington, DC: Author.

Asperger, A. (1944). Die autistischen Psychopaten im Kindersalter. *Archiv fur Psychiatrie und Nervenkrankeiten, 117*, 76–136.

Bachevalier, J. (1994). Medial temporal lobe structures and autism: A review of clinical and experimental findings. *Neuropsychologia, 32*, 627–648.

Bailey, A., Bolton, P., Butler, L., Le Couteur, A., Murphy, M., Scott, S., Webb, T., & Rutter, M. (1993). Prevalence of the Fragile X anomaly amongst autistic twins and singletons. *Journal of Child Psychology and Psychiatry, 34*, 673–688.

Bailey, A., Le Couteur, A., Gottesman, I., Bolton, P., Simonoff, E., Yuzda, E., & Rutter, M. (1995). Autism as a strongly genetic disorder. Evidence from a British twin study. *Psychological Medicine, 25*, 63–78.

Bailey, A., Phillips, W., & Rutter, M. (1996). Autism: Towards an integration of clinical, genetic, neuropsychological, and neurobiological perspectives. *Journal of Child Psychology and Psychiatry and Allied Disciplines, 37*, 1, 89–126.

Baron-Cohen, S. (1988). Social and pragmatic deficits in autism: Cognitive or affective? *Journal of Autism and Developmental Disorders, 18*, 379–402.

Baron-Cohen, S. (1989a). Are autistic children behaviourist? An examination of their mental-physical and appearance-reality distinctions. *Journal of Autism and Developmental Disorders, 19*, 579–600.

Baron-Cohen, S. (1989b). Perceptual role taking and protodeclarative pointing in autism. *British Journal of Developmental Psychology, 7*, 113–127.

Baron-Cohen, S. (1989c). The autistic child's theory of mind: A case of specific development delay. *Journal of Child Psychology and Psychiatry, 30*, 285–297.

Baron-Cohen, S. (1991a). Do people with autism understand what causes emotion? *Child Development, 62*, 385–395.

Baron-Cohen, S. (1991b). Precursor to a theory of mind: Understanding attention in others. In A. Withen (Ed.) *Natural theories of mind* (pp. 233–253). Oxford: Basil Blackwell.

Baron-Cohen, S. (1991c). The theory of mind deficit in autism: How specific is it? *British Journal of Developmental Psychology, 9*, 301–314.

Baron-Cohen, S. (1994). How to build a baby that can read mind: Cognitive mechanisms in mindreading. *Cahiers de Psychologie-Cognitive [Current Psychology of Cognition]. 13*, 513–552.

Baron-Cohen, S., Leslie, A., & Frith, U. (1985). Does the autistic child have a "theory of mind?" *Cognition, 21*, 37–46.

Baron-Cohen, S., Leslie, A., & Frith, U. (1986). Mechanical, behavioural and intentional understanding of picture stories in autistic children. *British Journal of Developmental Psychology, 4*, 113–125.

Barth, C., Fein, D., & Waterhouse, L. (1995). Delayed match-to-sample performance in autistic children. *Developmental Neuropsychology, 11*, 53–69.

Bauman, ML. (1996). Neuroanatomic observations of the brain in pervasive developmental disorders. *Journal of Autism and Developmental Disorders, 26*, 199–201.

Bettelheim, B. (1967). *The empty fortress: Infantile autism and the birth of self.* New York: Free Press.

Bleuler, E. (1911). Dementia Praecox oder Gruppe der Schizophrenien. In *Handbuch der psychiatrie.* Leipzig: Duticke.

Bosch, G. (1970). *Infantile autism.* New York: Springer-Verlag.

Brauner, A., & Brauner, F. (1978). *Vivre avec un enfant autistique.* Paris: Presses Universitaries de France.

Bretherton, I., & Beeghly, M. (1982). Talking about internal states: The acquisition of an explicit theory of mind. *Development Psychology, 18*, 906–921.

Bryson, S. E. (1996). Epidemiology of Autism. *Journal of Autism and Developmental Disorders, 26*, 165–167.

Bryson, S. E., Clark, B. S., & Smith, I. M. (1988). First report of a Canadian epidemiological study of autistic syndromes. *Journal of Child Psychology and Psychiatry, 29*, 433–446.

Charman, T., & Baron-Cohen, S. (1992). Understanding drawings and beliefs: A further test of metarepresentation theory of autism. *Journal of Child Psychology and Psychiatry, 33*, 1105–1112.

Courchesne, E., Chisum, H., & Towsend, J. (1994). Neural activity-dependent brain changes in development: Implication for psychopathology. *Development and Psychopathology, 6*, 697–722.

Creak, M. (1961). Schizofrenia syndrome in childhood: Progress report of a working party. *Cerebral Palsy Bulletin, 3*, 501–504.

Curcio, F. (1978). Sensorimotor functioning and communication in mute autistic children. *Journal of Autism and Childhood Schizophrenia, 8*, 281–291.

Damasio, A. R., & Maurer, R. G. (1978). A neurological model for childhood autism. *Archives of Neurology, 35*, 777–786.

Damasio, A. R. (1994). *Descartes error: Emotion, reason and the human brain.* New York: G. P. Putnam.

Dawson, G. (1996). Neuropsychology of autism: A report on the state of the science. *Journal of Autism and Developmental Disorders, 26*, 179–184.

Dawson, G., & McKissick, F. C. (1984). Self-recognition in autistic children. *Journal of Autism and Developmental Disorders, 14*, 383–394.

De Myer, M. K., Hingtgen, J. N., & Jackson, R. K. (1981). Infantile autism reviewed: A decade of research. *Schizophrenia Bulletin, 7*, 388–451.

Dennett, D. C. (1978). Beliefs about beliefs. *Behavioural and Brain Sciences, 4*, 568–570.

Eisenberg, L., & Kanner, L. (1956). Early infantile autism 1943–1955. *American Journal of Orthopsychiatry, 26*, 556–566.

Elia, M., Musumeci, S. A., & Ferri R. (1995). Clinical and neurophysiological aspects of epilepsy in subjects with autism and mental retardation. *American Journal on Mental Retardation, 100*, 6–16.

Fernyhough, C. (1992). *Ideology and dialogue in the development of higher mental functioning.* Unpublished manuscript. Cambridge, England: Department of Experimental Psychology, Cambridge University.

Folstein, S., & Rutter, M. (1977). Infantile autism: A genetic study of 21 twin pairs. *Journal of Child Psychology and Psychiatry, 18*, 297–321.

Folstein, S., & Rutter, M. (1988). Autism: Familial aggregation and genetic implications. *Journal of Autism and Developmental Disorders, 18*, 3–30.

Freeman, B. J., & Ritvo, E. R. (1984). The syndrome of autism: Establishing the diagnosis and principles of management. *Pediatric Annals, 13*, 284–305.

Frith, U. (1989a). A new look at language and communication in autism. *British Journal of Disorders of Communication, 24*, 123–150.

Frith, U. (1989b). *Autism: Explaining the enigma.* Oxford: Basil Blackwell.

Frith, U. (1991). *Autism and Asperger syndrome.* Cambridge: University Press.

Frith, U., & Happè, F. (1994). Autism: Beyond theory of mind. *Cognition, 50*, 115–132.

Frith, U., Morton, J., & Leslie, A. M. (1991). The cognitive basis of biological disorders: autism. *Trends in Neurosciences, 14*, 433–438.

Gillberg, C., & Coleman, M. (1992). *The biology of the autistic syndrome.* Mackeith Press.

Gillberg, C., & Steffenburg, S. C. (1987). Outcome and prognostic factor in infantile autism and similar condition: A population based study of 46 cases followed through puberty. *Journal of Autism and Developmental Disorders, 17*, 273–287.

Gillberg, C., & Wahlstrom, J. (1985). Chromosome abnormalities in infantile autism and other childhood psychoses: A population study of 66 cases. *Developmental Medicine and Child Neurology, 27*, 293–304.

Goshen, C. E. (1963). Mental retardation and neurotic maternal attitudes. *Archives of General Psychiatry, 9*, 15–18.

Grattan, L. M., & Eslinger, P. J. (1992). Long-term psychosocial consequences of childhood frontal lobe lesion in patient DT. *Brain and Cognition, 20*, 185–195.

Happè, F. (1994a). An advanced test of theory of mind. Understanding of story characters, thought and feelings by able autistic, mentally retarded and normal children and adults. *Journal of Autism and Developmental Disorders, 24*, 129–154.

Happè, F. (1994b). *Autism: An introduction to psychological theory.* London: University College London Press.

Happè, F., & Frith, H. (1996). The neuropsychology of autism. *Brain, 119*, 1377–1400.

Harris, P. L., & Muncer, A. (1988). *Autistic children's understanding of beliefs and desires.* Paper presented at the Annual Conference of the Developmental Section of the British Psychological Society, Coleg Harlech, Wales.

Hermelin, B., & O'Connor, N. (1970). *Psychological experiments with autistic children.* Oxford: Pergamon.

Hobson, R. P. (1986). The autistic child's appraisal of expression of emotion. *Journal of Child Psychology and Psychiatry, 27*, 321–342.

Hobson, R. P. (1987). The autistic child's recognition of age- and sex-related characteristics of people. *Journal of Autism and Developmental Disorders, 17*, 63–79.

Hobson, R. P. (1989a). Beyond cognition: A theory of autism. In G. Dawson (Ed.), *Autism: Nature, diagnosis and treatment* (pp. 22–48). New York: Guilford.

Hobson, R. P. (1989b). On sharing experiences. *Development and Psychopathology, 1*, 188–206.

Hobson, R. P. (1990). The origins of self and the case of autism. *Development and Psychopathology, 2*, 163–181.

Hobson, R. P. (1993a). Through feeling and sight to self and symbol. In U. Neisser (Ed.), *Ecological and interpersonal knowledge of the self.* New York: International Universities Press.

Hobson, R. P. (1993b). *Autism and the development of mind*. East Sussex: Hove.

Hobson, R. P. (1993c). Understanding persons: The role of affect. In S. Baron-Cohen, H. Tager-Flusberg, & D. J. Cohen (Eds.), *Understanding other minds*. New York: Oxford University Press.

Howlin, P. (1997). Prognosis in autism: do specialist treatments affect long term outcome? *European Child & Adolescent Psychiatry, 6*, 55–72.

Hunt, A., & Dennis, J. (1987). Psychiatric disorder among children with tuberous sclerosis. *Developmental Medicine and Child Neurology, 29*, 190–198.

Huttenlocher, J., & Smiley, P. (1987). Early word meanings: The case of object names. *Cognitive Psychology, 19*, 63–89.

Kanner, L. (1943). Autistic disturbances of affective contact. *Nervous Child, 2*, 217–250.

LeDoux, J. E. (1994). Emotion, memory and the brain. *Scientific American*, 50–54.

Leekam, S., & Perner, J. (1991). Does the autistic child have a metarepresentational deficit? *Cognition, 40*, 203–218.

Leslie, A. (1987). Pretense and representation: The origins of "theory of mind." *Psychological Review, 94*, 412–426.

Leslie, A. (1988). Some implications of pretence for mechanisms underlying the child's theory of mind. In J. W. Astington, P. L. Harris, & D. R. Olson (Eds.), *Developing theories of mind*. New York: Cambridge University Press.

Leslie, A., & Frith, U. (1987). Metarepresentation and autism: How not to loose one's marbles. *Cognition, 27*, 291–294.

Leslie, A., & Frith, U. (1988). Autistic children's understanding of seeing, knowing and believing. *British Journal of Development Psychology, 4*, 315–324.

Lord, C. (1984). The development of peer relations in children with autism. In F. J. Morrison, C. Lord, & D. P. Keating (Eds.), *Advances in applied developmental psychology* (pp. 165–229). New York: Academic Press.

Lord, C., & Garfin, D. (1986). Facilitating peer-directed communication in autistic children and adolescents. *Australian Journal of Human Communication Disorders, 14*, 33–49.

Lord, C., & Hopkins, J. M. (1986).The social behaviour of autistic children with younger and same-age non-handicapped peers. *Journal of Autism and Developmental Disorders, 16*, 249–262.

Lord, C., & Magill, J. (1989). Methodological and theoretical issues in studying peer-directed behaviour and autism. In G. Dawson (Ed.), *Autism: Nature, diagnosis, and treatment* (pp. 326–345). New York: Guilford.

Loveland, K. A., Landry, S. H., Hughes, S. O., Hall, S. K., & McEvoy, R. E. (1988). Speech acts and the pragmatics deficits in autism. *Journal of Speech and Hearing Research, 31*, 583–604.

Luria, A. R. (1966). *The higher cortical functions in man*. New York: Basic Books.

Mahler, M. (1952). *On child psychosis and schizophrenia: Autistic and symbiotic infantile psychoanalytic study of the child* (vol. 7, pp. 286–305). New York: International Universities Press.

Mahler, M. (1965). On early infantile psychosis. *Journal of the American Academy of Child Psychiatry*, 554–568.

Minshew, N. J., & Goldstein, G. (1993). Is autism an amnesic disorder? Evidence from the California Verbal Learning Test. *Neuropsychology, 7*, 209–216.

Mundy, P., Sigman, M., Ungerer, J., & Sherman, T. (1986). Defining the social deficits of autism: The contribution of non-verbal communication measures. *Journal of Child Psychology and Psychiatry, 27*, 657–669.

Mundy, P., Sigman, M., Ungerer, J., & Sherman, T. (1987). Non-verbal communication and play correlates of language development in autistic children. *Journal of Autism and Developmental Disorders, 17*, 349–364.

National Society for Autistic Children (NSAC) (1978). NSAC definition of the syndrome of autism. *Journal of Autism and Childhood Schizophrenia, 8*, 162–167.

Neisser, U. (1988). Five kinds of self-knowledge. *Philosophical Psychology, 1*, 35–59.

Neuman, C. J., & Hill, S. D. (1978). Self-recognition and stimulus preference in autistic children. *Developmental Psychology, 11*, 571–578.

Ozonoff, S. (1995). Executive functions in autism. In E. Schopler & G. B. Mesibov (Eds.), *Learning and cognition in autism* (pp. 199–220). New York: Plenum.

Ozonoff, S. (1997). Components of executive function in autism and other disorders. In J. Russell (Ed.), *Autism as an executive disorder* (pp. 179–215).

Ozonoff, S., Pennington, B. F., & Rogers, S. J. (1991). Executive function deficits in high-functioning autistic individuals: Relationship to theory of mind. *Journal of Child Psychology and Psychiatry, 32*, 1081–1105.

Perner, J., Frith, U., Leslie, A., & Leekam, S. R. (1989). Exploration of autistic child's theory of mind: Knowing, belief, and communication. *Child Development, 60*, 689–700.

Piven, J., Gayle, J., Landa, J., Wzorek, M., & Folstein, S. (1991). Psychiatric disorders in the parents of autistic individuals. *Journal of the American Academy of Child and Adolescent Psychiatry, 30*, 471–478.

Premack, D., & Woodruff, G. (1978). Does the chimpanzee have a theory of mind? *Behavioural and Brain Sciences, 4*, 515–527.

Reed, T., & Peterson, C. (1990). A comparative study of autistic subjects' performance at two levels of visual and cognitive perspective taking. *Journal of Autism and Developmental Disorders, 20*, 555–568.

Rimland, B. (1964). *Infantile autism*. New York: Appleton.

Rimland, B. (1971). The differentiation of childhood psychoses: An analysis of checklists for 2–218 psychotic children. *Journal of Autism and Childhood Schizophrenia, 1*, 161–174.

Rogers, S., & Pennington, B. F. (1991). A theoretical approach to the deficits in infantile autism. *Development and Psychopathology, 3*, 137–162.

Roth, D., & Leslie, A. (1991). The recognition of attitude conveyed by utterance: A study of preschoolers and autistic children. *British Journal of Developmental Psychology, 9*, 315–330.

Rumsey, J. M., & Hamburger, S. D. (1988). Neuropsychological findings in high-functioning men with infantile autism, residual state. *Journal of Clinical and Experimental Neuropsychology, 10*, 201–221.

Russell, J. (1997). How executive disorders can bring about inadequate theory of mind. In J. Russell (Ed.), *Autism as an executive disorder* (pp. 256–305).

Russell, J., Mauthner, N., Sharpe, S., & Tidswell, T. (1991). The 'windows' task as a measure of strategic deception in preschoolers and autistic subjects. *British Journal of Developmental Psychology, 9*, 331–349.

Rutter, M. (1978). Diagnosis and definition of childhood autism. *Journal of Autism and Childhood Schizophrenia, 8*, 139–161.

Rutter, M. (1979). Language, cognition and autism. In R. Katzman (Ed.), *Congenital and acquired cognitive disorders*. New York: Raven.

Rutter, M., Bailey, A., Bolton, P., & Le Couteur, A. (1993). Autism: Syndrome definition and possible genetic mechanisms. In R. Plomin & G. E. McClearn (Eds.), *Nature, nurture, and psychology*. Washington, DC: APA Books.

Rutter, M., Bartak, L., & Newman, S. (1971). Autism: A central disorder of cognition or language? In M. Rutter (Ed.), *Infantile autism: Concepts, characteristics and treatment*. London: Churchill-Livingstone.

Rutter, M., & Garmezy, N. (1983). Childhood psychopathology. In M. Hetherington & P. H. Mussen (Eds.), *Carmichael's manual of child psychology*. New York: Wiley.

Rutter, M., & Schopler, E. (1987). Autism and pervasive developmental disorders: Concepts and diagnostic issues. *Journal of Autism and Developmental Disorders, 17*, 159–186.

Schopler, E., & Mesibov, G. B. (1988). *Diagnosis and assessment in autism*. New York: Plenum Press.

Schopler, E., & Reichler, J. (1979). *Individualized assessment and treatment for autistic and developmentally disabled children*, Psychoeducational Profile. Austin, TX: PRO-ED.

Shaw, P. (1989). *Is the deficit in autistic children's theory of mind an artifact?* Unpublished manuscript, Oxford, England: Oxford University, Department of Experimental Psychology.

Sigman, M., Mundy, P., Sherman, T., & Ungerer, J. (1986). Social interaction of autistic children, mentally retarded, and normal children and their caregivers. *Journal of Child Psychology and Psychiatry, 27*, 647–656.

Smalley, S. L., Tanguay, P. E., Smith, M., & Gutierrez, G. (1992). Autism and tuberous sclerosis. *Journal of Autism and Developmental Disorders, 22*, 339–355.

Sperber, D., & Wilson, D. (1986). *Relevance: Communication and cognition.* Cambridge, MA: Harvard University Press.

Spiker, D., & Ricks, M. (1984). Visual self-recognition in autistic children: Developmental relationship. *Child Development, 55*, 214–225.

Spitz, R. A. (1946). Anaclitic depression in the psychoanalytic study of the child. New York: International Universities Press, 313–342.

Surian, L., & Frith, U. (1993). Prospettive della ricerca di neuropsicologia cognitiva sull'autismo infantile. *Età Evolutiva, 45*, 73–83.

Steffenburg, S., Gillberg, C., Helgren, L., Anderson, L., Gillberg, L., Jakobsson, G., & Bohman, M. (1989). A twin study of autism in Denmark, Finland, Iceland, Norway, and Sweden. *Journal of Child Psychology and Psychiatry, 30*, 405–416.

Swettenham, J. (1992). *The autistic child's theory of mind: A computer-based investigation.* Unpublished Ph.D. thesis, University of York, England.

Tomasello, M., Kruger, A. C., & Ratner, H. H. (1993). Cultural learning, *Behavioural and Brain Sciences*, 122–131.

Trevarthen, C. (1979). Communication and cooperation in early infancy: A description of primary intersubjectivity. In M. Bullowa (Ed.), *Before speech* (pp. 321–347). Cambridge: Cambridge University Press.

Van Berckelaer-Onnes, I. A., Buysse, W., & Dijkxhoorn, Y. M. (1997). *Autisme en een mentale handicap: geintegreerde zorg.* Leiden: Rijksuniversiteit, sectie Orthopedagogiek.

Van Berckelaer-Onnes, I. A., & Hoekman, J. (1991). *De Auti-R.* Lisse: Swets Zeitlinger.

Van Yperen, T. A., Van Berckelaer-Onnes, I. A., & Rispens, J. (1992). The classification of specific developmental disorders: Moving away from the hierarchical model in DSM and ICD. *The European Journal of Psychiatry, 6*, 223–235.

Wimmer, H., & Perner, J. (1983). Beliefs about beliefs: Representation and constraining function of wrong beliefs in young children's understanding of deception. *Cognition, 21*, 103–128.

Wing, L. (1980). Childhood autism and social class: A question of selection? *British Journal of Psychiatry, 137*, 410–417.

Wing, L. (1993). The definition and prevalence of autism: A review. *European Child and Adolescent Psychiatry, 2*, 61–74.

Wing, L. (1996). *The autistic spectrum.* London: Constable.

Wing, L., & Gould, J. (1979). Severe impairments of social interaction and associated abnormalities in children: Epidemiology and classification. *Journal of Autism and Developmental Disorders, 9*, 11–30.

World Health Organization (1992). *The ICD-10 classification of mental & behavioural disorders: Clinical descriptions and diagnosis guidelines.* Geneva, Switzerland: Author.

www.ingramcontent.com/pod-product-compliance
Lightning Source LLC
LaVergne TN
LVHW010649300926
849161LV00005B/1078